What people are

C000133958

A Sense of Sor

Beautiful, moving and richly-observed memoir...

Despite being an intensely personal account, *A Sense of Something Lost* examines issues that affect us all, and it feels very well-realised. Sue Wells has a wonderful sense of humour, a rich vocabulary, a deep understanding of, and compassion for, the human condition and a way with words that is often thought-provoking.

Alison Taft, author and creative writing tutor

A lifetime journey of the spirit told with warmth and honesty. This is powerful stuff, no doubt about it!

Angie Sage, international best-selling author

A Sense of
Something Lost

A Sense of
Something Lost

Sue Wells

BOOKS

Winchester, UK
Washington, USA

JOHN HUNT PUBLISHING

First published by O-Books, 2019
O-Books is an imprint of John Hunt Publishing Ltd., 3 East St., Alresford,
Hampshire SO24 9EE, UK
office@jhpbooks.com
www.johnhuntpublishing.com
www.o-books.com

For distributor details and how to order please visit the 'Ordering' section on our website.

ISBN: 978 1 78904 283 2
978 1 78904 284 9 (ebook)
Library of Congress Control Number: 2018961982

A CIP catalogue record for this book is available from the British Library.

Design: Stuart Davies

UK: Printed and bound by CPI Group (UK) Ltd, Croydon, CR0 4YY
US: Printed and bound by Thomson-Shore, 7300 West Joy Road, Dexter, MI 48130

We operate a distinctive and ethical publishing philosophy in
all areas of our business, from our global network of authors to
production and worldwide distribution.

Contents

Acknowledgements

I want to thank everyone involved for the various ways in which they have helped bring about this memoir I started writing over 30 years ago:

All the teachers – both spiritual and healers alike – that I have had the privilege of knowing: Ken and Elizabeth Mellor, the meditation teachers that helped as I stumbled along the spiritual path in search of answers, and especially Jean-Marc Mantel, Eckhart Tolle, Gangaji.

The healers I encountered especially Harold Klug.

The amazing mediums – including Marcus from Bristol and the lovely, late Jo Wainman.

My old primary school chums from Dunedin, New Zealand who offered valuable snippets and reminders of life in the early sixties: Alison Duke Wilson, Jock Irvine, Mary Caughey and especially the late Warwick Larkins and Claire, the postgraduate student he managed to find who kindly gave me her thesis on Victorian illegitimacy in NZ.

My cousin Murray MacKinnon who researched our family history so impressively.

The late Murray Ryburn for his ongoing inspiration.

The Early Settlers Museum in Dunedin.

Also dear friends whose interest in the memoir never faded where mine sometimes did – Vaughn Malcolm, Angie Powell, Patrick Thomas, Arpi Shively, Kate McNab and writing buddies Jo Suaju and Caroline Mitchell. Also Rowena Lamont; Sandra and Olwyn, Cathy and Annie.

Thanks to my mum and to my dad for teaching me what, looking back, I most needed to learn.

For my daughters Sarah, Anna and Sophie – most particularly my first daughter whose life was blighted by adoption but who has managed to turn her life around and enabled me to do the same.

Most of all, I want to thank my husband Martin for all sorts of things – his love and support, his professional insight and wisdom, his patience with endless discussions on long car journeys, his gentle encouragement and enthusiasm, especially over the last few years, to keep writing the book!

For anyone who has been affected by lifelong trauma – may you find freedom beyond your personal story.
This includes the thousands of young women whose trauma has often gone unrecognised when they were forced to give up their precious babies for adoption because they were not married.

Part I

Lost

Help! I Need Somebody...
The Beatles, 1965

Prologue

Bristol, England 2014

How much does a single trauma shape your life? Inhibit your true self, your sense of freedom? How could it possibly become your greatest gift, as a wise man predicted, your unique key to the freedom you seek?

I couldn't finish this story when I started writing it 30 years ago. I suppose I didn't really try. But now I know the ending. And it's not what I expected. The story itself began long before that, in the 1960s, maybe beyond. Who knows when the kernel of a seed starts to sprout? To incubate, before affecting or, in my case, infecting the entire being.

I didn't keep a diary back then, in the 1960s. I mean, who wants to record the worst time of their life? To have an ongoing dialogue with yourself reminding you of the shame and devastation you caused, bringing to the surface events that are best forgotten, but which have, nevertheless, lurked, like a long, solitary shadow, casting doubt and unworthiness over everything thereafter, so that the shadow itself appears to be who you are.

Now I am ready. Now the time is right when I can step back, observe and record my own demise from a different perspective. I have become aware that only by looking back can I, at last, weave together the fragments of my life – all the blind alleys and wrong turnings – into a meaningful, cohesive whole. A mosaic that finally helps make sense of the fragments. Like looking down at the earth from the moon and seeing your life all at once.

So I am not rewriting my story. There's no longer a need. I lost peacefulness at 17. I lost touch with myself, with the world. I became restless and stayed restless, unable to focus on anything or give myself to anything except a sense of emptiness.

Years later I went to see Harold a reputable healer about it.

'It's as if your brain has never told your body that you were relieved of a baby,' he said referring to the baby I was not allowed to keep. 'Your emotions are buried in the womb.'

This has been my challenge. My 'hill to climb', as he put it. To finally welcome myself, a little belatedly, back into the world, and in so doing, release myself from my own prison.

'To be peaceful,' he said. 'To be still enough to offer to the world the person that you are. You've got everything in place,' he added, 'brought up your kids well, finished work... and now it's time for your journey: a journey of healing.'

Chapter 1

Doing My Duty

Lambeth Social Services, Brixton, London 1981
I am 34 years old

There was a moment in the office when everything was still. No phones ringing, endless chatter across an acre of desks or bursts of reggae pulsating up from the street below. It was Friday afternoon, and the office was usually deserted unless you were unlucky enough to be on duty when anything could happen.

I lit a cigarette and leaned back in my chair watching the blue smoke curling upward towards the half-open window as if it too were escaping, bidding me a theatrical farewell.

I pondered on the client I had just visited for the first time. Mrs Brown, known to social services for over twenty years. File as thick as a house brick. She had made me feel uneasy. It wasn't the junk in her front garden – the bits of bike and cars and God knows what strung together with weeds like a giant's crazy necklace, or the mean-looking, murderous Alsatian baring its teeth, daring me to reach the front door, emitting a low growl as I approached. It was the brief conversation I had with her standing in the doorway of her front room as there was nowhere to sit, buffeted by wafts of stale urine and old socks.

'I see from your notes you've had a social worker for the last twenty years, Mrs Brown... I was wondering... has it helped?'

She rubbed her chin, raised her upper lip, as if she had also smelled something unpleasant and said: 'Nah, not really! I'm alright... don't really need nuffink.'

Back at my desk I couldn't get Mrs Brown out of my mind. Why wouldn't she accept the help offered, why stay the same? Living in that mess year in, year out with nothing changing. I inhaled deeply and wondered when her hopelessness had taken hold. Maybe it was growing up in care, poor thing, owing to her mother's neglect, having no one to look out for her, no proper role model. Anything might have happened to her; I shivered. Even so it was hard to understand why she wouldn't want things to be different, at least help with a good old clean-up and a skip or two.

I stubbed out my cigarette, crushing it into the ashtray. Why did it bother me so much anyway? It wasn't as if we had anything in common. I couldn't live in a mess like that, I'd had a lovely mum, I wasn't neglected. I stared out the window at the brick buildings opposite. It was me, I realised, who wasn't happy with the way things were; who wanted things to be different. Sorted, cleansed. At least Mrs Brown's crap was out in the open, nothing tucked away, nothing hidden. The irony made me squirm. It's not her that needs help for heaven's sake, it's me!

The peace and tranquillity of the office was hijacked by a loud, angry voice demanding to see a social worker. The only good thing about being on duty on a Friday afternoon meant that, if you were lucky and no clients came in, you finished earlier than usual, at 4.30 rather than 5pm. Otherwise anything could happen including finding yourself mostly deserted by colleagues eager to scuttle away from the office, maybe meeting up later in the pub. Today I was unlucky. It was almost 4.30. A large, red-faced man had ploughed into the office just as Barbara the receptionist was about to leave.

'Damn!' I thought. 'That puts me at least two brandy-and-Babychams behind her at The George later.'

Mr Reynolds was demanding I take his son Matthew into care.

'We've had enough of him!' he bellowed in the reception area before I managed to shoehorn him into the tiny interview room leaving the door slightly ajar as a silent signal to any stray colleagues.

'He's skipping school, staying out late, mixing with the wrong sort of boys, refusing to do as he's told... he'll end up in trouble, you'll see!' He waved a menacing forefinger in my direction... 'We need a bloody break from him!' he shouted having wound himself up like a coiled spring so he was unable to ease himself into the crappy little armchair in the interview room.

'He's driving us bloody mad!' he shouted turning an unattractive shade of puce, and hammered his fist down on the low table in front of him causing me and a glass ashtray to jump simultaneously.

'We can't just take him into care,' I explained as gently as I could, wondering where the hell everyone else was, 'because from what you're saying he's not in any immediate danger.' Not like me I thought smelling his sweat and his rage and possibly alcohol if I was foolish enough to confirm it by leaning closer to him.

'No more than lots of kids his age,' I continued. 'So many parents find this age really difficult. You're not alone.'

He fumbled for his fags, lit up and inhaled deeply, as if he was imbibing the burden of his family's problems, then exhaled in a gust all over me. I could feel my eyes watering and hoped he didn't mistake it for misguided empathy.

After he calmed down a bit, I explained how we helped families in similar situations and what that would involve, suggesting we meet together as a family in the next few days and see how we go.

Mr Reynolds eyed me dubiously but eventually agreed, after I alluded to the time, late Friday afternoon, ironically now a help to me, explaining how difficult it would be to access his son's school, assuming of course that was alright with him. He nodded in agreement, softening slightly when I deferred to him about contacting the school and eventually left after receiving some empathy and support, hopefully feeling marginally less burdened and maybe even a little optimistic. But I did wonder how come he thought he could simply march into the office late on a Friday afternoon and expect to dump his son. Heartless bastard!

Mr Reynolds brought my own father to life, from wherever he was buried. I imagined he was much the same: always shouting to be heard, blaming everyone else, insisting he was right, demanding certain action. Always getting his own way. Never listening to what anyone else might want. I could still see my father watchful in his chair behind the newspaper or hunched at his place at the head of the table or brandishing his leather strap to maintain authority. He had a tabletop temper too but I was usually ready, braced in anticipation. I could still feel my father's presence, always at a distance, for he was not a demonstrative man in the positive sense. In fact, I can't recall any displays of affection towards my mother, or us – unless we were sick when he just might buy you oranges or grapes. Come to think of it, I can't remember him ever greeting me, saying hello or even smiling. Maybe he did and I wasn't looking.

I never thought of my father as someone like other people, who would eventually die. To me he was immortal, powerful, controlling and fearful; he decided everything and that was that. I thought he was flawless and it was me, not him, who was flawed. Part of me still resisted the finality, the simplicity, of his death, reluctant to acknowledge a straightforward, mortal image of him, as if by doing so, I might lose part of myself. Part of the past, where memories can easily get lost, dissolved by time. What else did I have to hang on to? Instead, I needed to recall those childhood scenes, or should I say teenage years, with the same crisp clarity I'd always done, to reassure myself that this is how things were – that there was nothing I could possibly have done to change anything. Nothing at all.

Unlike Mr Reynolds, my father would never have sought help. Never! Especially not for me. Or even admit there were any flaws or cracks in the family, never mind the craters I had caused. Dad's knee-jerk reaction to treat me as if I was no longer part of my family but simply an adjunct to be segmented off and discarded made me wonder about Mr Reynolds. Was he seeking help for his family or trying to get rid of his son for his own needs?

The passage of a decade or so without my father's physical presence on this earthly plane was a minor detail. He was as alive as ever in my head to offer criticism at will.

'Bloody waste of time,' he'd have muttered prosaically about my trying to help families like the Reynolds in this way.

Although I was lacking in paternal care and affection, I had witnessed the expression of a different kind of love, political and impersonal. My father's profound concern for the underdog. Well, a certain type of underdog, not just any old underdog. It was this love, no doubt influenced by his own family's experience of anti-Semitism about which both sides of the family conspired to remain silent (especially the Presbyterian side), that fuelled my own passions and had culminated in my belonging to the 'helping' professions. So I guess something of him had rubbed off. But I've often thought it was ironic that my dictatorial father had created within his own family the very hierarchical system that, with his socialist background, he purported to abhor.

Thinking about the Reynolds family, I could only guess at the source of Mr Reynolds' bitterness. Unlike my intransigent father who no doubt carried with him the legacy of his parents' pain and misery of the murderous racism and prejudice which caused them to flee the pogroms in Poland before the turn of the 20th century, to be banished from their homeland and forced to emigrate; first to England, then on to New Zealand, to endure the grief and loss of the only home they'd ever known, to always be haunted by injustices and hatred and then face the indignities and feelings of worthlessness that probably accompanies most immigrants, especially Jews.

At least Mr Reynolds seemed willing to try and sort things out with his family, trying to make things better. But then I wondered, maybe uncharitably, if there were other things going on at home that had got beyond his control, facing him with a loss of power. Things that might require him to acknowledge something in himself, like his own vulnerability. Perhaps this was his way of trying to regain his power and control. His way of dealing with problems by simply getting rid of them – like his son. Perhaps he was more like my father than I realised. Trying to solve the problem by disposing of it.

Maybe I was also being a little uncharitable towards my father, lacking the compassion I felt for most of my clients, by minimising the burden of his family history and suffering that must have infused and contaminated his childhood like a disease, so that dealing with unpleasant problems like me automatically triggered in him some kind of extreme response unlike most kids' fathers. It was a lot to try and fathom.

Chapter 2

The Confession

Dunedin, New Zealand June 1964
Aged 17

Meeting Mr Reynolds catapulted me back to 1964 so quickly that I had no time to prepare myself, repress the memories. I was on my way back to our house, having dared to make a dramatic escape to the beach to get away from my parents. I thought of the scene at the dining table. It was still very vivid. Like a painting that refused to fade years later even in the harshest light, where every single detail remained embossed, every sense reawakened, as intense as ever.

My father sat, as always, at the head of the table. My mother sat on his left with my older sister beside her and my twin brother sitting reluctantly on his right. It was his turn. I had the privileged position of being slightly out of sight of my father with my brother sitting between him and me. Our seating arrangement was a carefully thought-out strategy. I think it was the only thing we ever cooperated on together.

'Take your elbows off the table!' shouted my father to my brother and at the same time forced him to do so by jabbing them with his own elbow causing my brother to jolt the table and fall forward into his soup. The impact caused everyone else's soup to spill in perfect harmony on my mother's clean, white tablecloth. This, in turn, caused me to stifle a giggle. No one ever saw the funny side.

'Now look what you've done!' shouted my father as my brother slid from the table terrified, slipping past Dad in a trice.

'You come back here, you sooky,' he shouted, 'or you'll be eating your meals off the mantelpiece for a week!'

That always struck me as odd, since our mantelpiece was so

11

narrow you couldn't have placed a cup on it never mind a plate, but it was always shouted in anger so it was never the right time to question it.

The rest of us stared at our gaily coloured blobs of soup which were beginning to soak simultaneously into the thick, white damask tablecloth, straining the liquid from the vegetables as it did so.

'I wish you'd just leave him alone,' Mum said in a low, flat voice, no doubt trying to distract my father from the defiant bang of my brother's bedroom door.

Suddenly I felt an overwhelming urge to be sick and, as if to upstage my brother, scraped my chair back against the wall, which was strictly forbidden, in an attempt to get up, and was unsuccessful in preventing a long, low, colourful projectile of homemade vegetable vomit, still steaming, on to the ill-fated cloth. The situation was further aggravated as I was trapped between the table and the wall. This was the only factor that would allow my brother the compromise of swapping seats. Sometimes it was necessary to be able to make a quick getaway.

My sister screamed, then choked and coughed in a faint simulation of what had just taken place directly in front of her.

'God!' she shouted. 'I don't know why I bother coming back! Nothing ever changes!' and stormed through to the kitchen for a glass of water and, no doubt, some fresh air.

'What the hell's going on here?' my father shouted getting up from his chair. 'Look at that mess!'

It was difficult to ignore and I noted the shape spreading out from my 'deposit' looked rather like a map of Australia. The diced carrots defining little towns in the outback, the tomato seeds illuminated dwellings dominated by an Ayers Rock mountain of red lentils.

'I'm sorry... really, I am,' I said quickly when I realised they were looking in my direction. 'It just came over me,' I said as I moved my bowl to cover 'Australia'. There was an unfamiliar hush in the room.

My mother, who was always gentle, quiet and kind, stared at me and said, 'This is the second time you've been sick today, isn't it? I heard you in the toilet earlier.' My sister returned to hear this remark and there was another unfamiliar hush. I dare not look at my father who had thrown his spoon disconsolately into the remains of his soup. I wondered how it was that my mother had heard me being sick. I thought I had become skilled at mingling and muffling the retching with the exact synchronisation of the toilet chain and remembered feeling grateful at the geographic isolation of the toilet at the back of the house.

'You're not pregnant, are you?' asked my mother expressing some of the terror I was beginning to feel.

'I think I'm going to be sick again. Let me out! Let me out!' I lunged forward, pushing against the table with a force that surprised me and escaped through the kitchen to the sanctuary of the toilet.

I made loud and exaggerated vomiting noises in the hope that it might elicit some sympathy and for a time tried to ignore what was about to happen, as if my body were stoutly protecting me from a kind of impending annihilation.

They were waiting for me. Nobody asked how I was feeling as I stood close to the door of the sitting room. A shaft of late afternoon sun fell almost timidly on the carpet, then sort of twinkled conspiratorially. But the room was cold, chilled by suspicion. They were all standing together in a line, my sister's arms folded across her chest ready for action. I noticed for the first time that they were all more or less the same height which strengthened them against me as they stood united and impenetrable.

It was my sister and not my father who launched the first attack. She stepped out in front of my mother as if to protect her and shrieked, 'You can't possibly be pregnant! You're only 17!' and if that wasn't enough she added, 'I'm 21 and I'm still... what are all my friends going to say?' she sobbed and, receiving no comfort, slumped on to the small, tangerine sofa and continued abusing me in a tearful rage.

My parents stood before me, separate yet united for the first time I could remember. Father, short, lean, dark, his Jewish features highlighted by the slim shaft of sun, giving his face a scarily pointed look. His hands were clasped behind his back. For the first time in my life I got the feeling he was actually unsure and somehow this strengthened me. He was standing slightly behind my mother, who, uncharacteristically, dealt the first blow, and said simply and bluntly, 'You're pregnant, aren't you!' summing up so simply all the preceding weeks of denial and devastation. It was finally out. Paradoxically a weird sort of relief. Like at last squeezing a troublesome pimple that suddenly erupted all over the mirror.

I was terrified about what would happen next. I couldn't bring myself to speak.

My father looked at me with undisguised disgust. There was a pause like when you're waiting for a firecracker to go off. And off he went.

'I told you this would happen, didn't I?' he raged. 'Spending all hours with that bloody boyfriend! You've always been the same... done exactly as you wanted! Well now you'll just have to take the consequences, won't you!'

He paused in triumph. Wasn't this what he had predicted? Hadn't he said a thousand times, 'That girl will end up in trouble!'

I couldn't speak.

'There you go! Typically stubborn,' he shouted as if proving a point. In the past that sort of comment would only serve to strengthen my identity but now it gave him the licence to launch into a vicious attack, one I'd heard many times before, but whose impact was nevertheless powerful. His dark skin flushed with the energy expended in flailing his arms and punctuating the air

14

with his forefinger. He paused for a moment.

'Take her to the doctor first thing tomorrow!' he shouted at my mother. Then, without consulting her he added, 'We've got no choice. She can't stay here. She'll have to go away!'

Mum began to cry and turned towards my father for comfort. He didn't notice. If only he would put his arms around her, around all of us. Tears bit my eyes and I ran towards her so we might draw some comfort from each other. But my father darted in front of her and stood with his hands palms-outwards in front of him and said in a low, contemptuous voice, 'Leave her alone. You don't deserve her love!'

I turned and fled towards the door, colliding with my brother who, no doubt, felt safe enough to emerge from his room, now that it was no longer his turn.

Chapter 3

After the Confession

Dunedin, New Zealand June 1964

After the confession, my mother took to her bed for a whole week. This wasn't anything out of the ordinary, but it was a very sensitive time. And no amount of denial on my part could avoid confirming my father's correlation of 'what I'd done' with my mother's absence. Here was the irrefutable proof and he was not to be deterred from proving himself right on numerous occasions. I guess this was what attracted him to the legal profession, although the odds on winning in court were no doubt greatly reduced compared with home. Perhaps that was why he eventually quit the profession and relocated on the domestic front.

'Look what you've done to your mother!' he would say angrily as he waited for his dinner to be served, punctually, as always, at six o'clock as if I was solely responsible for all the bad things that happened in our family, including my mother's poor health. Meal times were always the worst, because this was my father's forum. After he'd listened to *The Archers*, a British radio programme about other odd families at war, boring each other to death in strange accents in the English countryside.

Meals took the form of a ritual. Everyone, apart from my mother when she was up and about, had to be seated at the table and the meal ready to be served, before he would deign to sit with us. The food would then be passed to him first, then us and my mother would often have whatever was left over. It was especially important to continue the ritual at the moment for two reasons: first, he would experience as little disruption as possible, particularly having his dinner ready at the same time each evening and thereby avoid drawing attention to my mother's absence. Second, to ensure that none of his authority was usurped.

He would then sit hunched over his meal, cooked solely to account for his taste. We had to endure boiled cabbage, boiled potatoes and boiled chicken, or meat. On a good day this would be fillet steak or maybe freshly caught oysters or crayfish given to him by a local fisherman in exchange for some past legal advice, I think. But usually the food tasted of old shoes. Whatever the meal, it was invariably plain, monotonous and boring. He would then work himself, and us, into a nervous frenzy. The meal would in turn become doubly indigestible, unless you had developed the skill of surreptitious gulping and occasional 'discarding', for which a discreet cat (my little furry friend 'Thomas') and the prized seat were a prerequisite.

I had developed an acquired indifference to the food and was able, when called upon, to display perfect table manners. This required a lot of concentration and a certain amount of luck. With my mother out of sight, the rules of the game were less clear-cut. Less predictable, especially since my efforts to replicate the dull food usually resulted in an incomparably bland imitation. I'd have forgotten to add salt or the vegetables were mysteriously limp.

Today, things were different. Father seemed to be preoccupied. I glanced at him without lifting my head, but he was eating in his usual mechanical way. I thought I caught a glimpse of sadness or despair. It was difficult to tell. Perhaps he felt he had failed in some way, or the plans he had made for me had been thrown into chaos, beyond his control. Or maybe he was wondering how to tell his own family, who would no doubt blame him. In any case, the meal passed without any comment, save for my brother asking, 'Who cooked this garbage?' in the full knowledge it was me.

I hadn't been to college all week because I had assumed the role of little housewife and was working hard to alleviate my guilt by doing lots of extra jobs for my mother, like cleaning out neglected cupboards.

'It's lovely, you helping me like this,' she said. 'I just haven't got the energy for it these days.'

I think she enjoyed me waiting on her, bringing her wee treats and cups of tea and doing endlessly boring, meaningless jobs around the house, like tidying and vacuuming and more tidying and vacuuming. It was no wonder she was taking so many pills for so many ailments. The tedium and pointlessness of repeating the same unremitting chores in an endless effort to ensure everything was done well before Dad got home, creating an illusion of cleanliness, order, peace and tranquillity. If only things could've stayed like that, nice and peaceful like my friend Sandra's house. Her mum probably did the same housework but it all seemed so different. When her dad came home, her parents would have a sherry in tiny glasses, so it must have been a powerful drink. Sandra's mum would have put on her lipstick. And she kept a nail file handy in case of an emergency, so she was always manicured and wanting to look perfect for him. It was so romantic. They even held hands when they went out walking together and for some reason it made me feel good, sort of proud. My parents never held hands or kissed or anything as if my mum's love always went unrewarded.

But I loved my mum in a special kind of way. I didn't even need to say anything, she just knew it. I don't know if Sandra felt that way about her mum or not. But a lot of things at home went unspoken. My mum didn't mention the pregnancy, except to express concern and anxiety by blaming herself for my 'going off the rails', as if she was responsible for what I'd done, as if I was somehow an extension of her, still part of her.

'What sort of mother am I to let this happen to you?' and she turned her face away to protect me from some display of emotion, feeling guilty having failed me. 'What will people think of me?'

19

It felt as if we were both trapped at the centre of the family, both feeling the same way and yet not quite understanding how it had come about. Both of us feeling guilty, full of shame and feeling responsible: me about what I had done and my mother about what she hadn't done. The difference between my mother's attitude to 'what I'd done' and my father's was that, at least my mum could express disappointment at what I'd done whereas I *became* the disappointment where my father was concerned. 'What I'd done' became me. It *was* me. I *was* the disappointment. I think that's the main reason I still feel so much shame. Will I ever be enough?

It was me who had failed and I carried that failure with me: to be a good daughter, please my father, appreciate how much harm I had caused my mother, be truly feminine, even though I never would be if that meant confining myself to domestic doormat duties like cooking and sewing and staying at home, forever compromising myself trying to be calm and quietly tranquil.

This stagnating, stifling lifestyle was everywhere. It never felt right, just being at home all day waiting on the family. I didn't know anyone whose mother worked outside the home. And we were expected to do the same. Most certainly not exploring, taking risks or having anything to do with boys!

I think education was important. I'm pretty sure Dad was pleased when I did well at school even though he never actually said, and would always focus on the B pass. I guess it's hard to find fault with an A pass. Maybe that's why I never felt pleased with my own efforts. I was doing the same thing to myself, expecting high standards, never questioning the value of individual achievement and the competition that surrounded us, pitting one child against another as if winning was all that mattered. Instead, I found myself fault-finding until I eventually realised it meant having to be perfect. So I tried to change the record, put a stop to it and become more of a slob. It took years.

Whatever I did back then felt as if it was never good enough – I was never good enough.

'If I try a bit harder and do a bit better, do my very perfect best, Dad might like me more,' I told Mum.

Dad's opinion was powerful, maybe more than my mother's. I don't know if that was because her love was unconditional whatever I did and his wasn't. It was as if his opinion alone counted for everything – who I was, what I was. Until I discovered that my best was not good enough either. Even when I had to sit my University Entrance exams, unlike most students who were accredited with a pass if they'd worked well during the year. It had a really low national pass rate of around 10 per cent.

'I passed!' I shouted to Dad waving the envelope triumphantly, '… Only three of us in the whole of Otago! And guess what? I came top!'

'Make sure you do better next year,' he muttered.

I think he had plans for us to go to university like he did. And his brother and sister who both excelled, his brother winning a scholarship in mathematics to Cambridge, for heaven's sake, and one of his sisters gaining a Master's in philosophy during the war which always struck me as rather bizarre timing, bearing in mind what was going on elsewhere. The only one who didn't study, Aunt Hypatia, was forced to stay at home to look after their parents, boil kosher chickens and knit horrid jerseys for the rest of her life.

I fetched my mum a hanky while she continued to berate herself for not being a good enough mother as if her illnesses were somehow avoidable.

'I should've been here when you needed me,' she cried, 'instead of being sick all the time.'

'Mum… It's not like that,' I protested.

'You're just trying to make me feel better,' she said, then added quietly, almost whispering, 'I'd hardly kissed your father before we got married…' She gazed at the huge copper beech tree outside her window and said wistfully, 'I had to almost beg him for children.'

I pretended not to hear what she said. I didn't know how to respond and I certainly didn't want to dwell on the image. It was too horrible and made me feel sick. And even more guilty. But how could I possibly make it up to her? I didn't know how I would ever put things right. Or what I needed to do, except go away and return without the baby. And try to pretend it didn't happen by never breathing a word about it. But maybe nothing I did or said would ever make it right ever again. Even if I stayed at home and learnt how to knit horrid jerseys forever. Everything was broken, undone.

I knew I couldn't rely on my brother to defend me. Or my sister. Not even in the smallest ways. My sister had aligned herself firmly with our parents and apart from screaming, 'How could you?' refused to talk to me. She wanted me out. Maybe that's what she'd always wanted. Me and my twin brother. After all she'd recited often enough how, at aged five, she'd been sent away to stay with an aunt, returned home some time later to find 'two hideous pink things in the front room!'

Poor girl. It was like she never recovered from the shock. Never forgiven us for being born and never forgiven our parents for sending her away. Banishing her like that! Now it was my turn.

Fortunately, I suspected Mum couldn't bring herself to discuss the pregnancy, or worse, the birth which was a great relief. Or the baby. No one ever mentioned the word 'baby'. That was a taboo word, even to myself. I suppose it was my mother's way of helping me pretend there wasn't a baby. Not an actual baby. A real living, growing baby that was connected to us all. Instead, how much easier it was to see it all as a transgression, one that meant I would be exiled for a while and return as if nothing had happened. Excuses would be made because everyone had to be protected from me, the truth about me. What I'd done. And as for the baby, well… it didn't exist.

Chapter 4

The Family Scapegoat

Brixton, London 1981
I am still 34

This was the first time I had seen the Reynolds family all together. They were offered an appointment after Mr Reynolds had stormed into the office late on Friday afternoon the previous week demanding I take his son into care. They all looked a bit grumpy when I went to greet them in the reception area as if no one wanted to be there. The parents were slumped opposite each other with Mrs Reynolds leaning slightly towards her son as if to protect him. Her face was devoid of any expression or animation; the daughter looked indifferent as if she, too, had been dragged reluctantly along to the meeting. No one made any attempt to hold eye contact with me. I smiled benignly and led the way to the interview room, the only one available. I didn't like working in it as it was cramped with barely enough space to house five armless low chairs placed in an erratic circle like an old people's home or an addiction meeting, plus a random, old lacerated leatherette armchair. The windows didn't open so cigarette smoke hung in the air like a dank, sulphurous cloud. And you could often hear what was being said from outside this particular room especially if people raised their voices. I anticipated things would thaw a little when we did the introductions. Wrong. The parents had hardly sat down before they started arguing.

'I'm sick to death of him!' shouted Mr Reynolds already red-faced to his wife as if he was still in his sitting room. 'Either he goes or I go!'

'Yeah, well, no loss there then,' she shouted back impressively quickly.

Eleven-year-old Matthew eyed me dolefully as he bounced

up and down in the shabby old armchair, grinning awkwardly at me between his parents, while they carried on rowing about him in a blazing attempt to prove that each of them was right. Their fourteen-year-old daughter Sharon had moved her chair slightly out of the circle, as much as the space would allow and sat with her arms folded firmly across her chest staring in obdurate fashion at the blackened Brixton terraces beyond them wearing what looked like a 'here-we-bloody-go-again' look on her face. Both children in familiar ringside seats, a reluctant audience.

This was not a good beginning. Far from the tutoring and textbook guidelines I had diligently and earnestly absorbed and practised in our training group. And I had barely introduced myself never mind the details of how we might work together including working out a 'contract', as it was known, that would act as a guide in our sessions.

'Why don't you just ask *me* what the problem is instead of asking them what's going on and what they'd like to be different?' demanded Mr Reynolds. 'I've already told you!' he said suddenly turning in my direction. I swung my head sharply towards him in response and managed to whack myself in the face with one of my long, heavy, solid silver earrings. No one noticed me nursing my face as no one was looking, except perhaps Mr Reynolds.

'Well, I'll tell you again, shall I?' he boomed without giving me a chance to respond and repeated what he told me about Matthew's impossible behaviour.

'Never begin by asking a family what the problem is,' boomed my textbook. I could see why. It was like opening the floodgates of hell, a question to be avoided unless you wanted a catalogue of accusations accompanied by screaming, shouting and scarlet faces as each relived their own particular grievances. A bit like what was going on in front of me right now.

After the parents had finished yelling at each other they just stared deliberately and blankly at the walls opposite, like a conductor might do, signalling the end of the music to the orchestra. It was as if I became the focus of their anger. Sharon's arms still folded firmly across her chest, Matthew still bouncing nervously in the armchair until Mr Reynolds' second sudden outburst.

'I don't know about all this family therapy stuff,' he shouted, glaring at his son. 'The only thing I want to be different is for him to go to school! We've tried doing everything until we're blue in the bloody face! Walking him to the school gates, waiting outside in case he reappears, threatening him with God knows what, depriving him of his pocket money, bribing him, punishing him – even trying to be nice to him for Christ's sake! Short of dragging the little bugger by the hair,' shouted his father red-faced and furious, 'what else can we bloody do?'

The little bugger grinned uncertainly.

I could feel myself recoiling from his anger and hoped the family hadn't noticed. I suddenly felt vulnerable, afraid he might do something to me, drag me by the hair like I suddenly remembered seeing a girlfriend's father do to her years ago in a fit of rage, dragging her from her bed while she screamed out in pain and I stood helplessly by. Or he might attack me as if I were part of his family, responsible for escalating this drama, trying to dismantle him somehow, threatening his position. But what was most scary was that I actually felt pulled into their conflict as if by some magnetic force, as if they were my own family.

'Perhaps,' I said as calmly as I could, trying to get their attention and keep my voice as even as possible, 'perhaps Matthew thinks he's doing you a favour by bringing you all here.'

Matthew stopped his bouncing. It was then that I thought I noticed a bruise on his face and hoped I was mistaken. He frowned at me clutching the arms of the chair with whitened knuckles and looked shocked by what I'd said.

'It sounds to me as if he's actually worked very hard at getting you all here… together,' I ventured, 'to try and sort things out. As a family.'

Their mouths dropped open as they all stared hard at me frowning. And even Sharon was jolted into holding brief eye contact as they stood up and, without a word, followed Mr Reynolds out.

In those days I would probably have laughed off this fiasco defensively, geed it up a bit, dined out on it. Shared it with colleagues in our local pub. The five-minute family therapy session! But something stopped me. The humour I might have seen looking back at this scenario evaporated. Nudging me just beneath the surface was a deep discomfort I couldn't identify, a faded memory like pale ink, a sense of something lost.

Chapter 5

The Reynolds, the Riots and the Winds of Change

Brixton Social Services, London 1981

My mate Maggie and I had just sat down to eat lunch in a cafe in Brixton tube station, about to enjoy that rare privilege of actually having lunch and a natter, when two cops came bursting in, ordering us out because of a suspected bomb threat.

'But we haven't had our lunch yet,' I protested pointing pathetically at our plates of soggy sandwiches.

'Out!' they shouted in unison, 'Out!' as we slowly and reluctantly gathered up our bags and coats and sandwiches and left, with them trying their best to frogmarch us as seemingly decently as they could towards the exit. It was a tense time but somehow we didn't feel vulnerable. I guess that's because we saw ourselves as part of the community.

I wasn't able to share my anxiety about the Reynolds family with Maggie, tell her that although I empathised with them, especially with Mrs Reynolds being married to such a bloody bully, I also found them hard to engage with; they made me feel awkward, inadequate, but mostly how intimidated I felt by Mr Reynolds. My confidence seemed to evaporate around him, ebb away from me... and there was something about them, the way they related to each other... I ended up feeling vulnerable, almost raw, for heaven's sake. Maybe my feelings about them were more to do with me, how I personally perceived them; I was left with the feeling I had just made things worse, as if I was getting in the way. I'd have to wait till Friday night to talk to Maggie although we wouldn't be meeting at The George. It had been petrol-bombed.

'Perhaps delaying talking about it suits me,' I thought, my

way of trying to escape having to face the prospect of what might happen next, what did happen next. So instead of taking responsibility and behaving like a grown-up by discussing it properly with Mike my supervisor, or Maggie, I kind of froze inwardly and managed to avoid dealing with it altogether.

Later I was waiting for my weekly session with Mike when I was jolted back again to my first session with the Reynolds. I had sat for a while, rather stunned and humiliated in the wake of their explosive walkout, wondering how you actually encourage parents to love their children, listen to them, value them... and each other... and although we were supposed to be experts in what was regarded as acceptable parenting, how could you do this satisfactorily with your own emotional baggage weighing you down?

I became aware that the same smouldering, inexplicable tension in the Reynolds family had been mirrored outside a few days earlier. A community torn apart. The Brixton riots, a tsunami of fury that swept through the neighbourhood and taken hold, with mainly black youths, fed up with the heavy policing of their community, sparking riots that resulted in injuries to both police and locals – burning cars and buildings, including our local pubs The Windsor Castle in Leeson Road and The George in Railton Road. Both were petrol-bombed and completely destroyed. I suppose we could easily have been at either one of them as it was Friday night, pub night. And the first petrol bombs had been thrown at 6.30. Our drinking time exactly. But somehow we didn't turn up. And curiously, we didn't feel vulnerable. We were all on the same side, bar the cops, weren't we?

What wasn't acknowledged at this stage was a deep desire for change. But, like the Reynolds family, I don't think that could be easily articulated in the midst of all the turmoil – not by the kids, families or the community... people wanting things to be better, easier, to feel valued, worthwhile. To have a voice, autonomy. And retain their own identity.

It felt like that same desire for change was smouldering right here, with the Reynolds family. Maybe the riots symbolised exactly what Matthew was unconsciously doing, trying to draw attention to problems that needed outside help.

'If things go well for him and the family therapy is effective,' I told Maggie enthusiastically when we were able to talk later, 'hopefully he won't continue to be rejected or banished by his family. They'll be able to face their own demons, deal adequately with their own problems. Maybe they'll even recognise that Matthew's behaviour was simply a role he was playing at the time and that that role isn't who he really is! He cares about them!'

'Well... sounds a bit optimistic, Susie. He seems to have accepted the scapegoat role,' said Maggie, 'he's certainly giving it his best shot!'

'It's just what everyone's dumped on him, projected all the family ills on to him,' I heard myself say with feeling. 'Well, his father certainly has,' I added.

'Mmmn... still, perhaps it's hoping for a bit much, the family being able to see Matthew causing all this chaos to get help for them,' said Maggie doubtfully.

'Well, if the therapy doesn't work well, and the family refuses to see his behaviour as a cry for help on their behalf, he'll cop the lot. And all the responsibility for the family's problems will be projected on to him,' I said, hearing my mournful tone.

And what about that bruise? Did I imagine it... shall I say something to Maggie, to Mike? It was quite small...

'I heard the father ranting in the office earlier... you poor thing. How are you managing him?'

'Not very well. He's such a bully! Reminds me of my father,' I said. 'Perhaps I don't feel very optimistic. Maybe he'll continue blaming Matthew, banish him to care, discard him, whether or not we think it would benefit him and his family...'

It mirrored what was happening in Brixton. Not to mention

what happened in my own family! Some people were attributing all society's ills on to its 'disaffected black youths' holding them responsible for virtually everything: the poverty, high unemployment, poor housing. When I think of Matthew it felt like a parallel process of powerlessness. In his family and in mine.

It was amazing making these links, bringing alive the social anthropology from my university days where theories were translated so vividly into practice – the way beliefs and values of particular groups were being played out in real life – seeing how one group threatened, or felt threatened by, another. Like my father, I thought, gripped, like so many other parents in the sixties, in the belief that marriage and the family was sacred, to be preserved, whatever the choices, whatever the cost. Why hadn't I seen it this clearly before?

It made me wonder if Mr Reynolds, like Dad, felt forced to make a choice, one in which he felt justified in trying to get rid of his kid, dump him in care, using duress to force a particular outcome... Ostensibly, of course, for the greater good of the Reynolds family (I still think he's a bastard!).

'OK,' said Mike smiling. 'So what happened in the first session with the Reynolds?' He rubbed his hands together as if he were striking a deal, then leaned back in his swivel chair, pushing his glasses up his nose and peered intently at me, eyebrows raised expectantly. He had fair, shoulder-length curly hair that framed his face and brown eyes, sort of velvety. Quite cute, really. He was full of enthusiasm, really keen on this way of working with families.

'Most things can be mended,' he had said once. 'Even families.'

You'd have needed superglue to mend mine, I thought.

But his attitude was infectious. He firmly believed Family Therapy was effective in enabling family members to be heard, to have a voice, to work together as a team and empower them to make their own decisions.

'Reconnecting them,' as he put it.

I was trying to do the same thing with the Reynolds. I realised my own personal experience provided a valuable apprenticeship, and although the games were different, the rules were the same: the power of the parents cannot be usurped. Unless, of course, you are a social worker.

Chapter 6

Ponderings on the Profession

Brixton, London 1981

What was it, I wondered as I sat waiting for Mike, that drove me to become a social worker in the first place? Shame, perhaps. Oh, not one's own shame, of course. This was kept at bay by feeling someone else's shame or grief or sense of injustice – immersing oneself in theirs thereby unconsciously avoiding one's own even in the face of those clients whose problems frequently and uncomfortably mirrored one's own (how on earth does that happen!).

I had become quite an expert on the subject. Often it was the shame, humiliation and powerlessness that many women felt, like those I saw experiencing domestic violence, separation, divorce, family breakdown, forced adoption. One could say it was my business – I'd made a career out of it. After all I had the necessary breeding. My parents, united on very little else, would have resolutely declared my personal experience in morally – never mind physically – reprobate behaviour equipped me better than most to spot it in others.

As a social worker I could immerse myself in other people's lives, gleaning vicarious and sometimes voyeuristic glimpses which sustained my interest and fed some insatiable need in me. Why else pursue such a peculiar profession? It was, after all, naïve to hope that I had any real power to make positive changes, alleviate distress bar the most superficial, measurably improve the quality of people's lives, protect children adequately or return them to their parents.

Looking back, maybe becoming a social worker was a form of self-styled reparation, born of despair, unworthiness and powerlessness. I sometimes wondered how you could be effective as a social worker if you, too, are coming from the same place of powerlessness as your clients. Especially if your own traumas remained unresolved.

But at the bottom of it all, there was always a deep desire to help others, to try and put things right. Perhaps it was a secret way of seeking forgiveness. On the other hand, maybe something more sinister lies beneath. And our motives, my motives, are more mixed, ambivalent and less clear-cut. That daunting thought only occurred to me after talking to Rachel, a friend who was a psychotherapist.

She had worked with social workers, and had made some amazing, or should I say, disturbing, observations.

'There are often clear links between the social worker's conscious desire to help vulnerable children and their own unconscious past childhood traumas,' she told me. 'It's often the cumulative effect of having to face violence and abuse on a daily basis that will resonate with old situations that are filled with emotions such as fear, dread and helplessness,' she said. 'They're re-enacting this over and over through their clients until they can't take it anymore and become stressed, burn out or leave.'

Argh, who knows what the hell drove me to become a social worker!

'So... any thoughts about the function of Matthew's behaviour?' asked Mike, jolting me back to our session. 'Staying home from school, perhaps being school phobic?'

The phone on his desk rang again and he cast his eyes upwards.

I think I'll hold back on the big family walkout at this stage, I thought, shifting uneasily in my chair at the thought of having to tell him what had happened in my very first session with the Reynolds. Don't want to distract him from his train of thought. Mind you, this is exactly what the family did, wasn't it? Walked out to avoid any challenging discussions. Mmmn, that particular pattern of escapist behaviour was sounding familiar. Uncomfortably familiar.

What would have been different for everyone in my family, I wondered, if I hadn't been seen as the problem, hadn't become the scapegoat for all the family's ills? If, instead, my father hadn't assumed that everything would be OK again, that some sort of harmony would be restored once he had sent me away. If my parents had been able to pick up the signs of my distress, seen my behaviour as a way of trying to communicate something to them that could, and did, affect everyone. I laughed to myself imagining the absurdity of the scene: my father sitting round the table, showing concern, anxious to resolve things, make things better. Being accountable – I don't think so! Maybe that's Mr Reynolds' problem too; he wouldn't make himself that vulnerable by exposing his true feelings either. It was the total opposite to his way of behaving. Like Dad, he needed to be in charge – or at least believe he was.

All this hanging around waiting for Mike, feeling saturated in the subject of families, soggy, like a biscuit dunked too long in a cup of tea. Maybe the discomfort was around being forced to think of my own family. Although there were shades of similarity between them and the Reynolds, there was one profound, potentially life-changing difference. Something that was available to them but not to me or my family. Aside from the Reynolds being offered help to fix what was broken, it was in the context of a system where the child is not regarded by the social worker as **the** problem! Maybe it was more about feeling sorrow than soggy, realising that this way of seeing things, responding to things, could have made a radical difference to my life, my family's and maybe my daughter's.

'At least if this way of working is successful, he won't be made to feel like the black sheep, labelled for life as the problem,' I thought, not like me.

I knew Mike would want to explore what was behind the

unacceptable behaviour... What did Matthew's behaviour signify? What did mine signify? What did those young black guys' behaviour signify?

It made me think of the deep unrest in Brixton, now linked in my mind to the Reynolds family who somehow represented a microcosm of what was going on there: where the black community was regarded by some as the source of all the problems, where they were being scapegoated, like young Matthew, and all the difficulties in the community were attributed to them, just like other visibly different groups before them – and no doubt after – single parents, teenage pregnancies, juvenile crime, Jews, Indians, West Indians... all vilified in this way throughout history.

And, for me, closer to home, the determination of some folk to dictate to others how they should live their lives, based on beliefs and prejudices, including stamping out 'bad moral attitudes', a phrase for me that has echoed down the ages – all the way from those devout Scottish Presbyterian ministers, early settlers in New Zealand clutching in their hearts and fists a Utopian view of society, right through to exactly the same comment made by a British Conservative MP just after the riots.

I thought of my father's father imposing his communist views on him; my father imposing his views on me, regardless of mine. I thought of my now 17-year-old daughter's views and wondered if she ever thought what mine might be – or had been, about her adoption. To be forced to give your daughter away to strangers because you weren't married. How could she ever reconcile what happened to her with what was regarded as best for her? Best for me?

Everyone had a view about the riots especially those of us directly affected by them, living or working in Brixton at the time.

'Part of the problem is that we can get too focused on the

symptoms,' said my (second) husband Martin in one of our many conversations with friends and workmates about the riots, 'instead of looking at the causes... whether it's to do with families we're working with or communities. We should be asking what lies behind their riotous behaviour, what did it signify, symbolise? But also what had caused such extreme behaviour?'

'Maybe every family and every society need its scapegoats,' I said hoping they wouldn't notice the tension in my voice. 'Ways we project things on to others so we don't have to face those things we're all responsible for... don't have to acknowledge and respect different ways of doing things, or bear the blame for others,' I said. 'Actually, I've been reading up about scapegoating. It goes back to biblical days. According to the Old Testament, on the Day of Atonement, a priest would confess all the sins of the Israelites over the head of a goat then drive it into the wilderness symbolically bearing their sins away. So the poor old goat cops the lot and is subsequently banished. Sound familiar?' I said, giving Martin a meaningful look.

The scapegoat still has its place. So did the 'fallen women' of years gone by – including 'fast girls' like me – accused of causing moral decline (never mind the men!) and at this moment it is the turn of disaffected black youth in Brixton, held up as being responsible for the high crime rate there. But heavy-handedness and ignorance never really work – in families or in communities. Especially where folk feel discriminated against. And powerless. It can be a recipe for violence. Or lifelong sadness and grief and a sense of loss.

'Sorry about that,' said Mike, 'bit of an emergency. Anyway, back to the sessions with the Reynolds family. Where were we... oh, yes, any thoughts about the function of Matthew's behaviour – staying home from school, perhaps being school phobic? It's often that the child who presents a problem expresses something that can't be faced in the family.'

Or a secret, I thought. Sometimes it was a bit chilling dealing with other people's families especially when something triggered a discordant poke at your own past. Often it was like being faced with a curious jigsaw puzzle that required a particular perspective trying to work out how all the pieces fitted together into a cohesive whole, the bigger picture, one that didn't only focus on the piece that no longer appeared to fit.

That night a dream transported me home to New Zealand. I was sitting with my family in a small marae, a Maori meeting house, somewhere in the South Island. My whole family was there, all together for the first time ever, both sets of grandparents, the Scottish and the Jewish all dressed up in traditional gear. Kippahs, kilts and sporrans... They looked wonderful and bright, full of colour and energy and vigour. The scene was saturated with a sense of profound meaning that was somehow humbling. I thought how fine and proud they all looked. It made me want to cry – for them and for me. A reminder of what had been lost... and taken. I thought I could hear a baby crying but I couldn't work out where the sound was coming from.

My father David and his brother Harold looked quite cute in their kippahs... particularly my father. It suited him, as if he belonged to it. And their sisters Hypatia and Beryl wearing long, dark skirts and cream blouses. And my Scottish grandfather John MacKinnon whom I never met, wearing his tartan kilt, bagpipes over his shoulder, standing tall and proud. My paternal grandmother, Esther, usually the epitome of misery habitually sitting immobilised in her chair by the fireplace was actually smiling, even laughing with her daughters, looking quite beautiful with her glowing, dark complexion and her grey, curly hair. What **was** she wearing? Then I spotted my mother Catherine and her two sisters Marion and Mary wearing long tartan skirts and white blouses, giggling while they danced a sort of jig together around their mother, my grandmother also called Catherine whose long grey hair was not restrained in its customary tight bun but braided with pretty pink flowers. All us kids sat dotted around the circle gazing at everyone.

No one spoke. Then I noticed a Maori elder sitting among us. When I looked more closely I saw it was Mike. He was wearing a feather cloak and a black bandana woven in reds and yellows.

'Differences between us are only costumes,' he pronounced in a gentle, low voice. 'The stories that are woven into them can also cause separation and conflict. It is these very differences, by which you believe you identify who you are, that mean your view of the world cannot include both sun and moon... Enjoy and celebrate the differences... rich cultures coming together all contribute different things to each other,' he said gravely.

'Stop identifying with your costumes and find out who you truly are. Always remember, the rose and the daffodil are different but arise from the same earth,' he added in a slow, measured way, staring intently at each member of the family in turn – including all the kids, as if he could read into our very souls. We all sat in silence feeling the privilege of his presence.

'All living things possess whakapapa – it is our heritage from the gods to the present time,' he said in a low voice. 'We all carry with us a deep connection to the land and to our ancestral roots – our history, our beloved whakapapa...' he intoned.

'As the wisdom of an ancient proverb goes, "When the petal falls from the flower, it is separate",' he said gravely, '"but does it stop being flower?"'

Chapter 7

The Power of the Parent

Dunedin, New Zealand June 1964
Aged 17

After the 'confession' had been dragged out of me my father was apoplectic with rage and no doubt disappointment, but mainly rage. But what could he do to me? What else could he take away from me? He had forbidden me to see my boyfriend as if John was totally responsible for what had happened and began treating me as if I were a stranger, ordering me around even more forcefully than usual but with an edge of indifference as if he didn't care about what was happening. He was completely closed to me, as opposed to almost completely, and just wanted 'it' sorted out and dealt with. He had simply decreed that I was not to see John and, furthermore, my brother was to inform him should any evidence to the contrary become apparent. All contact was to cease. There was to be no argument about it. That was that.

Dad had threatened to see his parents to 'try to sort this mess out,' and I wondered in what way they could possibly help. John was the oldest of eight children, a large Catholic family, and I was always pleased Dad never commented on that fact because some people seemed to think that Catholics were different to everyone else. They kind of were because they had their own schools and only Catholics could go to them. And lots more children than anyone else. And all sorts of rules and beliefs like having to go to church every Sunday, otherwise it was a sin. But that didn't seem to matter because they could just go and confess to the priest they hadn't gone to church plus all the other bad things they'd done. And then everything would be all right. If only... But I think if I'd had a priest, I wouldn't have confessed anything to him, even though there was no one else to talk to or ask for any sort of help. Instant forgiveness didn't feel quite real, quite right. Or very helpful.

I was glad it was Wednesday as Dad always went out sharp at 6.30 to the private radio station he ran in his spare time. 'Radio 4XD, Dunedin… the oldest private radio station in the southern hemisphere,' he repeatedly announced when the station came on the air at 7pm exactly, before playing some dreary music that probably no one ever listened to, including us. I always enjoyed switching him off.

This was the one night of the week John and I could always guarantee to be together and I couldn't bear the thought of not seeing him. The problem was how to convince my mother and brother that this routine should continue unabated. It wouldn't be too difficult to persuade my mother of the important need to see him 'just for an hour or so', using the threat of impending banishment as an emotional prop. But it would have to be a secret shared three ways and convincing my brother presented more of a problem.

Although we were twins, any similarities stopped there: for him, there'd be no end of bribes and brownie points to score off me, but he was quite a different matter. I would not consider myself bad by comparison, only more curious. This characteristic naturally required more in the way of activities outside the home which were usually unacceptable, bad or forbidden. However, a lot of the rules were unwritten, unspoken. One could therefore plead ignorance, except perhaps in extreme cases, like this.

I hadn't seen John since the day my parents found out. During that time we'd only exchanged a few, furtive phone calls. Prior to this, we were constant companions and had been for one year, seven months and five days. We'd met on a train going to a pop festival in Brighton, just outside Dunedin. Curiously enough, this meeting confirmed, a week or so later, that I needed glasses. John turned out to be the same handsome Christian Brothers' schoolboy we used to lust after, hanging out of our sixth form upstairs window at Otago Girls' High School where such unseemly behaviour was quite at variance with the rules. Every aspect of behaviour was carefully anticipated, mirrored and monitored: navy serge gym frocks were to hang discreetly three inches below the knee, the back of one's hair could not touch the white collars of our blouses and shiny, patent leather shoes were strictly forbidden, based on the unreliable but interesting rumour that boys might see your knickers reflected in them. The reason this rule never made a lot of sense is that we were forced to do our gym in those same navy-blue knickers, often outside in full view of the roving eye of any passing male who happened to walk by the rather low perimeter hedge.

I was not averse to John attempting, within reason of course, to inspect these knickers from time to time and this often took place in a secluded churchyard during the lunch hours. This required some planning as leaving school during lunchtime was strictly forbidden. Unless you had a note signed by a parent. We'd also meet every day and most evenings when Dad was out and walk hand in hand along the beach, later nestling in our favourite hollow in the sand dunes. He was very loving and passionate and I often wondered where he learnt it all. Perhaps he made it up. If so, his imagination was even more vivid than mine.

I became obsessed with the idea of seeing him and switched off the radio blaring *Do Wa Diddy Diddy* to concentrate. He was the only person I could share my real feelings with, although my girlfriends had suffered along with me. But he was special and I loved him. I wondered if he had told his parents.

It occurred to me that the oldest bribe in the world was money. My brother was saving for something or other and would surely be amenable to a bit extra. The amount was difficult to determine, but perhaps he'd be open to negotiation.

I switched the radio back on, turned down the volume and set about preparing dinner. I felt cheerful for the first time in days, regenerated. I made Dad his favourite steamed date pudding, then lit the fire for him.

'I'll set the table,' I called out almost cheerily to my brother, hoping my magnanimous gesture would lay the groundwork for later bartering. I had picked some flowers and set them in a crystal vase on the table, then noticed I was overdoing it and took them through to my mother.

'Dad's late tonight,' I said as I placed the vase on her bedside table.

Dad was never late. Dad was always early, honking the car horn if you kept him waiting for a single minute which only served to increase his waiting time as you then flew nervously round the house grabbing whatever you needed. That's if the honking didn't make you forget what you were looking for so you took even longer.

'Don't say anything to him, will you,' said my mother quietly from her bed. 'Just let him come in the door.'

My father came in, grunted and sat down with the newspaper. After a few minutes, he got up and came out into the kitchen while I was drying up some dishes.

'Yes?' I said, puzzled. My father never came into the kitchen.

'That doctor you saw, MacAlpine,' he said. 'I spoke to him today.'

I froze. Dad had never really spoken to me before, not like this anyway.

'He's lined up somewhere for you to go.'

I stared at him, frozen with fear.

'There's some bloke up north, a friend of his. He and his wife have got some domestic problems. Apparently they could use a girl like you.'

With that he left the kitchen and returned to the sitting room to read his paper. I stood where I was, still clutching the tea towel. I don't know how long I stood there. Minutes may have passed. I became aware of the banging inside my chest. Then tears of terror. I ran into the sitting room and fell on to my knees at his feet.

'Please, please don't send me away,' I begged, weeping. I flung my arms around his knees and hugged and squeezed them. I don't remember ever touching him before. His knees felt hard and bony and my tears left traces on the trousers of his suit. I hoped he wouldn't notice them.

'Please let me stay! I'll look after you and Mum!' I cried. 'I'll stay inside so no one will see me. Please, Dad, please!'

He got up awkwardly from his chair nudging me to one side with his knee and stood by the fireplace with his back to me, looking out the window.

'You'll have to go away. I have no choice. Your mother's not strong enough and I have to take care of her. She's upset enough already. If you stay, it'll kill her!'

I could not get up off the floor. I looked at him with sudden loathing. He was abandoning me, throwing me out like unwanted rubbish. As quickly as he could. I was an embarrassment to him.

The familiar music of *The Archers* infiltrated the room. Dad's favourite programme, signalling the customary silence. He continued to stare out the window, shoulders hunched, his hands habitually jangling the change in his pockets. He was clearly planning ways in which they could all carry on as usual, with as little disruption as possible, acknowledging my plight as a minor hiccough. An inconvenience. He was tossing me to the wind.

I picked myself up off the floor and calmly announced on my way out, 'You can get your own dinner.'

Chapter 8

No Way Out

Dunedin, New Zealand June 1964

I walked out of the house in a daze. Obedience to my father had become vital at the moment, in order to be seen to perpetuate dependence on him. He liked that. Under normal circumstances, my father would not have permitted such an easy escape. But I knew he wouldn't give chase this time. Such an act would lack dignity. And what would it have accomplished, what else could he do to me I wondered as I headed swiftly towards the beach? Punishments had taken various forms over the years, but this one was unique. It was not like 'a good hiding' – a threat as regular as breakfast. His turn of phrase to merit the enormity of the crime committed, which could be the slightest misdemeanour. It was not like being sent to your room until 'big daddy' finally gave the all-clear, or being deprived of your pocket money which barely purchased a packet of fags. This was a death knell. And there was no escape.

I found myself breaking into a run, unable to contain my terror of what he had said and must have run the quarter mile or so without stopping for breath. I found our secluded hollow in the dunes and threw myself into it, exhausted. After a while I became aware of the sound of the surf crashing and fizzing on the shoreline and sat up, wriggling to remould the sand firmly around me.

I stared for what seemed like hours at the sea, its rough, white surf smashing on to the rocks below, its anger dissolving as it reached the shoreline. I nestled instinctively into the tussock grass where clumps clothed the dunes and defined the worn tracks of picnickers and lovers.

It was still warm and there was no wind. Summer had long

gone and there was no one was on the beach now, not even the surfers who seem to have retired after an interminable season. I was glad. A solitary gull flew overhead and I watched its easy, effortless drift down to the rocks below. My gaze took in the familiar lace line of bubbling surf, curving scallops that stretched the half mile or so from St Kilda to St Clair. I loved those names, they reminded me of part of my family history, blurred in the Scottish past. The other part, the Jewish part, felt scary, dark and secretive by comparison and not a lot to do with us. Except for the biscuit-y Jewish bread 'matzos' which Dad kept sort of secretly in the hot water cupboard. I'm not sure if that was because it was a warm place or a hiding place. But they were yummy spread thick with butter and Vegemite.

Just below the far end of the promenade, I could almost make out the milk bar. But I wasn't hungry. And I hadn't brought any money with me. And it was deserted anyway.

We loved this beach as if it were our own, a part of us. There were lots of other beautiful beaches around Dunedin, beyond the harbour, so remote you could gallop a horse down the untrammelled sand and shout and scream at the top of your voice and no one would hear you. I knew a girl who did that once, a quiet, shy girl whom hardly anyone knew. She was at Teachers' college with us. I heard later that she'd been admitted to Cherry Farm, our local mental institution whose very name suggests insanity. So screaming down sand hills after that didn't seem so safe. But I wished I could behave as she did and rip down these hills without inhibition, purging my soul in a long, piercing, primitive scream that would cleanse the very essence of my hateful being and change me back into a dutiful and desirable daughter, the virgin queen I longed to be.

I didn't want to return home. I didn't know what to expect. And the beach felt safe, special. It had always been our playground, our second home. It had an anarchic quality about it – anything went. It was everything to us as kids – rousing, exciting, liberating – and later, romantic. It gave us a kind of silent permission to do as we pleased.

I remember the day my friend Sandra and I wagged Bible Class when we were aged about 10, and flung our hats over the back of the stables which were right by the beach. We soon discovered that 'stables' was a euphemism for knacker's yard and we were full of horror after discovering a dead horse hanging upside down from huge chains, its innards hanging out and covered in flies. After that, we always bought them sugar lumps out of our pocket money. We felt sorry for those poor, magnificent creatures hanging around the barbed wire enclosure waiting for their lives to end, waiting to be slaughtered. Now I felt the same.

Nobody at the stables seemed to mind us taking the horses out for a canter. We didn't know if they just didn't care, preferred to sit around smoking and drinking beer or had some amazing faith that all would be well. They couldn't have observed us very closely, clinging on precariously, tilted almost side-saddle, in excited terror as the horses shot off under us along the beach to our tentative command with us pulling hopelessly on the reins, dizzy with danger and delight at our own power. And the rush of freedom that sang in my veins! Amazed that these great beasts were actually under our control!

Afterwards we made a poor job of drying out our clothes. They'd become soaked after splashing our way on the horses along the water's edge. That was the day we came across a man playing with himself in the sand dunes. I had never seen a grown man's willie before and was horrified. We were glued to the ground in front of him, clutching each other for protection, unable to move. It was as if he had some power over us until we were able to break the spell and flee for our lives. Later we had christened him with a special code name known only to us and swore we'd never, ever reveal our secret to anyone. Especially our parents. That way, nothing would change and we could keep going to the beach. The 'secret' bound us even closer together and we sort of hoped we might chance upon him again, but from a safer distance.

The beach was also a sanctuary; I felt safe here, protected at this very moment when I needed it. I nestled instinctively into the tussock grass that curtained my hollow of sand. I remember hiding here once before, like a small, crazed criminal when I was aged about eight or nine. I had cowered in the dunes until the last, long shadows disappeared with the sinking sun. I had stolen a pound note from home to buy my favourite, Caramello chocolate. Lots of it for Sandra and me! But the old bat at the news agents told my mother who simply said, 'Wait till your father gets home!' She knew how to use him against me, though thankfully didn't do it very often. Then I would hide under my bed, listening out for his car to turn into the driveway. The worst bit was when he came storming into my bedroom shouting my name and would pull me out from under it. But at least you knew it would soon be over. Not like now.

The ritual that followed always took the same form. Dad would shout and bellow and all protestations of innocence would invariably be overlooked. The ensuing crescendo would then justify the only course of action open to him. He would pluck the thin, leather buckled belt from its hook behind the sitting room door and drag you screaming and shouting through the kitchen to the bathroom. I suspect that the bathroom meant that in spite of its echoes, always a personal challenge, it was out of sight of my mother. This was a father's work – a duty I came to suspect he rather enjoyed.

Suddenly the beach began to feel menacing and hostile. A wind had whipped up from nowhere and the surf quickly became rough and frothy white. Dark silver clouds made an appearance. I got up and watched the sand being flung about in the short bursts of wind. The clumps of tussock grass that dotted the dunes were waving about in unison. I felt cold and stood up, turned and faced the sea. It was choppy, loud and unfriendly. I focused on the darkening water, drew a deep breath and thundered down the sand hill towards it, emitting a piercing, primitive scream as I went, hoping the raging water would swallow me up. I'd go mad like the girl from college, or else a great big hole would trip me up and I would disappear forever.

I lay face-down on the wet sand by the water's edge panting for breath. I wanted to stay like that, to die or be rescued. And then I felt ashamed. Not of myself but of my father. I got up, trembled a little, held back my tears which formed a fist in my throat and headed for home. I found myself welcoming the thickening mist that blurred my vision. I didn't want to find my way back but knew I had no choice. There was no way out. I walked slowly until I reached our front gate but decided against opening it as the noise of the latch was sometimes impossible to stifle. The house was set back a few yards from the street and hidden by two enormous trees, a copper beech outside my parents' bedroom and an umbrella tree outside mine. A concrete path wound its way between them to the front porch. My parents' bedroom was on the left, mine on the right. It might as well have been miles away.

I could see my parents' bedroom light was on but the rest of the house was in darkness. A strip of light escaped from under the blind where it didn't quite meet the windowsill. I took off my shoes and inched my way up the front path towards their window. I bent down and peeped into the gap. I could see my mother in bed with a facecloth over her eyes and my father was pacing round the room wringing his hands together, but seemed curiously silent. She seemed not to notice. I felt sorry for my mother and had always been inclined to join with her on those occasions of sadness and despair she experienced so often, usually on account of my father. If only I could rush in and embrace her, like I usually did, maybe even embrace my father which I never, ever did and proclaim that all was well, there was nothing more to worry about. It had been a false alarm. Mum, at least, would have found it in her heart to forgive me. And my father could have continued to make plans for my future. Whatever they were.

I shivered a little and blinked at this cameo before me. My parents thrown together in shock and anger, inflicted on them by me. But there was something about the atmosphere in that room, the sight of them drawn together by circumstances that permeated beyond the room to the outside. Although they were united in grief and anger and disappointment, they seemed unable to resolve anything together. I'd heard them arguing many times, my mother's low tones against my father's loud attacks. But I'd never before observed them as clearly as this. I expect we were too busy trying to distract them in some way, divert their attention elsewhere in a bid to rescue our mother. It was at that point my sense of detachment gave me the courage I needed to go inside.

I slipped round to the back door which was always left unlocked. It was shut firmly against me. There was no sound except a moth whirring and butting against the deceptive welcome of the outside light. It occurred to me that there were two clear courses of action:

Either I could stroll in, closing the door in a casual manner to indicate a confident, almost friendly return, my bravado throwing my father off-guard and thereby eliciting a more positive response to me, perhaps even a little tenderness, or, at worst, expressing relief that I was finally home. Alternatively, I could sneak in unheard which required practised stealth, avoiding the creaking floorboard somewhere near the middle of the hall floor and pray that my bedroom door wasn't shut; slip into bed and immediately feign a deep sleep from which I could not be woken should Dad come in to check.

I stood there deliberating, but secretly knew this was a sham. My father was not known for his tenderness unless you were sick. But my sickness did not warrant treats or sympathy. My sickness was an outrage and no one was going to give me anything. I didn't deserve it. Least of all from my father.

Suddenly the urgency of choosing a plan ebbed away and the desire for self-preservation receded. I turned the handle of the back door with a quiet indifference and walked swiftly but noiselessly to my room. I got undressed in the dark and got into bed. I could make out the neat, carefully-picked hole in the white, embossed spotted wallpaper by the light of the moon through my open blinds and set to work on it, below eiderdown level, prepared at the flick of a switch to fall into an unshakeable sleep.

Chapter 9

For Your Own Good

Dunedin, New Zealand July 1964

The morning after my father's announcement that I was to be sent away my mother was up and dressed and carrying in a tray with my breakfast on it.

'How are you feeling today, dear?' she asked as if I was recovering from a bout of flu and placed the tray on my lap. I wondered whether I should tell her how miserable I felt, how none of it felt right but decided against it. She had enough to worry about.

'OK,' I said. 'Thanks for the brekkie... but I'm really not hungry.'

She pulled up the blinds to let in a harsh sunlight but lowered them a little when I grimaced. Dust danced where the sun caught it.

'I thought I might go into town and meet John for lunch. I haven't seen him all week. Hope that's alright.'

She sat on my bed and sighed. It was hard for her to go against my father.

'I'd rather you didn't,' she said with a hint of ambivalence.

'Dad's got everything arranged!' I said, bursting into tears. 'He's sending me up north to strangers... And won't even let me see him before...'

My mother lifted the tray of untouched food off my lap and put it on the dressing table. Her face was twisted with tears. She knelt down and put her arms around me.

'I didn't know,' she whispered.

We stayed like that for some time, each nursing our own private grief. Eventually she got up.

'You'll be OK,' she said stroking my hair as if to reassure

herself. 'And you'll be back before you know it.'

She looked at the tray, paused and feigned a smile as she went out.

'You'll feel better when you have something to eat,' she added looking in the direction of the tray.

I couldn't eat, I felt sick, waves of nausea floating over me. I had a bath, got dressed after struggling with the zip of my trousers, then left the top button undone concealed by my big black fisherman-knit jersey and set to work on my face. Pale foundation cream, black eyeliner, black mascara. When I finished, I flopped on to the bed, exhausted, and could see my reflection in the triple mirror of the dressing table. I wasn't in the habit of gazing at myself but noticed without satisfaction that I looked unusually pale, deathly pale even more than we all strived for – but there was no evidence of a carefully made-up face. Instead, the black eyeliner encircling my eyes was too heavy, my eyelashes too spidery. I looked like a panda. My short, dark hair sat teased out, defying gravity with the aid of hairspray. I couldn't be bothered to straighten it with the iron. I'd forgotten the chalky lipstick (or 'white' as my mother would quietly observe without fail), but decided it would make very little impact.

The trolleybus slid silently to a halt as I ran towards the bus stop, clutching my stomach. A sharp pain prevented me from climbing further than the first step.

'C'mon, darling, this isn't a tram, ay!' grinned the driver, but I was unable to move. I smiled, then sucked in my breath, indicating the pain with a nodding motion by way of explanation. I glanced down the bus. Several ladies dotted the seats and were looking quizzically at me, moving their heads from side to side to negotiate the poles that were obstructing their view. I managed to free up one hand and fumbled for my fare.

'Don't worry about that now, ay,' said the driver and leapt out of his seat.

'Let me give you a hand to sit down,' and he hooked his arm through mine as I continued clutching my stomach and steered me towards a seat close to the front whilst the ladies continued staring at me. He then plopped me down gently, grinned and gave a wide, sweeping bow to the assembled ladies to indicate the show was over.

But the ladies, not to be deterred, chorused a kind of group, 'Ooooh,' as they whispered audibly, 'Wonder what's wrong with her... mmmn, maybe she should see a doctor?' Did they suspect? Could they tell? Maybe I shouldn't have clutched my tummy now that I was starting to show.

I tried to concentrate on the view as the trolleybus whirred along its familiar route, Musselburgh Rise and down Anderson's Bay Road, allowing snatches of harbour views between the faceless warehouses. Everything looked different, greyer. We eventually stopped at the Exchange. The pain had subsided. I had derived a strange kind of comfort from the driver which created an invisible bond between us. I caught his eye in the large rear-vision mirror as the doors hissed open, smiled at him, raising my thumb in a gesture to indicate all was well.

There was an air of decay about Dunedin, a stagnancy, that seemed to permeate the old buildings – the Savoy, the Bank, the City Hotel. They looked drab, lifeless where the sun failed to catch them. I noticed the Grand Hotel needed a coat of paint. The kilted doorman looked unbecoming in his fine uniform. Perhaps it was his slouch, or air of indifference. I'd automatically have wondered which clan the tartan belonged to, thinking of Grandma MacKinnon and her Isle of Skye roots, but today I didn't really care.

I wandered up to the Octagon, through Moray Place where my lovely uncle Bill had a wee jeweller's shop, but this time I didn't pop in. His shop was very near the doctor I saw, whose words still rang in my ears.

'What *are* we going to do with all you young gals?' he had

asked rhetorically, like an out-of-work actor.

Afterwards I wanted to say you know exactly what you are going to do... 'Get rid of us like some dirty stain. Send us away so we can all pretend nothing's happened to upset the adults' apple cart...'

The Octagon felt like the centre of town, midway between Princes Street and George Street. It was a good place to meet, a circular, grassed area fringed with trees cut through by the city's main street and dominated by a deified statue of Rabbie Burns. That's if you liked his poetry, whisky and could identify with his Scottish heritage. Seats clustered reverently around him, so that should he cast an earthly glance, he would be satisfied, especially on a sunny day like today. The same might also be said of Burns nights, when poetry and alcohol became inextricably mixed.

Most of the seats were occupied by middle-aged ladies wearing a variety of hats, giving the appearance of a colourful competition. Mum always dressed smartly to go to town. She had a range of hats, some a bit crazy, like her 'Baker Boy' phase, but the hats were usually quite conventional just like the Queen Mother's. I think that's how their mothers dressed too. No danger of me following suit, whatever happens.

I spied a seat beside a large, florid-faced lady wearing a red 'Baker Boy' beret and matching suit splashed with green. She looked like a tomato. A useful tomato though, because John would be able to spot me straightaway. I smiled politely and squeezed on to the seat. The tomato made shuffling movements to accommodate me.

It was pleasant sitting there in the sun. It was winter but the sky was blue and there were no clouds. I wondered how long it would last. People ambled around the Octagon and along George Street in their lunch hour. Young couples hand in hand, students in their duffel coats, businessmen in suits. Not my father. He drove the three miles home every lunchtime, arriving at exactly the same time every day. Quarter past twelve. There were no surprises about him, or my mother for that matter.

We saw each other at the same time and waved. I got up and ran towards him. He stood stooped, his arms outstretched as if I was a little girl. It always made me blush and laugh when he did that but secretly I liked it.

He looked so different in a suit. A real grown-up. Tall, slim, sophisticated. This was the uniform of his own private world of work and I noticed it irritated me slightly.

'Let's go to the coffee bar, then the beach!' he said, squeezing my hand. 'The boss' given me the afternoon off.'

'Why's that?' I asked, suddenly feeling a bit peeved. 'You haven't **told** him, have you?'

I withdrew my hand sharply. John didn't reply which instantly confirmed he had gone and blabbed.

'What did you have to go and do that for?' I hissed. 'He probably knows my father!' and stalked off ahead, knowing he would follow, but not deigning to confirm it.

I was overtaking people at an accelerated pace, weaving in and out like I was running an obstacle race. I could hear him parroting my movements in a sort of slipping motion. Suddenly he ducked in front of me and was facing me, skipping backwards so as not to break contact.

'I had to tell him,' he said, the words jerking out of him in time to his step. 'I'm sorry, darling. But he knew something was up.'

With that, he did a fancy double-skip, enabling him to turn round, then slipped his arm confidently through mine. He leaned over and pecked my cheek and we synchronised our walking.

We were heading for the Little Hut, our usual coffee bar along George Street. I was hungry now and had decided to have a double-decker sandwich and a cream meringue or a brandy snap to follow. I gave John's arm a squeeze and returned a quick peck. Food could be good! Especially right now.

We descended below ground to the coffee bar. It was quite

crowded, but nothing compared to Friday nights when it was taken over by trendy teenagers and students. We would cluster together at tables, smoking profusely and imbibing endless cups of coffee for the sole purpose of establishing which parties would be the best to gatecrash. As well as eyeing up the talent. The square mile or so of student flats nearby were potentially open house, provided you were equipped with the statutory brown paper bag of Dominion Bitter, or its equivalent.

We sat down and held hands.

'How are you feeling now, darles?' He leaned over to kiss me. 'You looked a bit pale earlier on.'

'OK,' I said and withdrew my hand. 'I'm starving,' and lunged at the double-decker sandwich he bought me.

He ate in silence for a while, then said, 'I told my parents last night.'

'Oh,' I said after a while. 'How did they take it?'

'They were really good about it – and very upset for you.' He reached for my hand.

I could feel myself bubbling with anger. I liked his parents, especially his mum who was always ready for a chat and spoke to me as if I were a grown-up.

'You're lucky,' I said with my mouth full. 'I suppose that's the difference, being a boy!'

Chapter 10

An Unlikely Proposal

Dunedin, New Zealand July 1964

We finished our lunch without saying any more.

'Let's go to the beach,' John whispered. 'We can be alone there.'

We left the coffee bar and managed to get a bus quite quickly to St Kilda. We sat quietly, close together. I didn't feel like talking. John was always sensitive to my needs, intuitive. Maybe it was having all those sisters. And a lovely mum. He was kind-hearted and knew how to take care of me, pamper me, always buying me little presents he could ill-afford, caring and full of compliments about how I looked – as well as a reliable audience for my jokes. He was easy to be with, equable. I often wished I could take care of him in the same way he took care of me. But that didn't feel so easy now.

We got off the bus at St Kilda and walked hand in hand along the promenade and down towards our private place in the dunes. There was no one about. A wind sprayed sand lightly on my face and I shivered. He took off his suit jacket and placed it around my shoulders. I began to cry. He turned me towards him and kissed my tears, then my eyelids.

'Dad's sending me away,' I wept. 'Up north, to a friend of that horrible doctor I saw.'

'The old bastard,' he whispered and held me tight. I could hear the seagulls squawking loudly overhead as they wheeled and encircled us as if in sympathy.

After a while he released his hold on me then held my shoulders. His eyes were bloodshot.

'Why don't we get married?' he said suddenly. 'And to hell with your old man!' He cupped my face in his hands and looked straight at me.

He was beautiful. His dark, straight Beatles haircut hair fringed his blue eyes and his small, sticky out ears. He was cute. I looked at his face. A tear had escaped and was beginning to trickle down his cheek. I wiped it away with my finger then licked it and pulled him towards me in a hug.

I hadn't thought of marriage, but I couldn't hold his gaze, and instead responded to the rhythm of the sea. How come I hadn't thought of marriage? I loved John and clearly it was the solution. That way, we would be in control. We would decide what happened. Not Dad. Or the doctor. Or anyone else who thought they had a right to do so.

We snuggled down into the hollow of sand staring out at the sea. Then John loosened his tie and slipped it over his head in a mockery of seduction. He got to his feet, whirred it round and round and let it fly off. He did a little dance thrusting one hip forward, then the other, then slowly undid each button of his shirt at the same time showing his smooth, tanned chest. He pouted his lips and, swaying towards me, ripped the jacket from my shoulders and flung it on the sand of our hollow. Then he nuzzled my neck and growled like a wild dog in my ear.

'Come on, Mrs Hamilton,' he smiled. 'Come with me,' and grabbing my hand we plunged back into the hollow.

'You must be hot in that jersey,' he whispered. We lay pressed together letting the distant rhythm of the surf wash over us.

'You mean everything to me,' he said in a soft voice as if he might be overheard. 'You're a part of me… we belong together.'

I propped myself up on my elbow and began to trace his profile with my finger over the broad forehead and dark eyebrows. I liked the way they almost joined together in the middle separated by a few black hairs that stood out assertively and protected his deep-set eyes that were inky blue like the sea. Most of all I liked his snubbed nose, small and slightly turned up with cute little nostrils, perfectly moulded triangles. He giggled as I ran my fingers lightly across his lips that never failed to excite me with their generous full curve upwards as if he was about to smile. I traced his chin which was pointed like his mother's, with a hint of amusement set round a defiant dimple. I combed his dark hair with my fingers. It felt soft and straight. I never tired of looking at him and leant across to kiss his nose.

'That's better,' he murmured as I held him. 'I love you and your little body.'

I sat up. John stroked my back affectionately. I gazed down at the beach. A lone man was out with his dog. He stopped and bent down to pick up some driftwood and flung it so it landed near the edge of the surf. At the same time the dog barked loudly and ran off anticipating where he would retrieve it barely before it had left his master's hand. I put my jersey back on and stood up brushing the sand off me.

'Dad would never agree,' I said eventually. 'And we would need his permission, wouldn't we? Besides,' I added. 'He has plans for me. And they certainly don't include a baby!'

John went to put his arm around me.

'Don't!' I snapped. 'Just leave me alone,' before issuing the final crushing blow. 'What's it got to do with you, anyway?'

He stopped in his tracks. Then grabbed my arm.

'What d' you mean?' he demanded.

Chapter 11

Secrets and Lies: the Reynolds' Family Tree

Brixton Social Services 1981

'So... how did it go doing the family tree together?' I asked smiling at the Reynolds after they had finally settled into the office armchairs. They were ominously quiet. Their body language suggested it was not a happy experience. I could already feel myself tensing, getting hot and my skin pricking, like a worm in a jersey. Was this going to be a repetition of the first session when they got up and walked out? At least they're here, I thought, trying to reassure myself, keep myself calm. Although persuading them to come back had been a bit like trying to budge an elephant.

'It felt like they pulled ranks against me,' I told Mike.

'Well, in a way that's a good thing... it showed unity,' he said.

Yeah, I thought later, and it feels like they're using the same process to exclude Matthew.

'Doing it together?' echoed Mrs Reynolds almost spitting out the word 'together' like it was a grape pip or something. 'Mmmn, well... actually, I wouldn't put it quite like that,' she said crisply looking directly at her husband. 'Let's just say there were some surprises... things me and the kids didn't know,' she added in a rather grim voice.

Mr Reynolds was uncharacteristically silent, looking at the floor.

She and the children waited for him to speak. Sharon sat slumped in her chair, stared at the floor and fiddled with her fingers while Matthew squirmed. Then she suddenly sat up and blurted out, 'Dad's father killed himself!'

There was a heavy silence.

Mr Reynolds looked crumpled, vulnerable... all the bluster

was gone.

'Oh... I'm really sorry to hear that,' I said. 'What a tough thing for you to have lived with.'

No one was looking at anyone as if it had nothing to do with the rest of them in spite of being family. Sounds familiar, I thought.

'And now to share this with your family...'

He nodded slowly and continued staring at the floor. The rest of the family remained mute and Mrs Reynolds looked unsympathetic.

'How difficult and painful for you all.' The remark hung in the air like a dirty big dust cloud. Another, shorter heavy silence.

'Yeah... well, the worst thing is he told me he died of a heart attack... now I find out he lied to me!'

Hardly the worst thing, I thought.

No one spoke. I felt drawn into their discomfort, sharing the tremors before the earthquake.

'Sometimes,' I said slowly and deliberately, trying to regain solid ground, 'people feel they have to hide the truth to protect the family... from... from fear and shame.' I heard myself stumbling over the words, swallowing quickly, feeling taut, tense. Where the hell did that come from? I paused and looked at them. If only they knew! They all kept their eyes fixed on the floor. Were they even bloody listening?

'It must've been a heavy burden to carry,' I empathised with Mr Reynolds and wondered if they could hear the hint of bitterness in my voice, or was it sadness...

'Yeah, well I don't know about all that,' said Mr Reynolds suddenly. 'It happened when I was a kid. And no one spoke about it ever again.'

I wanted to agree, to shout out that's how families are, just when you need them! Need their support... when something terrible happens. But their reaction is often the exact opposite!

I looked at Mr Reynolds. He was wearing a crumpled,

navy jumper and dirty-looking jeans. His hair was greasy and he looked as if he had been sleeping rough. The smell of stale cigarette smoke clung to him and made me feel slightly queasy.

'Sometimes it can feel dangerous to reveal a secret like that,' I said quietly. 'Especially if people think their family might suffer. Maybe that's how your mum felt at the time... that she didn't really have a choice.'

I was suddenly plunged back into my teenage bedroom and found myself echoing the exact words my mother had whispered to me after I told her what Dad had said.

'He's sending me away,' I had cried, 'up north to stay with strangers...'

'He didn't tell me,' she whispered, embracing me, 'but you know we... have to do this... for the family's sake...'

The others started to fidget and wriggle. Mrs Reynolds twisted the strap of her shoulder bag then untied and retied her scarf.

'So many families find it difficult to deal with the truth,' I said feeling the need to fill the awkwardness having thrown myself off balance, 'and to accept what has happened. They think it's easier that way... hiding the truth but usually it isn't – secrets can sometimes end up dividing families.'

'You still could have told **me**!' shrieked Mrs Reynolds as if his father had been a close relative. 'I'm supposed to be your wife!'

'As if you care!'

'What do you mean?'

'Since your mum died you've hardly looked at me!'

'Looking is about all you're good for these days!'

Death can touch you that way, I wanted to say. Like my lovely mum dying not long after I had returned home empty-handed as instructed. Engulf you in a kind of paralysis from which you feel you might never recover, a numbness you can't articulate, leaving an almost imperceptible scar to the outside world, a great, gaping wound within.

There was another awkward silence. Prickly. I was aware that my breathing had become shallow and I felt a lump forming in my throat. There was something magnetic pulling me inexorably into this family's drama. I needed to get a grip. I was supposed to be helping them for heaven's sake, not quietly disintegrating. No one looked at anyone.

'Sounds like... things have broken down between you at the moment... and each of you is blaming the other. But maybe it's the opposite! Maybe you're both doing the same thing: feeling hurt and keeping things from each other,' I ventured.

'Yeah... well, she's just shut down...'

'Tell the young lady yourself why that is,' she said, 'go on!'

'You've never spoken to me about your mum, not since she died... and that's about a year ago!'

There was another unfamiliar hush. Sharon breathed in and out loudly a few times in succession and Matthew wriggled around in his chair; even Mrs Reynolds was seduced into silence.

'It seems that you're both going through the same thing... I mean, the reason you're both unhappy is the same – you're both grieving,' I said hoping for a little eye contact then relieved to notice there was none. 'It's just that it comes out in different ways.'

I wanted to look at the parents to reinforce what I was saying but found I couldn't.

'It probably won't feel like it right now,' I said, 'but you might find it's a bit like wearing different costumes in the same play... Know what I mean?'

They looked dubious, the whole family wore the same expression.

'That's so often the case when it comes to men and women,' I continued as lightly as I could in a possibly vain attempt to get them to see they were both feeling the same way. In the meantime the family's fascination for the floor continued unabated in much the same way as my persistence and enthusiasm to help.

Chapter 12

The Felling of the Family Tree

Brixton 1981, Supervisor's office

'Sorry to keep you waiting,' said Mike. 'How are you?' he asked smiling at me.

'Good,' I replied, 'but a bit blown off-course by the Reynolds family news.'

Mike nestled his chin in his hand, like he was preparing for an interesting chat.

'During my last meeting with them, there was some rather sad news that came out as a result of doing the family tree,' I said. 'Sharon dropped a bombshell and blurted out that her father's father had killed himself. It was quite difficult... all a bit delicate... Mrs Reynolds seemed more furious he hadn't told her about it... that he'd lied and said his father had died of a heart attack.'

'Mmmn,' said Mike, 'so she was more concerned that he lied to her, not that his father had committed suicide?'

He looked thoughtful.

'So, what's your main concern?'

'I suppose it's for Matthew, mainly because Mrs Reynolds was very unsympathetic towards her husband,' I said. 'And he's now exposed his vulnerability by telling them the truth, but not getting the sympathy he expected from his wife... He sees Matthew aligned to her so I'm worried he might take his anger out on him.'

'Maybe deep down he didn't really expect her sympathy because that's the story of his childhood, that's how it's always been,' said Mike. 'I don't expect anyone ever listened to him, how he felt about things, so he learnt that expressing his feelings was pointless.'

'But how would his wife know that?'

'Well, perhaps she was just expressing what he unconsciously expected all along... a replay of his feelings being ignored since childhood.'

'What... you mean that this sort of thing set down a pattern for his whole life?'

'Yes, it can do, so the current family becomes a replica of his original family,' said Mike.

Wow – this is almost too much to handle. I need to go away and digest it all... Am I doing the same thing? Have I recreated my own family of origin, my childhood stuff into my current family? According to Martin I sometimes relate to him as if he were my father! 'Hell,' I remember him recently saying to me after a good old ding dong, 'I'm not your father!' Not only that, there's the 'not expecting to be heard' theme to digest as well!

'So...' I said, recovering from the shock of what Mike had just said, tucking it away for later, 'this whole scene fits with the rather sad story of his life then, even sharing his darkest secret, though I assume he was hoping for something different?'

'Yes,' said Mike. 'I guess it's hope that keeps us all seeking, ay?'

Gawd, I almost shivered, he's beginning to sound like a sage or a Maori elder, full of amazing wisdom...

'But underneath all that surely he must've been hoping to win her over,' I said puzzled. 'I know I would if I'd shared a secret like that.'

First I'd have to trust them with the information about what happened and hope they'd accept it, but most of all I'd be trusting them with my feelings, my innermost feelings. How could he possibly step back and try to deal with all that? I could feel tears pricking my eyes, and wondered if I was sounding too passionate.

There was an awkward pause.

'I feel even more worried about Mr Reynolds now,' I said

anxiously. 'He might become more defensive and angry and take it out on Matthew. It's like it's all backfired on him, hasn't it? And after what you said, instead of scoring some sympathy and maybe affection from his wife by opening up to her, he now feels humiliated and has made himself vulnerable. It's like he's suddenly closed down again. Snapped shut. And I expect he won't trust her, or himself, for a long time, if at all.' Or me, come to think of it.

I shivered, imagining how Mr Reynolds must have felt dropping the bomb, the secret he had harboured forever. Did he plan it, had he spent years dreaming of such a moment, sharing this dark, secret part, hidden from view, even from himself? To finally be released like a wounded animal now rehabilitated springing back into some strangely unfamiliar but natural place. Or was it simply an impulsive response to the 'homework'? And another alarming thought – did that mean it was all my fault since I set the homework?

'Mmmn... I suppose he must be pretty wound up,' said Mike rubbing his chin thoughtfully. 'So we need to think a bit more about Matthew – is he safe now that all this has happened?'

'I'm not sure... It feels like Matthew is even more vulnerable to Dad's temper; more unprotected since Mum seems to have her own agenda. Maybe it's not safe for him to be there at the moment.'

I could suddenly feel tears pricking my eyes again and my voice trembled slightly. What the hell was going on, I wondered? Maybe I was over-identifying with Matthew, reliving my own fear of my father. Wanting to be separate from him, to feel safer. But filled with a fear I couldn't articulate.

Then I heard the tea lady's welcome singsong, 'Who wants my lovely tea?' sung full throttle in the corridor. Paula, with her perennial Spanish naranja suntan and matching tea, seemingly without a care in the world.

'Actually, on reflection, I'm wondering if one way of helping them cope is to give them a break from Matthew,' I said to Mike suddenly remembering the bruise on Matthew's face.

'Well... that's a possibility but we also need to be careful we don't reinforce the notion that Matthew is the problem. Families have a tendency to project their problems on to a scapegoat... so something that looks like protecting Matthew may accidentally collude with the need for someone to carry the blame. I've seen it happen before and it's usually around fear and shame... all the stuff that's going on there at the moment.'

'Right,' I said, wondering how the parents would accept our interpretation. It felt like stirring up silt at the bottom of a very murky pond.

'Unless the father speaks about his problems, faces them, shares them with the family, he's going to have to carry on repressing and controlling them... as well as having a boy who's out of control.'

Same as me and Dad, I thought. Nothing was ever aired or shared, so nothing ever changed including Dad's penchant for power and control. The more independent he saw me becoming, the tighter his attempts to control...

'Do you think his wife's afraid of him? I remember from the notes that she's left him once before because of violence,' I said. I had worked for a while in the women's refuge in Wandsworth in the late 1970s. It was one of only a handful of 'safe houses' in the UK with loads of traumatised women and kids squashed into a couple of terraced houses. All topping and tailing on mattresses everywhere. A measure of their desperation. But a place of safety. A place to start again. The staff, too, seemed desperate, constantly 'energising' as one worker described it, always on the go, focusing mainly on practical issues. A lot of the women did very little, sat round the kitchen table smoking and talking, usually about husbands, housework and their kids. Some were more involved in helping run the place answering the phone and so on. But mostly there was apathy and despair and not much in the way of solidarity. My task was to offer them some groups on assertiveness and dealing with depression, two major issues but there was often the feeling that it was the men who were solely to blame. And then there was the problem of domestic violence that all the women had in common, not yet a criminal offence. Tension was always tight. I often secretly felt as fearful, restricted and hopeless as they did – always needing to be on my guard, careful never to divulge the address and most especially never to let a MAN into the property, always sniffing out danger, alert as a guard dog. And then the police turned up one day to drop off a violent husband previously cautioned for attempting to kill his wife, bearing flowers.

Chapter 13

The Power of Shame

Dunedin, New Zealand 1964
Aged 17

The enormity of what I had done was not only getting pregnant, which was bad enough; it was about the shame that accompanied it. The shame I had brought on the family, just like Mr Reynolds' father had done by committing suicide. Mine was a family built on courage, hope and optimism and a political ideology to sustain them, even if it wasn't always played out. All underpinned by fear, rejection and a deep desire to fit in. Where both sets of grandparents had been persecuted, banished, forced to leave or to flee their homelands to survive and try and make a better life for themselves. And their families.

'It's strange we know so little about our family history,' I remarked to my brother during a trip home a few years ago. 'I don't remember either set of grandparents ever mentioning their past to us, their history, their roots... their losses. I mean... what must it have been like leaving behind everything that was familiar and dear to them?'

'Maybe it was too painful for them to talk about,' said my brother.

'Or maybe they felt some sort of shame and didn't want to define us with their history,' I said, thinking of Mr Reynolds. 'I think Dad's parents were part of a large-scale exodus who fled as young people from Warsaw to London. It must've been in the late 1800s at the time of the pogroms.'

'Do you think they feared just up and leaving their friends and family and familiar places?' asked my brother. 'And what about their parents? Our great-grandparents. Were they forced to leave them behind or do you think they urged them to flee without them? Believing that was best for them?'

'It doesn't bear thinking about. It's so hard to imagine... especially living with all that fear every day – of the police and neighbours keen to denounce you; hiding and skulking and being afraid for themselves and their families,' I said. 'What would it be like saying goodbye to each other in the morning and never being sure whether they would see each other again?'

We each pondered on this piece of family history that was completely outside our own privileged experience.

'I wonder if they carried this fear and shame in their genes and passed it on to their children and to us? Maybe that's why they never said anything,' I said thinking of my poor daughter receiving a double dose of shame. Could I be mirroring some of their experiences?

'What would it be like to be branded, publicly shamed, made to wear those armbands stamped with the Star of David... labelled forever as unworthy, fit only for banishment? It's unthinkable!' said my brother. I shuddered. No, it wasn't, it was right here beside him – his twin sister! But my brother seemed oblivious.

Were they, too, deprived of their children, their babies, stolen or murdered in front of them? Along with the right to work, banned from certain areas of towns and cities, and ultimately their own homes. Were they able to manage the degradation, accept their lot, maybe even ultimately to forgive the perpetrators and move on? Is that what I should do? Or did their repression secretly ferment and turn them into victims of bitterness and resentment, blaming others for what happened to them, forever shrouding themselves in a mould of misery?

'Perhaps they didn't tell us anything about their early lives because they were trying to erase all the memories, in the same way that the Nazis had later tried to erase other Jews and their families... or maybe they brought their memories with them and they stayed buried inside them like some friends' fathers who had been Japanese prisoners of war,' I said.

'Who knows... I wonder if they knew themselves,' said my brother.

'Well, maybe they were trying so hard to integrate, assimilate into the mainly Scottish Presbyterian society that greeted them – can you imagine it! That they were prepared to fit in at any cost, including losing their own identity and beliefs. And would they have lost sight of what was really important, been prepared to lose everything, including their own child in order to fit in?' I wondered.

My Scottish grandparents had more in common with my Jewish grandparents than I ever realised. I always thought of them as being from totally different worlds, set apart by culture, language, religion and beliefs. They looked different, they spoke differently, behaved differently and ate different food (porridge and black pudding versus beetroot and boiled kosher chicken). One lot lived in an old weatherboard house high up in Mary Hill with beautiful coloured glass surrounding the front door that splintered lights of blue and red, had bagpipes, a mangle, a coal range and bunk beds in a sort of outhouse bedroom.

The other lot lived in a large, brick house down by the university, opposite the River Leith that meandered through the grounds. It had wide sweeping front steps that led to a sunless veranda, a swear box with Yiddish writing on it that remained forever on the mantelpiece suspiciously empty, a beautiful old violin that no one played any more, hundreds of books later donated to the university library and the New Zealand *Truth* newspaper always hidden from us under a cushion on the sofa. Both houses were kind of exciting, mysterious and full of potential which we were not allowed to explore.

In spite of their differences both sets of grandparents had been banished from their homelands, both sets determined to seek a better life, safe, secure and free from persecution. The more I discovered about the banishments, the more chilling the comparisons became and the more I identified with their plights: giving people no choice about their lives, others deciding where or how or if they lived; exploiting, scapegoating and rejecting targeted groups of people whose lives and property were entirely at the mercy of the monstrous power of the landlord or the military. Forcing those who had outlived their usefulness to 'relocate' elsewhere. Many felt they had no choice but to emigrate to the 'new world', including New Zealand, amid all sorts of rumours including Maori wars and the unsettling prospect of cannibalism.

I hadn't realised that banishment and the shame that accompanied it was woven so strongly into our family history. Maybe it was passed on in our genes, who knows? Am I guilty of passing on the same thing?

I felt enormous empathy for both sets of grandparents as each had echoes for the other. And both had echoes for me. It made me wonder how they decided to manage their banishment, the loss of their homes and their freedom especially after reading a statement by the young men of Sutherlandshire, near Skye, about the oppression and suffering of their community at the hands of their feudal masters. It brought alive the respective histories of both sets of grandparents.[1*]

We have no country to fight for as our glens and straths are laid desolate, no wives nor children to defend as we are forbidden to have them. We are not allowed to marry without consent... the result would be banishment. Our lands have been taken from us and given to sheep farmers and we have been denied any portion of them and when we apply for such or even a site for a house we are told that we should leave the country.[2*]

Did this apply to my grandparents forced as young people to

comply, to start from scratch after being banished... Is that what I should be doing? Beginning again? I can't start again, it's in my history. I know I've attempted to but it doesn't work... maybe it's in my genes. Look at the Reynolds and the disastrous effects of denial, of a secret told too late. It's like their experiences forced me to face my own demons, to see there's no escape, no starting again by pretending it never happened.

But why wouldn't you share your story with your family? Maybe they did. But it was as if their past counted for nothing, as if the present had no connection with the past and, in turn, nothing to do with us. Maybe that was how everyone managed their traumatic histories and that's what I should to do. Live in the present.

My grandfather Mark managed his history of persecution and banishment by fighting for social justice. He had fled with his family from Warsaw to London as a child, attended the Jews' Free School in the East End and later trained as a cabinetmaker. He became a socialist and, inspired by New Zealand's reputation as a 'workers' paradise' he emigrated to Dunedin in 1904, aged 19, followed later by his young, socialist bride Esther, my grandmother, where he quickly became a political activist, very involved in the trade union movement and was one of the founders of the New Zealand Labour Party. He was described as 'Dunedin's most radical socialist'. How cool is that? And spoke and wrote widely from a socialist perspective. He became a city councillor, mentor and champion of workers' rights and was later appointed a Director of the Reserve Bank of NZ. I know most of this because I read it in a book. And as a child I always remembered being fascinated seeing a cartoon of him dressed as a banker and a carpenter planing off pound notes. It made me feel proud of him, connected to him. I still remember him even though he died when I was aged four.

The trauma of injustice in his own family history led him to fight for justice for others. I guess I have padded along in his wake – a much milder version. He inspired me, maybe prompted me, driven me to eventually find my voice and stand up, fired by my own experience of injustice.

Both sets of grandparents carried with them their own agendas for a better world, their own histories of banishment, fears of discrimination, poverty, survival, uncertainty, losses, all flecked with hope converging on the long and dangerous journey to New Zealand, and in the process risked their lives to make a better one for themselves and their families. Then look what I go and do.

1* Footnote: The statement was made in response to a campaign to enlist them in the Crimean War.

2* Footnote: John Prebble, The Highland Clearances, *1963, p. 302.*

Chapter 14

Banished

Dunedin, South Island, New Zealand July 1964
Aged 17

I was sent away in disgrace. Banished. That was my punishment for bringing shame on the family. Shame so powerful that all acts of parental decency and duty were suddenly flung aside – cast off, along with me. Not to mention the baby. Nothing was the same after that. For any of us.

After extracting a 'confession' I was promptly disposed of, put on an aeroplane for the first time ever and sent up north to strangers. I think they were friends of the doctor I'd chosen randomly from the phone book. All I knew was they had a double-barrelled name and two or three children.

I had never been to New Plymouth. In fact, I had never been to the North Island. Nor had anyone else I knew. It might as well have been Timbuctoo. I had to look at a map to see exactly where it was. The middle of nowhere. On the west coast. Perdition. I did not want to 'discuss' the matter with my mum. I had no wish to communicate with anyone and confined myself to my room. What did it matter where I was living anyway? They had already made it clear they wouldn't be visiting, so what difference did it make?

I spent my last few days mostly at the beach. I didn't seek anyone's company and had instructed my mother to tell John that I was 'unavailable'. I knew that she would cushion my absence more discreetly, but I didn't really care.

When I was at the beach I was drawn each time to the cliffs at the far end of the promenade – clambering along the steep sides trying not to look down at the waves crashing against the rocks below. No one walked in this perilous place called Lawyer's

Head unless they were crazy or contemplating suicide.

My girlfriends had arranged a farewell get-together. It was to be a Jane's house on my final night. There would be the six of us: Joy, Cathy, Annie, Patricia, Jane and me. Our friendship was firmly rooted in high school days. We had shared our discoveries of ourselves, the world, exchanged ideas, gossip, intimacies. We accrued status by our radical behaviour at school, quietly defying the rules, days of blatant truancy, that had almost culminated in suspension.

I was 17 and it was six months since we had all left school. We had fantasised about sharing a flat together, going to university, staying single, travelling to England. I decided to become a teacher or social worker, then travel to the UK. My ambition was to live in London by the time I was 25. Which coincided with our school being 100 years old, or was it 150 years old? Whatever it was, it had become a very long way off.

Now all I felt was detached from them, from everyone, everything. From the aspirations we had shared. There was nothing up ahead anymore, no future. Just emptiness. A void. I no longer fitted. I had been set adrift, set myself adrift and might easily drown. Nothing in my life was the way I thought it was going to be.

But any feelings of alienation were quickly dispersed at our little farewell gathering. I was hugged and greeted in a special way. I had been nervous about seeing Jane's parents, what they might say to me and how I'd conduct myself. But they were out. We sat round drinking coffee and eating lamingtons Jane's mother kindly made for us. We talked about college and varsity, the gossip of the past couple of weeks, the demise of the art lecturer, Joy's job, a friend's car accident. We talked about Cathy's parents, Patricia's new boyfriend, apartheid in South Africa, the price of shoes. But we didn't talk about me. We didn't talk about pregnancy and childbirth, banishment, strangers, isolation or despair.

Then it was time to go. I couldn't imagine what it was going to be like without them – and John – for three whole months. My father was collecting me, as he usually did. And we drove home in silence as we usually did.

John had rung several times apparently. And my mother had ensured that she answered the phone.

'He's very upset,' she said when she came into my room to say goodnight. 'Perhaps you should ring him in the morning... before...' she hesitated and looked away.

'I thought you didn't want me to have any contact with him,' I said.

'I know, but he was so distraught. And he's a nice boy... in spite of what's happened.'

Mum packed my suitcase but said she couldn't come out to the car to say goodbye, it was too much for her.

'It's all too upsetting,' she said and looked as if she was going to cry. I kissed her at the front door then picked up my suitcase which was very light and my duffel bag, and walked down the front path. I shut the gate and turned round to see if she was still there but she'd gone inside.

Dad drove in silence except when he was cursing other motorists all of whom were in the wrong while I cried quietly in the front seat beside him. We went past the park at the end of our road. I could see the empty swings moving lightly in the breeze, the jungle gym we used to swing from like monkeys, the merry-go-round where we screamed our lungs out and held on for grim death if someone made it go too fast, usually a boy. We drove to town along the familiar route that Dad used to take me to school, past the King's High School boys on their bikes sporting short pants and hairy legs which weren't funny today. We drove on past the Caledonian sports ground where I had represented the school sprinting, hurdles and long jump. It seemed so long ago. Past the Oval cricket ground where some girlfriends and I had an unfortunate car accident (no one held a driver's licence), after celebrating the end of school. Dad then deviated without explanation to Leith Street near the university where his mother and sister lived. He had obviously decided to just pop in – unheard of with me on board. We usually preferred to keep away, except for the odd obligatory Sunday afternoon.

'Why are we going to Grandma's?' I asked.

Dad made no reply.

'Do you think I'm not coming back – is that it?'

Still nothing.

'It is, isn't it. You think they might never see me again...'

It felt a bit like a final goodbye – a 'just-in-case-she-doesn't-make-it' goodbye. Maybe Dad genuinely thought I might not be coming back, so they might never see me again. Or maybe it was a way of demonstrating that I couldn't really have been absent for around three months should they later remark they hadn't seen me for ages. Or it was possibly a deception designed to protect me and this was how it was going to be from now on: making excuses, duping friends and family. And I was part of the conspiracy. I felt sorry for them being deceived by their own son and brother to keep them ignorant of what I had done and shield them from the truth about me.

I had a sudden, unfamiliar surge of affection for them, with their manicured lawn and straight concrete paths dividing a large vegetable garden from the house which was filled with beautiful wooden furniture that always seemed to exude its own soft rosy glow; furniture that my grandfather had made, including a mahogany book-lined study that we were not allowed to go in.

We drove back through town and all the drabness I saw the other day had faded away. Everything looked bright and busy with people scurrying confidently about their business, cheerful, safe and secure.

'Please don't send me away,' I implored Dad again. 'Please let me stay. I promise I'll be good.'

He didn't respond, just stared hard at the road ahead which took us up over Saddle Hill that led to the long, straight, boring road through the Taieri Plains.

'What's say there's a plane crash?' I cried. 'Would you still not care?'

Dad continued driving in silence.

'I'm frightened, Dad... frightened about... the plane,' I cried. 'I mean, how does it stay up?'

'Should've paid closer attention to your studies instead of gallivanting around with that boyfriend of yours,' he said.

I wanted to say I was sorry and I would try and make up for it by doing exactly what he wanted but his message was loud and clear.

'You'll stay with these people then hand it over... and that'll be the end of the matter,' he'd said then added, 'Otherwise you'll never set foot in this house again! It'd kill your mother!'

When we arrived at the airport he got my ticket rather brusquely from the young woman behind the counter who was a similar age to me. I've never wanted to be someone else more than at that moment... a daughter my father could be proud of, sort of pure and holy and uncomplicated instead of one that embarrassed and shamed him, one he was trying to get rid of as fast as he could, almost pushing me through to Customs.

'Please, please don't...' I cried once more resisting, then turning awkwardly towards him as I tried to embrace him for the first time ever, his small, unfamiliar bony frame strangely similar to mine. People were looking as he turned and walked away.

I could see him through the small window of the aeroplane standing in a crowd outside the airport terminal as if he was bidding farewell to an old friend. Maybe it was his way of making sure I had finally gone. The engines started up and I was terrified. It was the first time in my life I'd ever wanted him to rescue me, save me, make everything all right again. He continued to just stand there, hands in pockets as if he was watching a cricket match or something, the only person not waving, as the plane rolled down the runway and I became more and more fearful, gripping the armrests as he got smaller and smaller.

Chapter 15

A 'Proper' Family: Married with Children

New Plymouth, New Zealand 1964

Doctor Hartley-Farrell stood out from the small crowd at New Plymouth Airport by his clothes. He was wearing a pinstripe suit and bow tie offset by a red carnation in his lapel, and to top it all, a wide-brimmed felt hat. Was he going to the races or a wedding later? He stepped forward confident of who I was with his hand outstretched.

'Hartley-Farrell,' he announced in a loud voice as if he was meeting someone important. 'And I assume you're Susan!'

He crushed my hand before I could confirm my identity and insisted on carrying my duffel bag, which he swung inexpertly into the air and across his back.

He was a short man and rather stout, but somehow managed to increase his stature by his manner.

'Trip OK?' he asked, turning to look for the baggage. 'Jolly good,' he said, lingering over the 'jolly' as I nodded in reply.

We stopped to wait for my suitcase with a handful of other passengers.

'And how's my old friend Mac?' he asked continuing to look around, maybe for a porter although I had only one small suitcase.

'We were at med school together, you know – in Dunedin. Best years of my life...' he sighed. 'Haven't seen him for years... surprised he stayed there actually. Not many of us did. Must be his Scottish origins.'

He smiled in my direction. We stood in silence and watched the porter unload the baggage. Then he reached over me as I went to pick up my case and swooped it skywards.

'Well, let's be off then,' he said loudly. 'I've got a busy schedule this afternoon.'

We went out into a harsh light and walked over to a big car that shone in spite of the grey day. He held the front passenger door open for me, mimicking a servant or something.

I wanted to tell him I didn't know his friend Mac and that was the reason I'd gone to see him. But the real truth was that I'd heard he'd helped someone who was pregnant, given her some pills to get her started. Maybe I'd gone to the wrong doctor. Or maybe he felt especially sorry for that girl, or knew her family.

I still shudder when I think of his dark, dingy waiting room in the centre of Dunedin, somewhere in Moray Place not far from my old high school, the ominous silence pierced by the loud, relentless rhythm of a ticking clock, the suspicious glances from the elderly receptionist. Did she know my mother? My parents? And then the doctor with his white, puffy face, horn-rimmed glasses. He tried to smile politely while asking me, 'How can I help?' When I told him I hadn't had a period for a while he had looked at me rather sharply and suddenly everything changed. His fat, banana fingers, commanding me to 'flop your legs apart', although I was already strapped into stirrups, having obeyed his gruff instructions and removed my 'lower half', scorched scarlet with embarrassment.

I felt sick. 'Flop'. Why did he choose that word? Perhaps all the ladies who were forced to lie like this had floppy pink thighs that fell apart like jelly on his command – one which was contrary to everything we'd been taught as females, and while some of us may have chosen to ignore the injunction on occasions, we'd nevertheless been enjoined to keep our knees firmly together. Enjoined... I therefore found it difficult to absorb the doctor's instructions without reiterating to myself that he was indeed a doctor and not a pervert and as such had a totally different view of things, especially female things.

Nevertheless, I had felt humiliated lying like that on his couch and very, very embarrassed. I watched him snap on rubber gloves, stretching his fat, podgy fingers with exaggerated movements to help ease them on. I turned my head away and faced the wall. I was incapable of flopping and his exhortations only increased my tension. I grabbed his wrist to prevent him from examining me any further and he muttered, 'Come on now, you must be used to this.'

I sat up suddenly and made as if to get off the bed.

'Just relax,' he said. 'I'm not going to hurt you.'

I could feel hot tears running down the sides of my face and was determined not to let him see them. Short of screaming, I failed to see how he would know whether or not he had hurt me and I didn't want to give him that satisfaction.

'Ach... not another one!' he sighed, casting his eyes to the ceiling and pronounced the words I was dreading to hear. I was pregnant. All this unpleasantness because, he assumed correctly, that at age 17 I was unmarried.

I can still remember the look on his face when he confirmed I was over five months pregnant and somehow it had deterred me from having the courage to ask for pills. Afterwards he had sat behind his big, mahogany desk, clasping his fat, white hands together and peered myopically at me as if somehow I'd transmuted into a different person from the one that came in. Then he had shaken his head and sighed, asking, 'How many more of you young gals?'

I had stared at the floor and blushed. The gas fire hissed quietly in the blocked-up grate and reminded me of the one in our old headmistress' office. So did being here, the way the doctor had frowned disingenuously at me across the desk and then shook his head, in spite of having all the facts. I could feel his disapproval stabbing at me. It almost felt as if he was waiting for me to apologise.

'I'm sorry,' I could have said. 'I'm sorry for being in love. For getting swept away. For not knowing about The Facts of Life. For getting pregnant. For being independent. For being a female!'

Instead I said nothing and concentrated on the hissing gas fire.

I couldn't convey to Dr Hartley-Farrell how much I'd been dreading the moment I saw his friend Mac and put off going in the hope that it might all go away. I'd deliberately cross the road to avoid walking past his surgery as if to confirm to myself that I had no need to see him. And then it was all happening just as I imagined. But worse. It hadn't occurred to me I would have to get undressed or be examined in that way.

'For heaven's sake, girl,' I could still hear him saying sarcastically when I showed my reluctance to lie on the high white bed in his pokey little back room. 'How can I possibly examine you when you're standing up fully clothed?' I'd felt foolish and angry with him but mostly terrified.

I didn't particularly dislike him or his fat, pale moon face and horn-rimmed glasses. Nor did I much care what he thought of me or my situation. It was something more powerful that had led me to submit and endure this humiliation. I was afraid. I was helpless. But what was worse, I felt I needed him. Now it seemed as if I needed Hartley-Farrell.

'Please,' he announced, lighting a cigar. 'Call me Gerald. After all, we are going to be living together for a while,' and he chuckled before loudly sucking in his cigar smoke. 'Can't have you calling me "doctor" all over the place, can we?!' And he chuckled a sort of, 'ho ho ho,' again to himself.

'What shall I call your wife?' I asked, looking across at him and quietly winding down the car window a little hoping he wouldn't notice. I felt sick and the cigar smoke made me feel worse.

'What shall you call her?' he repeated and grimaced round his cigar by gripping it with his teeth. 'Well, not the same as I feel like calling her sometimes,' he guffawed. 'That's if she's there,' he added solemnly, retrieving his cigar.

'You can ask her yourself soon, we're almost home. At least I hope she's there,' he mumbled.

I hadn't noticed anything on our journey from the airport but was left with a sense of flatness. I sat there wondering where his wife might be. Surely she knew I was coming. Dr Hartley-Farrell didn't offer any explanation. It seemed as if he wasn't sure himself. Perhaps she didn't really want me there cluttering up her house, invading her privacy and this was her way of showing me. Or her husband.

I became aware of houses spinning by and tried to work out what was different about them. They had a foreign appearance as if they belonged somewhere else. It was almost like being in another country. A lot of the houses were built of wood, not brick, like down south. But somehow everything seemed different, not just the houses. The trees weren't the same, or people's gardens. Some had huge ferns and flaxes that I'd never seen before. I fiddled with the identity bracelet John had given me, our names inscribed on either side, and wished I felt like a cigarette.

'Well here we are, young lady. Didn't take long, did it?' he said as if he'd just flown us across the Tasman. 'None of those damn Dunedin hills here! Flat as a pancake round here.' I gave a small smile to nothing in particular.

We turned into a driveway through some tall, open gates and stopped in front of a garage. I looked up at the house. It was huge. Much grander than ours. The outside was roughcast, painted white with small, squared windows jutting out of the roof, painted green like the doors. They were all closed. A large stretch of lawn ran alongside the driveway dominated by a rotary clothes line. Underneath it lay a basket of washing.

Dr Hartley-Farrell leapt out to open my door and led the way into the house, armed with my suitcase and duffel bag. He flung open the back door and without turning round marched inside. I followed apologetically in his wake as if somehow I was responsible for whatever was going on. We stepped over piles of laundry lying on the wash house floor and through a door that led into the kitchen. A smell of burnt toast hung in blue wisps in the air and dirty dishes lay on the table and scattered along the benches. Dr Hartley-Farrell dumped my bags on the kitchen floor and plucked off his hat.

'Damn, what a mess,' he exclaimed. 'This is typical at the moment, I'm afraid,' he said. 'Perhaps she's upstairs. Caroline!' he called and disappeared into the hall. 'Caroline!'

I could hear him bounding up the stairs and opening doors. I looked at the mess. Plates and glasses lay strewn around the sink, and several dirty pots and pans stood on the cooker. Breadcrumbs dotted the spaces in between. It looked like they'd been left from last night's dinner. I wondered whether I ought to start clearing up or pretend I hadn't noticed. It didn't feel right to stand at a stranger's sink and do their dishes for them, but I suppose that was what I was there for. And what if she returned to find a complete stranger clearing up her mess? It was embarrassing enough as it was. I could hear him returning and moved closer to the kitchen window to concentrate on the view of pine trees that flanked the side of the house.

'Sorry about this,' he said. His face was flushed and now matched his carnation.

'She must have popped out for something,' he said and scanned the kitchen in a last minute attempt to glean some telltale sign of her.

'I suppose I should've helped clean up but I was on call last night actually, and slept at the hospital.' He shrugged and smiled in my direction then started stacking some plates on the table.

'Actually, she's not very well at the moment,' he added.

I took off my duffel coat and placed it on the back of a kitchen chair. He didn't offer any further explanation and it didn't seem right to ask.

'Please, let me help,' I said as cheerfully as I could. 'I'm good at doing dishes,' and went over to the sink. I thought of my twin brother and the daily rows we had over doing the dishes. We took turns at washing up and with this came the guarantee that the other one would chuck back most of what had been washed on the grounds that they needed to be done again.

'That's very good of you, I must say. And you've barely arrived. Goodness knows what you must be thinking of us. Not much of a welcome, is it?'

'Oh, that's OK. Perhaps your wife forgot the time, or had to pop out for something. I don't mind, really.'

I had seen him glancing at his watch while I filled the sink. He came over and cleared a space on the bench beside me, plonked some more dishes on to it, mumbling apologetically, then looked more pointedly at his watch, adjusting its position as he did so.

'My goodness, I really will have to go or I'll be late for my clinic. I suppose all you can do is wait for my wife. She's bound to be back soon. She often dashes out in the middle of things,' he said with a sardonic laugh. 'Probably down at the dairy with the baby.' He sighed and added, 'I expect you'll be a pleasing sight to her though… God knows, she needs some help these days. Oh, but don't worry,' he added, 'you don't have to clean all this up,' and lightly touched my shoulder as he brushed past to retrieve his hat and coat and was gone.

I watched the bubbles of Sunlight soap slowly disintegrate in the sink as they clustered together, translucent rainbows refracting light from the kitchen window. There was no sound anywhere. I hurried to finish the dishes watching the street and wiped the Formica table and benches, but left the pots on the oven so Mrs Hartley-Farrell wouldn't feel totally usurped.

I hadn't had anything to eat since I left home and would've liked a cup of tea, but didn't know where things were kept. I sat down and stared at the faceless rows of kitchen cupboards that lined the walls above the benches and thought of our own sky blue kitchen at home where I knew where everything was kept, where everything belonged. I wished I was sitting at our red Formica table waiting for my mother, not someone else's – a complete stranger with a mysterious illness which caused her husband embarrassment. He had apologised for the mess, and although he'd expected his wife to have cleared up, had nonetheless felt responsible. It was as if her illness was his fault. Maybe it was. Maybe he'd driven her mad.

I rested my head in my arms on the table and cried. It was all becoming horribly clear. I had been asked here to keep an eye on her. The doctor was embarrassed by his wife's condition and couldn't rely on a neighbour to help because of gossip. He had his position to think of. So he contacts his old friend Mac, whom he says he hasn't seen in years, for help. For a girl like me. According to Mac there were plenty of us to pick from. Being an outsider, I was the perfect minder. Totally dependent on their goodwill for a few months. Well, for a significant sum for board and lodgings I found out later, in return for the privilege of looking after their children and doing all the housework for three months. This way the doctor could satisfy his good name and enjoy being seen as benevolent at the same time.

Suddenly I became aware of a baby crying and a door opening. I jerked my chair back and stood beside the table. I could hear her trying to pacify the child in a faint, high-pitched squeaky voice. She emerged into the kitchen with her back to me, a wailing baby on her hip slightly preceding her. She extricated the child with the promise of a drink and plopped him on the floor. Then she stood up, turned round and gave a little scream at the sight of me which she stifled by clapping her hand over her mouth. Her eyes widened in shock as she seemed to register who I was.

My fantasies about her began to disappear. She was much younger than I expected, was tallish and slim, almost girlish with shoulder-length fair hair, most of which was scooped up carelessly in a pink ribbon on the top of her head so that her hair sprouted out like a small palm tree. The stray strands framed a pale, oval face, almost old-fashioned, the sort that artists painted in the last century. She wore a short, gathered skirt like one of my sister's and a bulky jersey that didn't quite match. But it was her eyes that first held my attention. She had suddenly screwed them up like a child peeping during a game of 'hide and seek', and as she released her hand from her open mouth, she lowered her face so that it was dominated by her big, pale blue eyes fringed with dark lashes. She reminded me of my walkie-talkie doll Rosemary whose eyes opened wide like that and at the same time synchronised with a squeak from somewhere inside her body.

Then she giggled.

'Oh dear, you must be Susan.'

Her hand flew back to her mouth for a moment.

'I'm terribly sorry I wasn't here when you arrived,' she sort of tittered. 'I was out and completely forgot the time.' She wiped her forehead with the back of her hand as if she were hot and continued talking in the same high-pitched squeak. 'Golly, I'm hopeless!'

The child continued to wail while she carried on talking.

'I expect Gerald looked after you properly and –' she broke off and swung around to look at the benches behind her. 'Don't tell me you cleaned all this up?' she said and blinked several times in quick succession at me. 'I bet Gerald wasn't too pleased!'

She giggled again, bent down and plucked the baby from the floor.

'By the way, my name's Caroline, though most people call me Carrie.'

I smiled at her as she plopped the child in the highchair. She seemed so friendly and young, although she must have been quite old to be married and have three children, at least 30. I had expected someone quite different after meeting Gerald and then witnessing the chaos of her kitchen. Someone large, loud and raucous. But she wasn't at all frightening, as I had imagined, or stuck-up as you might expect a doctor's wife to be. She wasn't even solid and sensible. Perhaps she'd changed after having children and that was why Gerald appeared to be so cross with her.

'I'll just give Simon a drink, then we can have one... to celebrate. I expect you're famished as well,' she said and clapped her hands together.

She filled Simon's bottle then poked him playfully in the stomach as he continued to wail.

'How about a little sherry. That'd be nice.'

She paused in the doorway, smiling at me. I was starving and the thought of alcohol made me feel nauseous, especially sherry which I knew smelt sickeningly sweet. I couldn't remember drinking alcohol at two o'clock in the afternoon before and certainly never with an adult. Dad would not permit alcohol in the house. According to his beliefs, based on some ancient sect called the Rechabites, alcohol was nothing short of evil which had made it more attractive but my experience only extended to beer. I sensed she might be disappointed if I asked for tea and nodded in agreement. I could hear her rummaging around in the next room while the child snuffled on his bottle, his eye fixed on the doorway. He was quite sweet now that he wasn't crying, with straight, fair hair that stood up in a crew cut and velvet brown button eyes that gave him the appearance of a little hedgehog.

Caroline returned and set the glasses down firmly on the kitchen table. I wondered if her hand was shaking as she poured the drinks. Perhaps she was nervous with my being there in her kitchen. In her house.

'Well, cheers,' she grinned at me in a breathless squeak. 'Here's to us,' and drained her glass while I managed to swallow a sip as though I was enjoying it. I wished she would make me something to eat. I was starving and had been too nervous to eat anything on the plane. I was convinced we'd crash into the Alps and was half-hoping we would. That way, my shameful secret would have died with me and everyone could go on pretending that nothing untoward had ever happened – just like they were doing now.

Chapter 16

Incarceration

New Plymouth, New Zealand 1964

It seemed a long time before Mrs Hartley-Farrell showed me upstairs to my room. I hurried behind her, dragging my suitcase and duffel bag as she bounded ahead, her ponytail springing out the rhythm of her steps. She paused on the landing indicating the various rooms which she urged me to peep into as quickly as possible as she hadn't 'got round to them yet.'

There were four bedrooms all of which opened out on to the same landing. Simon had the smallest, she said, 'although more often than not he ends up in ours!' she laughed. 'Gerald gets cross if he's woken up by his crying and my mother says I should leave him to cry and then he'd learn who was boss – except he just carries on crying. She thinks I spoil him and so does Gerald. So I can't win,' she said with a mischievous smile.

'Bruce and Victoria's room is a permanent tip!' she said as I obligingly peered over her shoulder at the toys and books strewn all over the beds and the floor.

'So I tend to close the door on it,' she giggled and demonstrated closing the door.

'Gerald thinks I should keep it tidy and so should the children... But it hardly seems worth the effort. They only mess it up again. And Bruce makes such a fuss if I ask him to help! Which reminds me... it's almost time to collect them from school!'

She quickly pointed out her bedroom, then opened the door beside it into mine which she announced with an exaggerated gesture, 'And this is the guest room.' She giggled again and was gone.

The guest room looked like no one had ever stayed there. I wondered if it would look the same after I left. Maybe that was why she giggled. Guests made no impression on the room. It was small, accentuated by the low ceiling that sloped down to where the eves jutted out with a window set between them. There was a slightly stale smell as if the window hadn't been opened for a while. In the far corner was a bed covered with a faded floral bedspread that was rather crumpled, and opposite was a chest of drawers made of dark wood. On it sat a dusty old Spanish doll in national costume. The walls were blank and bare, with a faint pattern of rosebuds on the wallpaper that was faded like the bedspread. Beside the door was a built-in wardrobe.

I sat on the bed and gazed around the room. It had a toneless feel to it, washed out and colourless, bland, bleached, exhausted as if everything had lost its brightness all at once. I thought of my own room at home with the blinds slightly lowered against the sun and the bold, bright cerise and green curtains and bedspreads that my sister had made so cleverly along with the matching skirt disguising the drawers of the dressing table. I could see the familiar patina reflected from the warm wood of my wardrobe doors and I could touch the plain white walls that offset the colourful hues of the fabric. A gallery of Elvis' magnetic sneers remained above my sister's bed keeping vigilance with a single poster of the Beatles on my side, watchful spectators on our empty room. This room was the exact opposite. It wasn't a prison exactly because it had furniture in it, and curtains, but it seemed to signal the same sense of being bad, incarcerated in a cell somewhere, against my will… for a long period of time. I had never felt so alone in my life. This solitude, this grim, empty space… it felt like a death sentence. Nothing was going to help me now because all the precious things in my life were gone, and I was no longer precious to anyone.

I got up and opened the window to lean out. I didn't want to dwell on the fact that I had been exiled here by my own family.

It was the first time in my life I felt separate from them. I also felt separate from myself as if I was watching myself in a film or something. I looked down on the garden at the front of the house. It was large and laid mainly to lawn, its ill-defined edges snaked uneasily around it. Almost everything had died down except some clumps of flax, some ferns and a few conifer trees. Leaves lay in heaps where they'd been blown against the trees. A single red rose had defied winter and waved in the breeze. I could see Caroline pushing the baby down the road and watched her until they were out of sight. I closed the window and sat down on the bed again as there was nothing else to do. The house was filled with stillness.

After a while, I opened my suitcase. The first thing I saw lying neatly folded on top were the two maternity dresses that my mother had made for me. They looked ugly and home-made with green flowers on one dress, and brown and white flowers on the other. They felt as if they had nothing to do with me.

'Do they fit OK?' my mother had asked standing outside my bedroom door as I started to pack my suitcase.

'Yeah,' I replied without thanking her. I hadn't even bothered to try them on and she didn't say anything more. I pulled them out and hung them in the wardrobe then noticed how huge they looked – like the space in the wardrobe – as if they were both waiting to be filled. I snatched them from their hangers and shoved them in a drawer that smelled of mothballs. The coat hangers clanged out an eerie rhythm as they nudged each other conspiratorially. I slammed the cupboard door on them and folded away the rest of my clothes. I realised I had hardly packed anything, just two pairs of trousers and two jerseys in one drawer and my underwear in another. Nothing precious like the gold watch my Aunt Hypatia had given me or the perfume John had given me, only my silver charm bracelet with our names engraved on it, 'Sue and John... forever.' It was like I had no use for them anymore. Then I knelt down in front of the suitcase and stroked my precious piece of sheepskin that lay there before pressing it to my cheek to enjoy the warmth and softness. I wanted to sleep. I wanted to dream of my mother's softness and to wake nestled in her warmth like I used to. Instead, I lay on the bed with my sheepskin and wondered how it was that I came to get pregnant in the first place.

As worldly schoolgirls a few months ago none of us would have dared to ask such a question for fear of derisory laughter. Our little smoking circle, a visible red glow submerged in the secret darkness of the school basement, would have convulsed with mirth. Our sophisticated discussions about our experiences and fantasies rested on the certain foundation of such knowledge. It was our private time for sharing confidences and strategies. Mysteries known only to us, which had the effect of binding us close together. Our conversations in those days were mainly about boys, sex and our own emerging sexuality. We were in no way competitive where boys were concerned and were not averse to sharing them on occasions, in strict rotation, of course. They were a source of great amusement. We would compare some poor boy's ability to kiss with that of a horse or a brick wall. We had even devised our own, secret code words which usually pertained to those parts of the human anatomy that were not taught at school, like 'smosob', bosoms spelled backwards, and more daringly 'fffurball', pronounced with a stuttering 'f' and as if it were one word, which related to male tackle.

I had not, however, been forthcoming about my relationship with John. It was special, private and passionate. And I was sure our sexual activities exceeded my girlfriends', if what they revealed was anything to go by. I could not pluck out a moment of intimacy and objectify it for communal amusement or fascination for fear of losing some special magical ingredient of his love. And besides, it was a delicate matter. Looking back, what I hadn't realised was that one of the very things that drew John and me together would soon drive us apart.

But while the mechanics of sex was common knowledge, I had known nothing whatsoever about the nuts and bolts of conception. After all, who would tell us such a thing? We had no books, pictures or films on the subject, presumably because the adults were too embarrassed, or didn't know themselves. I remember my friend Janet had been asking her mother about tampons and she'd told her she couldn't use them until she'd emptied her bladder. She thought you peed from your vagina! We all roared with laughter falling on to our backs in the darkness of the dust and dirt of the school cellar, and I had to repress the urge to confess I had thought that as well.

But they couldn't all have been ignorant – our teachers, mothers, grandmothers, aunts and sisters. They were females too, just like us. Perhaps they'd learned about 'it' only when they got married. As part of the ceremony, or shortly beforehand, to preserve the secrecy from young girls like me, a kind of verbal form of contraception to stop us from doing whatever we wanted... whatever that was.

It reminded me of something my father had said to me before I left:

'You're behaving as if you think you're free to do whatever you like,' which hadn't made a lot of sense at the time. Maybe that's why it stuck in my mind. But 'free' of what was still not clear. What was clear was that my ignorance of nature had deprived me of a freedom it seemed I had no right to expect in the first place.

Chapter 17

The Things I Did Tell John

New Plymouth, New Zealand 1964

I still have some of the letters John wrote to me and a few that I had written to him although I don't remember how I came by them. I can't imagine he would have returned mine to me. Maybe I found them lying around the bedroom he shared with his brother and scooped them up quick as lightning, mortified to think someone else might read them.

It is only by looking at them now, years later, I can see glaring omissions. Ones that told a different story but needed to be concealed, like the baby, for fear of upsetting anyone.

August 23, 1964
Darling John,
I love getting your letters. I live for them! They're the only thing that keeps me going, connects me to you and my real life. Being here still feels like I've landed from outer space. Caroline doesn't seem to understand or appreciate how I feel about hearing from you – little does she know how long I spend looking for the postie out the upstairs window every day! I don't think she'd be very pleased. She can be quite strict on some things.

'I am particular about **some** things,' she said when I first arrived emphasising the 'some' as if I might've assumed she wasn't particular about anything very much (which is more accurate!). She said this when she was showing me how to iron her husband's shirts for heaven's sake! As if I didn't know how to iron a shirt!

It's nice to know your mum was asking after me. She's a lovely mum. I haven't had any letters or anything from home yet but it's early days I suppose. I'm glad your job is going well although I do wish you hadn't told your boss about me. He's bound to know my father! Or my uncle or grandfather!

Well, I better sign off and go and collect the little brat, I mean girl from school and her brother. I hope she's nicer to me today. She keeps asking why mummy can't collect her, then goes all sulky. I feel like saying I wish she would... but I also wish she'd be a bit nicer to me. It's daft to feel wounded by a 5 year old!

This comes with great big hugs and lots and lots of love and kisses.

Susie xxxxxxxxxxxxxxxxxxxxxxxxxxxxxxxxxxxx

August 30, 1964

Dear Susie,

How are you, my darling? I do hope you're not too sad, you sound a wee bit down. I hope you're taking things easy and she's not giving you too much to do. Do you get time off? And what exactly is she doing while you're doing all the chores?

I saw Annie and Cathy today. They were having lunch in the Oasis as I walked past and they both rushed out to ask after you and send you their love. So do I, darles. I'm persevering at night school and should be taking my exams soon.

And now for the big surprise! Guess what I've bought for when you come back? A car! A Ford and it only cost £100!

Guess what else I bought? The latest Beatles song *From Me to You*. It's fab! It feels like they've written it just for us! I was going to get it for you but didn't know if you have a record player there? Let me know!

Love you always and forever.

John xxxxxxxxxxxxxxxxxxxxxxxxxxxxxxxxxxxxxxxxx

September 4, 1964

Darling John,

It was wonderful hearing from you so soon. I'm getting to know the postie quite well although I don't think Caroline likes it. Not sure if it's getting letters from you or talking to the postman. Maybe she secretly fancies him in his big shorts!

I'm so bored! Nothing happens! No wonder Caroline's a bit odd, there's only housework and the kids and I seem to do most of it, like looking after them, walking them to school and back, cleaning up after them, doing the laundry, cleaning out the fire grate, carrying buckets of coal... not forgetting ironing all the husband's bloody shirts the 'right' way! Which reminds me – when he's here you'll never guess what! He leaves a list of chores for her to do that day! Can you imagine it!! She never does them, just ignores them so muggins ends up doing them instead. Maybe the list is really meant for me! Or maybe it's his way of reminding her daily how useless she is. Or maybe he's trying to tie her even more to the house – she does seem to disappear quite a lot – or else he's hoping to drive her insane!

Anyway, I'm not insane yet. At least there's an end in sight to living here although it doesn't feel like it... and I don't like to think about it.

Oh, I forgot to mention your car – does it have a running board like Owen's? Can't wait!

I need to sign off now.

I love you,

Sooz xxxxxxxxxxxxxxxxxxxx

September 9, 1964

Darling John,

Sorry to say I'm feeling a bit down today. It's dawning on me more and more that I'm only here to skivvy. And that's all anyone seems to care about. (And taking the baby.) It makes me feel like a slave and it's not just because I don't get paid. Of course I don't expect to. But it's as if that's all there is to me. The only thing she has said to me today is to tell me off because I put the spoons in the wrong section in the drawer. It's like when she's down, I get down and it's the same with the kids. But I was thinking, maybe in some ways it makes things easier, like helping me step back a bit, by not engaging with anyone, not even the kids. And especially not with their baby Simon. It's a bit like what's happening – or, at least what's expected to happen between me and poor little you-know-who. No engagement.

Must go.

Love Sooz xxxxxxxxxxxxxxxxxxxxxxxx

September 23, 1964

Darling John,

It was so lovely hearing from you – even though you should've been studying! That made me laugh – you writing to me in class and making it look as though you were earnestly taking notes!

It's pretty gloomy here. Caroline seems to disappear more and more. Sometimes she says she's going shopping but never comes back with any, or she'll suddenly go out without saying where she's going or when she'll be back. And when she is back she just sort of hangs around the house. It's like she's got a secret or something the way she behaves. She jumped and squealed when I walked into the kitchen yesterday just as she was standing on a chair reaching up into a high cupboard… like she was hiding something. Maybe she thought I was a burglar or her husband coming home unexpectedly, catching her out at something!

I miss everyone so much. It's so empty here. One day tends to drift into the next so I've decided the best way to tell one day from another is to mark it off in bright red pen on my calendar. It makes me feel even more like a prisoner but at least I'm not scratching the dates into the walls! Well, not yet!

Love you always,

Sooz xxxxxxxxxxxxxx

September 29, 1964

Darling John,

I feel so isolated from everyone being here, and now I'm feeling the same way in this house, with Caroline, I mean. Or should I say without Caroline. If she hasn't slipped out of the house. She spends her time doing nothing as far as I can see. Sometimes she just sits on the sofa staring into space. It's a bit scary 'cos I don't know what to do. It's like the more I do, the more helpless she becomes. And I don't feel I can say anything to her husband – he's hardly here anyway and the number of nights he spends away sleeping over at the hospital seem to be increasing.

Sorry, my darling, I don't want you to worry but I need to tell someone what's going on. I know I'm here to help, but I can't help worrying it's making things worse. Especially for the kids.

Longing to hear from you.

I love you so much,

Sooz XXXXXXXXXXXXXXXXXXXXXXX

October 4, 1964
My darling Susie,
Of course I'm worrying about you. I can't bear to think of you being unhappy and I can't wait for you to come home! I'm sure everything will turn out fine. Maybe she's just tired or something.

Took the car out for the first time today! My brother came with me and we drove along the esplanade and I thought of you and our times together nestled in our special place... and yeah, I got all excited and wished I'd worn bigger underpants!

I'm rushing off to night school now but you're always in my thoughts, darles.

I love you more than I can say,

John xxxxxxxxxxxxxxxxxxxxx

October 6, 1964
Darling,
It was so neat hearing from you again today – in spite of the sulky fallout from madam! I still don't know what to make of her. She says to call her Carrie – her friends do. I want to say

I'm not your friend but sometimes she behaves as if she is – like giggling and pretending to whisper things to me and being quite sweet. I feel sort of seduced into believing she genuinely cares about me. And yesterday she almost confided why she goes out so often – I think it's to meet up with some bloke! I didn't know what to say – part of me thought 'I don't blame you' and another part of me felt quite angry with her – I mean she's married and **got** her kids... I know it's none of my business but it's just so two-faced, hypercritical... it's like if you're married you can do what you like! Have kids, have affairs, have it all.

But today she has turned! So I'm keeping a low profile. I hope it's not because she's regretting half-telling me her secret. She's started making hurtful remarks when I get a letter from you, like, 'Hasn't he got anything better to do with his time?' or 'Fancy a bloke his age spending all that time writing love letters to his pregnant girlfriend!' And then snigger as if she's made a joke. And then not speak to me for ages.

Sorry to go on about her – there's not much else here to go on about. But this morning I didn't know what to do. It was like she'd switched herself off. She didn't speak to the kids at breakfast or say goodbye when we all left for school. And yesterday she didn't even come down for breakfast! I've noticed she likes drinking alcohol, sometimes in the morning. Yuk! It seems to make her worse. So I always offer to collect the kids after school and take the baby with me because I don't know how she'll be with them – one day their behaviour's acceptable and the next day the same behaviour isn't and she'll start shouting and screaming at them, poor kids – you can imagine how confused they must be. I think they're scared of her. Sometimes they flinch when she goes near them – reminded me of Dad and me.

She can be quite scary, especially after a drink – playing sort of mind games, teasing me. Sometimes it's hard to tell whether or not she's being genuinely nice or a wee bit nasty. And it's the same with the kids. She'll repeat back to them what they say to her, like, 'Can we have a drink, Mummy?' and she'll reply in a high-pitched mocking squeak, 'Can we have a drink, Mummy?'

Hope it's OK to tell you all this. It's like we're all at her mercy. Tell your mum I was asking after her. And would it be OK to ask you to ring my mum and see how she is?

All for now. Give Cathy and Annie and everyone my love when you see them. Can't wait to hear from you, darling.

Love and kisses,

Sooz XXXXXXXXXXXXXXXXXXXX

I can't find any more letters from John. And just one more from me, shortly before the baby is due.

October 12, 1964

Darling,

Brilliant to get your news! I'm so glad your job is going well and that you're enjoying working in the bank! I still can't get used to the idea that you wear a suit and go to work every day – just like a grown-up! Still see you as a surfie!

Caroline had an accident today – she tripped coming down the stairs and fell! Fortunately she was near the bottom but has sprained her ankle so she needs to rest (even more than usual!). But at least I know where she is!

When I went to sleep last night I was absolutely exhausted. I'm finding the kids quite hard work – they're very demanding, not like your little brother and sister, and she doesn't pay them much attention. But when I woke this morning I found myself in a different world. It was full of beauty, with the sun peeping through the curtains and a shaft of sunlight reaching across the room to my bed and me. I felt really special, sort of blessed. It was such a wonderful feeling being saturated in its warmth – it was like a sort of reminder that maybe sometimes nothing else matters... until I was jolted back into reality after hearing the kids banging on my door and shouting my name, back into this nightmare, estranged from everyone and everything – including you and... everything else. Need to go now.

Love you always,
Soos xxxxxxxxxxx

Chapter 18

The Things I Didn't Tell John

New Plymouth, New Zealand October 1964

It was becoming much less easy for me to pretend that the baby wasn't here inside me, even though that was what I was expected to do by ignoring the situation, or accepting other people saying things like, 'You can always have another one.' But it felt so wrong, unnatural, especially when I could feel it fluttering inside me like a little trapped butterfly. That was when I most needed to communicate with her because that's what the flutterings felt like, a real presence.

I knew I was having a girl, don't ask me how, I just knew. I remember not wanting her to be born, not wanting to give her up. I even rang my father and told him I was bringing her home and to hell with him! But the bravado soon crumbled. How could I manage with no money, no benefits, no entitlement to anything, not even my baby... dependent on a family willing to banish me or a boyfriend whose love might one day fade away?

Late at night when no one was around I would sometimes stroke her little body surreptitiously, talk to her in a whisper, tell her about her father, her family. She felt such a part of me, sometimes sympathetic to my sadness, nudging me with flailing limbs as if to reassure me. But at other times I lay terrified in my bed and could feel myself disengaging from those flailing limbs reminding me of the nightmare existence I had suddenly been thrust into and could do nothing about.

I didn't tell John how I really felt, how each morning I woke up more and more homesick, desperate for anything that was familiar, like my mum's voice on the phone, maybe even a few kind words from my father. I don't think John could have understood how alienated I felt from everyone and everything, how I was often overwhelmed, afraid that nothing would ever be the same again, that I would never be the same. It was already happening. When John mentioned seeing my friends, part of me was transported back with them laughing and having fun like we always did. But another part of me wanted to shut myself away in the horrible spartan bedroom, cutting myself off from all that was dear to me because I didn't deserve anything, I wanted to punish myself in the same way I suppose my family was punishing me.

All this 'protection' in which I was forced to participate seemed to matter more than anything else: protecting the baby from the scourge of illegitimacy, protecting me from the shame of being unmarried, protecting the family's good name so that we appeared untarnished. But to me it was meaningless; it wasn't what I wanted. I knew I wasn't doing this for myself, maybe that's how it was going to be from now on; I had lost myself and become this sort of person and I would never be able to do the things I wanted but instead take care of other people's needs, demands, wishes. And that would somehow be enough. Like my Aunt Hypatia knitting horrid jerseys for everyone forever.

I didn't tell John about the dinner party either. I think it would have upset him and made him feel more helpless than he did already. It still stands out in my mind. It was Caroline at her worst. I don't know if she meant to humiliate me in front of her friends. They had invited three rather glam-looking couples to dinner one Saturday night. I could hear them in the lounge, the women chatting and twittering, the men guffawing in unison. I was glad I could hide in the kitchen with Kamara, a lovely Maori woman they had employed to cook the meal. She wasn't a lot older than me but seemed really mature, wise. She was tall and serene-looking with long black hair pulled back in a black and white striped bow, soft brown eyes and a beautiful, friendly face. She was the only person who talked to me about my 'situation' the whole time I was there.

'So... what's happening with your baby?' she asked smiling gently.

'Um... well, it's going to be adopted...' I stuttered.

'Out of the family, y'mean?'

I blushed. No one had asked me before. It was just assumed that I would do what everyone thought should happen, the right thing, the only thing to do, according to parents, medics, social workers... the church as well. It was what was expected of me so I suppose I felt it was the least I could do to try and make amends. It didn't occur to me I had a choice. Or what that choice would be.

'Is that what you want?' she asked stirring some onions on the stove and looking sideways at me, frowning.

'I... umm... I hadn't really thought about it... I mean... I hadn't thought about what I want... It's not really up to me... I don't... umm... well, I couldn't I manage on my own...'

'But what about your family?'

'My family? Well, um... they sent me here.'

I know it sounds daft, but that was the moment when it really hit home. That what I was doing was profoundly wrong; it felt wrong; not natural. In spite of what everyone was urging. Could they all be wrong?

Kamara looked thoughtful and removed the pan from the stove.

'Y'know in traditional Maori culture the mother has no right to adopt her baby out of the family, ay. The baby belongs to everyone, the whole community, not just the mother.'

I could feel tears welling up, my throat tightening; I knew what she was saying was how things should be. She was talking about what was right, natural.

'Adopting the baby out of the family... giving it to strangers... it's so wrong,' she said shaking her head slightly, 'and it will be a burden for the rest of your life,' she added quietly.

I was completely thrown. What did she mean? It felt like a

curse. I gaped at her, wanting to know more. She saw I was upset and came over and put her arm round me.

'Maybe it's meant to be,' she said softly, then patted me lightly on the shoulder and went back to finish chopping the vegetables.

I became aware of the guests getting louder. I started to wash up some pots and pans but I couldn't get Kamara's words out of my mind. I couldn't imagine what it would be like to live in a situation where everyone thought so differently about having a child out of wedlock. The complete opposite! Where young women like me were free to keep their babies without shame or stigma to the mother or the baby. Instead, the baby was welcomed into its rightful family where it belonged. Not snatched at birth and given to infertile couples... The shame would be in giving the baby up for adoption! Not keeping her! It was hard to get my head around it: Maori had no choice about not keeping the baby and we had no choice about keeping the baby! Who makes up these goddam rules? And how come we obeyed them? And what if 'it's meant to be' as Kamara said. Does that mean no one has any control, least of all me... well that's true now.

I could hardly bear to think about the image of family life that Kamara created, where everyone shared everything, the children, the child care... living in the same world as me but one that turned everything upside down, where the land was like the sky – and like their children – everything belonged to everyone. For a moment I melted into it. It made my heart sing.

I didn't know whether I was invited to eat with the Hartley-Farrells and their friends or help Kamara so I stayed out of sight helping her in the kitchen until Dr Hartley-Farrell called out to me.

'Susan! Do come and join us for a while...'

He patted the seat of the empty chair beside him. For some reason I felt enormous that particular day, much bigger than usual. It was getting harder to hide the bump now and I self-consciously shuffled towards the chair before sitting down a little too heavily on it.

'This is Susan,' Gerald announced. 'All the way from good ol' Dunedin.'

They nodded and smiled politely. The women sat with glazed looks, wooden, bouffant hairstyles and too much make-up, as my mother might have observed. The men were all wearing dark suits.

'Yes, she came through Mac. You remember him, Rob... he was at med school with us – sort of podgy, horn-rimmed glasses, a bit of a swot, always wore a bloody suit.'

They all stared at me, observed me closely as if they didn't have any prior knowledge of me and why I was there. No one said anything to me. I guess they must have felt awkward too.

'Anyway... Susan – have a drink! What can I get you?' said Gerald, slapping his hands together.

'Excuse *me!*' slurred Caroline. 'Did you just offer her a drink?'

'Yes, m' dear. Are you objecting?' said Gerald without looking at her.

'Yes, I am! I most certainly am! You do realise she's underage!'

With that everyone burst into laughter. I blushed and didn't know where to look. I thought to start with that they were laughing at the irony of Caroline moralising about my drinking alcohol. But then she said loudly, 'As you can see,' she gestured exaggeratedly in my direction with a sweep of her hand, 'she may be too young to drink, but in case you hadn't noticed – she's not too young to...'

They all exploded again with laughter. It rang in my ears long after I managed to ease myself out of the chair, quietly making excuses to no one in particular, and, burning with embarrassment, waddled self-consciously out of the lounge upstairs to the sanctuary of my room.

Chapter 19

Within Me, Without Me

New Plymouth, New Zealand October 1964
Aged 17

The birth was the worst. Caroline dropped me off outside the hospital. I was hoping she might help me, maybe stay with me since she'd had three children. But all she said was she didn't like hospitals and drove off.

She had screamed at me earlier that morning, 'You're in labour, you stupid girl!' after my waters had broken, making an embarrassing mess on the bedroom carpet. I could see she was cross and wondered if that was the reason she left me standing outside the hospital with my suitcase. I wanted to ask what happens now? But she was sort of revving up the engine and then she was gone.

I had known nothing whatsoever about 'it' (giving birth) and had acquired very little knowledge at school on the subject save the habits of rabbits, which wasn't a great deal of use to me. The only book I ever saw on the subject was at my girlfriend Annie's house. Her father was a doctor and we acquired the book with great stealth and excitement only to become horrified at bloody scenes of thighs and dark, shady areas of childbirth. We returned the book rather sooner than we'd anticipated, and I remember feeling relieved that the pictures were in black and white. I also wondered if that lady had given her permission to photograph such... a... well, unsightly display and whether her husband knew about them.

I got the feeling that Mum didn't know much about 'it' either, or she didn't want to say. I remember the first question I think I ever asked her when I was aged about 10 or 11 and we were in her bedroom. She was standing by the open cupboard door of the walk-in wardrobe when I asked her a question.

'Mum, Sandra and I have been wondering something... you know when you make a baby with a man...' My mum didn't turn round but stayed stoically facing the inside of the wardrobe. 'Well, she reckons his... you know... finds its own way there but I think he has to put it there. Who's right?'

Mum then stepped forward right into the wardrobe as if she were frantically searching for something at the back of it, and stayed there for quite a while before stepping back into the room and contemplating me in despair.

'My goodness,' she said quietly, 'how do you know about such things?' and without waiting for an answer slipped past me into the hall with a funny look on her face, her mouth sort of twisted like after you put on lipstick then purse your lips in a particular way.

I took a deep breath and went inside the hospital. The staff was very pleasant to start with, inviting me to sit down, offering me a cup of tea, asking how I was feeling. I felt safe and protected for the first time in months. It made me aware of how unprotected I had felt ever since I was sent away, ironically 'for my own protection', according to my father. Until they asked me where my husband was. Then everything changed. No more tea or sympathy, no reassuring smiles. They still kept calling me 'Mrs' and it didn't feel right, although I never said anything.

They left me on my own most of the time in a small side room somewhere at the end of a long green corridor, which was more or less OK to start with; I didn't want to make a fuss. I'd caused enough trouble. But the worse the pains got, the more difficult it was not to call out. And when they got really bad, I couldn't help myself. I gasped, I panted, I panicked, I screamed. Quietly at first, then a bit louder, and then I didn't really care about the noise I was making, the pains were so bad. I thought I was going to die. Explode. Split apart. I couldn't breathe properly. And that was when a nurse finally appeared.

'For heaven's sake,' she hissed, 'we are making a lot of noise!'

'Please... please can I have something for the pain?' I whimpered.

'Bit late now I should think,' she said, then pursed her lips in an exaggerated way and added, 'No easy way out for you, I'm afraid.'

'When do you think I'm going to have it?' I whispered when the pain subsided.

'Think!' she exclaimed. 'Think! Good God, girl, I'm not paid to think!' And with that she swept out of the room.

I began to feel sick again, like I did when they gave me something called an enema, then told me to go straight to the toilet.

'We don't want doctor having to deal with anything unpleasant now, do we?' the nurse had stated, although inserting it hadn't been very pleasant. I had rushed to the toilet and sat on the seat, but ended up spinning round and round, unable to decide whether to be sick or to 'move my bowels', as they put it. I remember I couldn't decide. I had no control over either end and was really worried I might make a mess or be sick on the floor. I also remember catching sight of my shaved pubes and wondered why they needed to do that. I'd been beetroot-bright with embarrassment.

The more I screamed, the more examinations I seemed to have and the rougher they became. Different doctors, but always the same cold approach. Each examination was a blueprint of the previous horrible one. Usually the doctor never looked directly at me. Sometimes he would speak through the nurse, if there was one to spare, repeating the same instructions in a matter-of-fact way: 'Ask her to flop her legs apart.'

The nurse would carry out the instruction not looking at me either, and I would burn and blush with shame.

But by that time I was in too much agony to care. And then they moved me on to a trolley, bouncing me any-old-how along a brightly-lit corridor and into an even more brightly-lit theatre, where I remember shrinking from its antiseptic smell, yellow, sickly and tasting of fear. I was bundled on to a high, narrow table, still screaming. The lights hurt my eyes and made me hot. I felt faint like my life was ebbing away. I was convinced I was going to die. I just wanted my mum. My legs were pulled apart and once again strapped into stirrups. A sheet was draped over my upper body. I disappeared.

Occasionally I could hear the doctors talking – then laughing. I thought I was in a movie, slow motion where time had no meaning, or floating in and out of a bad dream. Perhaps this wasn't really happening. I was getting confused. The doctors were talking about golf. I recognised some of the terms because my best friend's parents played golf together every Saturday.

Suddenly I was slapped across the face. Then a voice shouted, 'That's enough now! Push!' And then they were all screaming, 'Push! Push!' They kept screaming at me in unison, encircling me. Their faces were strained, red with the effort, as if they, too, were giving birth. I hated them and their fat florid faces. When I wanted to push earlier, they had shouted, 'No, don't push!' and now they wanted me to push. But I had no more energy. My body was splitting in two. I thought I was dying in this horrible place surrounded by these screaming, scarlet-faced strangers. I'd had enough. I just wanted to go home. Make everything go away. Be back home with my lovely mum. And John.

Then someone shouted, 'It's coming! It's coming.' And another voice shouted, 'Don't let her see it! Make sure she doesn't see it!' Then they put something over my head. I think I passed out.

When I came to, it was dark. I couldn't breathe properly. I brought my hands up to my head and found a paper bag there. I was dreaming, floating, melting but I could still hear the nurses talking.

'Get the baby out of here... Make sure she doesn't see it... Then clean her up as best you can...'

I ripped the bag away and sat up. I saw a nurse wheeling a cot out through the double doors and I screamed. This time it was from the pit of my being – a deep, primal wail like I've never heard before. Like a threatened animal might make. The nurse stopped and looked round in surprise as I wrenched off the stirrups and leapt off the bed shouting, 'My baby! I want to see my baby!'

I grabbed at the cot and looked down at the baby in disbelief. All the mayhem of noise and trauma and confusion faded away and in that moment it was silent, still. She was perfect. Beautiful. A tiny child just lying there in a cot, staring at me. Dark hair, pencil eyebrows, blue eyes. My whole body ached for her.

'You ought to be ashamed of yourself!' hissed the nurse, leaning over the cot in an attempt to cover the baby with her body. 'Ashamed!'

I reached out to pick her up. But the nurse suddenly whisked her away. And she was gone.

Part II

Still Lost

Living is Easy with Eyes Closed
Strawberry Fields, The Beatles, 1967

Chapter 20

Go Away and Forget

Dunedin, New Zealand March 1966

It was easy to start with, going away and forgetting. I didn't want to remember. So I filled my life being busy with girlfriends and parties, boys and study. I decided to go to university and study subjects I was interested in, anthropology, psychology and education, even though I didn't know much about them.

University life suited me, helped me forget. Parties, boys, booze – who cared? At weekends the campus was like one big party, the old weatherboard houses that clustered round the university rented mostly by students were open house: Skid Row, Union Street, Dundas Street, provided you turned up with some booze – usually brown ale. Sometimes us girls just hung around giggling on the front verandas peering in to eye up the talent. Or we'd meet in one of the student pubs, usually the Captain Cook where you needed to ring the bell three times to get in after hours (six o'clock back then!) as opposed to once by the cops, which sent punters fleeing to the toilets.

I tried to make out I was still the same as other young women my age, having boyfriends, going to pubs, always out and about with friends. But it was a lie. I was not like them. My experience was unique. I kept expecting to be exposed. I worried that everyone knew I was a fraud, a miscreant, a sinner. Sometimes I felt like screaming from the rooftops just to get it all out in the open. Finally have done with it – the looks, the whispering, avoiding eye contact. Was I imagining it? Sinners like me need to repent their ways, not go to parties. They should spend their lives seeking redemption. But even if I never went to parties, could I ever be truly redeemed, the stain expunged from my character, everything unacceptable filtered out?

I tried to comply by forgetting but was faced with so many reminders, especially my body – the changes to my breasts and tummy which made me self-conscious especially in changing rooms, never mind anything else! Everyday things lost their glow – walking along the beach or gazing at the sea from the dunes, scuttling past the bowling green at the bottom of our road where we used to snog, seeing John's family, my family, neighbours, old friends from school. Almost everything.

I wondered how much longer I could carry on hiding the truth. Would it keep on reappearing, nudging me hard in the heart forever? I became aware of other groups of people who were also expected to forget their past, like friends' fathers who returned home after the war having been tortured by the Japanese, carrying memories of seeing friends and colleagues beaten, starved, killed; our own grandparents, forced to flee for their lives to escape terrible injustices they had witnessed; and then there were young women like me and my friends – five out of eight of us, all now at uni – sent away and not allowed to return home with our babies. We never shared our stories from the day we got back home. I was barely aware we'd been through the same experience. Maybe it was the same for those soldiers and for our grandparents.

Everyone seemed to just get on with things, keep moving forward, leaving their pasts behind them, the same message we echoed loudly when we sang our school song *The Chambered Nautilus* about a cute little sea creature who sails upright through life unimpeded along the Pacific Ocean floor. Each of its chambers is sealed off once it has outgrown them but at the same time they continue to provide it with the buoyancy it needed. It was supposed to symbolise a template for maturation from girlhood to womanhood, a natural progression from one stage to the next:

Year after year beheld the silent toil
that spread its lustrous coil
she left the past year's dwelling for the new...
and knew the old, the old no more.
Oliver Wendell Holmes, American poet

But I had lost my buoyancy, my joy, any sense or purpose in my life, nothing propelling me forward, and most certainly not my past, as if I were living in a haze, my natural flow interrupted. Nor was the past entirely sealed off. It leaked.

I couldn't reconnect with John and was glad he wasn't part of the student scene. Nothing was the same when I got back home. In many ways it was as if everything was still the same – I looked the same as I did before I left, but I wasn't the same. I'd never be the same.

I didn't want to talk about what happened; it made it easier to pretend the past didn't exist. It felt safer that way. I didn't know how to manage things or do as I'd been told and simply go away and forget her, pretend I wasn't sad, stop crying. It was the physical longing that wouldn't go away, hard as I tried to make it. How could John understand that? Or anyone else.

Maybe Paul from our primary school did, although it didn't seem like it at the time. He was a kid from the local orphanage. Everyone, aside from him, tended to avoid the subject of my being sent away. Like we were all carrying a secret that hung on the air, stagnant, infused with disapproval and made me feel even more ashamed.

I saw Paul in George Street not long after I got back. He had the cheek to say, 'I hear you had a daughter.' I wanted to shout at him to mind his own bloody business! How dare he mention that! I wanted to hit out at him. Instead I said nothing and walked away.

But the outrage wasn't because of what he'd said... It was

about giving her an identity, making her real... making her mine as if somehow she had belonged to me so that the loss of her was what I had chosen. And now it looked as if I was simply moving on.

When I finished telling a primary school friend Alison many years later about Paul, she disagreed.

'Maybe he did have an understanding, an acceptance of what you'd been through,' she said. 'Because for him it wasn't outside his own experience. He'd grown up in an orphanage and so he probably knew better than most kids of the pain of forced separation. It wasn't foreign to him, it was part of his own life. So it wasn't a taboo subject as far as he was concerned.'

I'd forgotten she was a psychotherapist. It made sense. If only I'd had this sort of help to understand things back then. Maybe there were others like Paul who had a similar experience to him and had witnessed the effects of separating newborns from their mothers as if it were something natural, like kittens or puppies or lambs or calves and had heard the mothers crying for them in the fields near the orphanage. Everyone secretly knowing that it wasn't right, it wasn't natural because it goes against nature... and those who heard the loss in their cries hoped the sadness wouldn't last long.

That was when Alison told me about her father's return home after the war and the trauma he suffered at the hands of the Japanese.

'Apparently my dad had been a brilliant pianist but he was forced to play in the Japanese prisoner of war camp where he was held... to keep the prisoners quiet.' She hesitated and looked tearful. 'Then when he came home he never played again,' she said and whispered, 'I never even knew he could play the piano...'

Did he too feel he had betrayed something or someone even though it was beyond his control? That a single event where you have been expected to go away and forget – for everyone's sake

– can forever shape your whole life?

Maybe her dad felt the same as me, slipping between two separate worlds with two separate ways of being: one ashamed, secretive, fearful, haunted and hopeless with no sense of a future, no real dignity or self-worth. And the other, light, happy-go-lucky, taking all sorts of risks, not caring in the slightest what happened to me. Unable to move forward as expected of you, each way of being held in check by the other so all you experience is impasse.

'Both sets of grandparents behaved as if nothing out of the ordinary had happened to them either,' I told Alison. 'You'd never have known they'd been driven off their lands, were persecuted, powerless, humiliated... and probably reduced to a mere shell of what they had once been,' I said.

Is that how I should live my life, too?

John had been very attentive and sweet, making sure everything was OK. He rang me every day to see how I was, offered to help me with anything and everything, wanting to see me all the time like we used to.

He had organised a surprise for me that should have melted my heart. He led me to a cute little secluded fairy tale of a cottage, a love nest, hideaway for hippie honeymooners and lovers. He made me close my eyes then led me through some trees to the door of the cottage, lifted me over the threshold and carried me through to the bedroom. A double bed dominated the room. It had been carefully made up, pillows plumped, brown and cream bedlinen, a bottle of wine and two glasses on the bedside cabinet. He stood behind me with his arms around my waist.

'So what d'ya think, Susie? It's ours for as long as we want...'

I knew I was going to disappoint him even before we went inside the little hut. I could imagine all the trouble he had gone to making it as cosy as possible, attending to details with love – the wine glasses, the bed all made up. We'd never spent the whole night together even though I had moved away from home.

'Oh... it's... fab...'

'Neat, ay!'

He started nibbling my neck. I wanted to turn round and hug him, kiss his wonderful soft lips, try and make things seem normal, the way it used to be. But I was finding it impossible to shake off the past, discard it. To forget. Instead I could feel myself trembling. I had a flash of an image seeing myself swear on a huge bible when I signed the adoption papers never to try and find her.

'I swear,' I can still remember whispering in a solicitor's darkened office organised by my father miles from home in the small town of Roxburgh in Central Otago so no one would recognise our family name, aware of the piles of files everywhere tied in crimson ribbon, having been instructed to repeat after the solicitor while placing my hand on a large black bible, 'I swear... never to make any attempt to look for or to contact my daughter from this day forward.'

Then I excused myself, went to the toilet, threw up, got on the coach and made the solitary journey home, our lives tied up in secrecy bound together with crimson ribbon somewhere in a solicitor's dusty office.

'Is there a kettle in the kitchen?' I asked and burst into tears.

I desperately wanted to forget, to move forward like everyone else. But in spite of the promise and the legal agreement, I had an almost defiant but natural need to remember, a need infused with guilt and regret that grew with time fuelled by a fear of forgetting as if someone or something bigger than a bible might try and blot out the past. Pretend it never happened. Perhaps part of me was trying to do the same. Melt into this collective madness.

The more I tried to forget the harder it became. Any small shred of a need to 'go away and forget' was choked by an increasing need to know. Like bamboo that has been scythed then smothered in concrete, continuing to grow, emerging, quietly at first, defiant then irrepressible so that even a supersonic scythe couldn't deal with it.

I desperately needed to remember her birthday. To remember how she had looked in those few seconds snatched straight after her birth. The cap of dark hair, the fine line of her eyebrows framing blue eyes. Her stare that I carried with me. What was she thinking, I wonder? Maybe she was asking me the same question.

What if that memory were blotted out like excess ink, and I had acquiesced, gone away and forgotten, left with nothing but a faded image, a faint trace of an image open to distortion that ebbed and flowed with the passage of years, steeped in uncertainty so that even I doubted whatever image I had managed to retain? If I ever forget her little face, or her birthday, I'll forget what hope feels like.

Chapter 21

The Day My Mum Died

Dunedin, New Zealand December 23rd, 1966
Aged 19

My lovely mum is gone forever. Two days before Christmas. I didn't know she was going to die. She was only 53. She wasn't able to say goodbye, otherwise I'm sure she would have. She'd had a stroke a few months earlier and wasn't able to be herself anymore. Maybe she'd had enough, found life too difficult to manage. Somehow arranged it with herself, even though it affected all of us, not just her. But I dearly wished I'd had some warning, a second chance. Like my mum had the first time with her stroke. Then I could have tried to turn back time, been the daughter I should have been. Not weighed her down with sorrow and shame. It was as if she, too, was suddenly taken from me, snatched away without so much as a bye or leave, echoes of my daughter. I could have made sure they both knew how much I loved them. And what happened was not her fault. But if I'd had that opportunity I know I'd never have let her go. Or my daughter. Maybe my mum knew that, knew how much I needed her, how important her love was to me. I wondered if she sensed she'd never see me again when I announced I was going up to Auckland for a working holiday... I wondered the same about my daughter the only time I saw her. Do people play a part in their own demise, their own destiny, their own deaths?

Bristol, UK 2014

I'm writing this more than 40 years later. I could never have done so back then. Losing my mum was too emotional, too numbing, too fraught with regret at what I did and didn't do. It wasn't a matter of letting bygones be bygones where memories might

133

begin to erode with time, able eventually to be digested. It's hard to shake them off, the sensations of feeling bruised, bereft. Christmas still carries with it a sense of emptiness, greyness although I try not to let it show. I've never really been able to talk or think about my mum without getting a lump in my throat, tears in my eyes. Even now. Such a private thing, grief. Hard to share. And the tears would always get in the way. I had cried for her almost every night for years after she died. Like I was a young child, I suppose. Except a young child doesn't know whether the grief could last forever or might recede, thaw a little, and that's when it can really hurt. Become raw and sensitive when exposed to warmth. So I never really shared my feelings about her with anyone. I found it hard until recently to get the words out.

Auckland December 1966

Two weeks before my mum died, I'd hitchhiked several hundred miles up to Auckland with a girlfriend. A new beginning, a new city, shedding the past, freeing me. I hadn't decided whether to return to university or not. I was all over the place. We'd taken our time after a couple of long car journeys and a tired truck that took us to Kaikoura on the east coast near the top of the South Island where we lay on the rocks with loads of seals we'd spotted from the truck, basking in the warmth of the sun. It felt strange being so close to such magnificent creatures, meeting their dark eyes, noticing their wet skin glinting and gleaming granite bronze, iridescent in the sunlight, their whiskers delineated like fine needles silhouetted against the open sea, their proximity making you feel like you were part of their existence and they were part of yours.

We crossed to the North Island on the ferry from Picton, a cute little town set out like an American Western minus the tumbleweed, and arrived in Wellington after a delicate, overnight crossing. Then we spent a couple more days hitchhiking to

Auckland.

I managed to get a waitressing job in a posh hotel as soon as we got there. I don't know if Mum objected to my leaving. I don't remember sensing anything. No one told me she might possibly die. I had no idea that this was the last time I'd ever see her. I was going up to Auckland, partly to meet up with a new boyfriend who called me 'bee's knees' because I wore stripy tights, but mostly to get away from everyone I knew. I had felt torn being there especially at home. It was impossible to please Dad, get things right, keep things going no matter what sacrifices I'd made or how much I tried to repair things, repay him for what I'd done. And I felt sad and useless and responsible seeing my mum so changed and helpless. I was starting to crumble, become passive, as if I were drowning, like my mum, yielding to a force that felt much greater than me.

Dad rang the hotel where I was working and the receptionist came and found me and suggested I take the call in a phone box in the lobby. I assumed it was because it was a toll call from Dunedin.

'I'm ringing to tell you your mother's dead,' he said almost abruptly.

Silence.

'Are you there?' he asked assuming we must have been cut off rather than realising the effect on me of what he'd just said.

'You bastard!' I shrieked. 'How dare you ring me up and tell me such bullshit!'

I'd never sworn at him before, never dared, but I didn't care about the consequences.

'Susan's gone mad,' I heard him say, presumably to my sister. 'Quite mad!'

I had slammed down the receiver and then noticed everyone was looking at me. I ran up the hotel stairs, packed my suitcase and caught a bus to Mount Eden where my boyfriend's mother lived. She was lovely. Kind and beautiful and good fun. I preferred her company to her son's. She took charge. She rang my father, then confirmed the news I couldn't bear to hear. She arranged the plane fare, took care of me and tucked me up in bed, which I discovered the following morning, to my absolute horror, I had wet during the night.

On the plane I found myself seated next to a friendly man who tried to strike up a conversation. It ended rather abruptly after he asked me why I was going to Dunedin.

'My mother's just died,' I'd said in a matter-of-fact way. 'So I'm going to her funeral.'

Dad decided I shouldn't see my mother's body. And that was that. No reason given, except, 'because I said so.' So all I had was a sense of absence. My mother's absence without knowing why or where she'd gone. It was as if she'd just up and left. And I, in turn, was left with a familiar sense of emptiness, incompleteness. I felt as helpless as she must have felt, always trapped in his wake.

My father had also decided that my mother should be cremated, even though she had always said she wanted to be buried. So that was that as well. I felt I had played no part in her leaving (except being seen by my father as the cause of her leaving), made no contribution, no giving thanks, no interaction. Nothing, really. She was suddenly just gone. No ritual or bidding farewell. Like me, walking quietly out of the hospital as I had done, away from my daughter.

The funeral passed in a haze. I don't remember much, except that for some reason I was sitting at the back of the church, not up the front with my family. Or maybe I'd imagined that as being my rightful place, the place I deserved, I don't know. After all, Dad had wasted no time telling me I was responsible for my mum's death.

'I hope you realise this is all your fault!' he'd bellowed at me. 'You're the one who killed her! You're the reason she's dead!'

I remember my father and sister shaking hands afterwards

and speaking with everyone who came. There were no tears, only a kind of maturity I knew I didn't possess. I was outside the church too but couldn't join them for crying. I didn't know where my brother was. And John had suddenly gone to live in Australia. Only one relative, my Auntie Shirley, came and spoke to me.

'Your mum was lovely... and she really loved you. I hope you know that.'

I've never forgotten that kindness and clung to it whenever I remembered it alongside another relative's comment – not even a blood relative – who came up close to me after the funeral and whispered in my ear, 'You've got no right to mourn.'

The memory of them stuck in my head for years. Part of me evaporated at the guilt I carried, unable to move forward. The other part remembers her love for me. For some reason I needed to remember both remarks together, one exonerating, the other punitive, locked in conflict between past and future. A pernicious impasse lodged in my memory.

But these days memory alone cannot be counted on. Recalling time and events is starting to become a bit less reliable and at some stage I expect things to be quietly dissolving, disintegrating and blessedly less clear-cut. Less limiting, less destructive in its power. In spite of that, some images and traumas can stay forever. And so do attachments. Looking back, it is less about memory and more about trying to make sense of things, not holding on to negative memories and images which serve no purpose, stop me in my tracks. So when I think about my mum, it's love that fills me up, love and gratitude flood through me, like lifting a sluice gate and allowing the rush and flow of water to go where it will. I now realise the most important thing is love, and love outweighs everything, so that is the memory I have chosen to absorb and retain. Reshape myself.

I had always enjoyed being with my mum, that's what I remember. And I'm sure as eggs she enjoyed being with me. I didn't need to search for clues, we liked being together. She was good company in a nice, quiet sort of way. She was gentle, kind and sweet-natured. She could be funny, especially imitating accents.

'Ach, canny make yer a wee cuppa tay?' she would say.

Now there were no more afternoon tea treats, cosy chats in bed, no one there to hug me when I came home. No one at home. And then, not long after, no home.

People liked my mum. But she was also quite shy, unassertive. She never insisted on anything for herself, so I suppose she wanted it like that. She was at the mercy of things, had no control over anything, and so was I, unable to help her. Especially her own health which often fluctuated from seriously ill to dangerously ill according to late night hospital phone calls... or her own happiness and her own freedom. It was like she adapted herself to suit everyone else as if any change was impossible and no one would take her seriously. I think she had more power than she realised but wouldn't have used it in case, perhaps, she felt we might no longer love her. The way things were, the way we lived was obviously best for everyone.

My mother's life had revolved largely around the house. She seemed quietly content at home as if she was unaware that there was another world out there, like it was natural to wait on us hand and foot, always slaving away and making sacrifices for us and never seeming to get fed up. Or rewarded in the smallest ways, like Dad noticing what she'd done or thanking her for something nice she'd baked. What pleasure was there in that? It was ironic that he had to pay all those horrible housekeepers to look after us every time Mum went into hospital, what with the liver and kidneys and brains and tripe they cooked... 'Today, tripe!' one would say and dump the dish down hard on the table where it lay inert and grey, unmoved by the impact, followed by tasteless tapioca puddings.

Although my mother appeared to be content, she didn't seem

particularly happy either, but it was often hard to tell what she was really feeling. Maybe she'd decided long ago that her situation suited her.

'I suppose marriage meant security,' she said when I asked her why she married Dad and told me about her impoverished childhood being one of five children whose parents emigrated from the Isle of Skye. Did they really live in a tiny cottage with a mud floor when the gold rush was on in Central Otago? She told me they didn't always have knickers and instead she would have to use a safety pin to hold her vest together, which must've made going to the toilet very frustrating. And dangerous. It was a strange link with marrying Dad. Perhaps he was the best she could hope for; or maybe she felt she had no choice, no power to shape her own future, no opportunity to ever be free to be herself. And just accepted the way things were. And that's how she became a humdrum housewife. It was a scary thought. Would I, too, become a second class citizen for very different reasons? Perhaps it was a sort of self-preservation on her part which evolved into self-annihilation. Maybe she had cut herself off from her real feelings a long time ago and tried hard never to reconnect with them. I shuddered. That is what I am supposed to do, go away and forget, focus on what is expected of me. Or perhaps she became ill because she lost her own power; her stronger impulse was to maintain us as children and her sense of self ebbed away in the process. Perhaps she thought this was how everyone else lived, this is what being a woman and a mother was all about. With some notable exceptions, like me. With neither a wedding ring, my child or a sense of self. Neither of us free to live our own lives.

Love, not her own sense of power, was all-important, even at the expense of being in touch with her real self or any sense of her own freedom. As if they were mutually exclusive. That it was natural. Maybe it was but its value got lost because she got lost. It made me feel confused because having a loving mum was the best thing; so I felt doubly guilty as if her sadness were our fault, especially my fault.

'Don't you ever get fed up being on your own all day with nothing to do?' I asked after waking her with her favourite afternoon tea of freshly-made pikelets piled high with jam and cream, then snuggling in beside her.

'Not really,' she said, murmuring how delicious the pikelets were.

'After all, I've got all of you to look after... and the house. And the garden! And when I've had my afternoon rest, I've got the dinner to get.'

'Yes, but Sandra's mother plays golf, sometimes all day, and she's a housewife.'

'I don't think your father would be very keen on my doing that,' she said, sipping her tea from one of her best bone china cups I'd chosen specially from the display cabinet, with her little finger extended. 'I'm sure he thinks that this is my proper place... not gadding about on a golf course. Besides,' she added, 'I wouldn't have the energy for that sort of thing.'

After that, our little conversation came to an end and I had the feeling what she really meant was she didn't feel she had any choice. She couldn't move away from the things that didn't suit her, like Dad. Or even move towards anything she did like, maybe playing golf like Sandra's mother. Maybe she believed the same as Dad, that her job was to take care of him and us so gadding about on a golf course all day wouldn't work. But how did it 'work' for Sandra's mother? Did taking care of everyone else automatically mean becoming trapped in an unhappy marriage? What sort of freedom is that? I wanted the freedom to love and to be loved even though I'd messed things up really badly, let everyone down, brought shame on the family. But in my darker moments I wondered if I, too, could ever be free to live my own life.

I hadn't seen these similarities as clearly before, neither of us free to be in charge of our own lives. And somehow, maybe unconsciously, it felt like I wanted to show her there was another way in spite of the chaos I had caused – and even though there was no roadmap, no template to guide her – or me. I had, on occasions, begged her to leave Dad.

'No one gets divorced,' she'd said, 'and what would people say, how would I cope financially and where would we live? Oh, and you've forgotten something else: where on earth would I possibly meet someone?' And I couldn't really answer those questions. Maybe she saw leaving Dad as exchanging one form of suffering for another. There didn't seem to be much hope, whichever way she turned, and it did make me wonder how she'd manage to live without him to protect her. She had no savings, no real skills and no security... just like me.

She stared relentlessly out of the bedroom window.

'I do love those trees,' she sighed, 'even when they're losing their leaves.'

I wanted to say that I was sorry about what had happened, sorry that I was a disappointment, rotten as those fallen leaves, that I had somehow dragged her into all this mess, that I was never going to be the kind of daughter that deep down I'm sure she really wanted, certainly not now! How could she feel free to hold her head up? She'd never stepped out of line, never truly been herself. Because those were the things that seemed to matter least: not being in charge of your own life, having a sense of self, happy in what you're doing, free to make your own decisions about your future. Or having any real hope or curiosity. Or confidence in yourself. Or even enjoying yourself! No, it was all about getting married and being respectable, taking over from our mothers as if there was no room for change. Why did I think my life would be so different? Hadn't I replicated the exact same scenario? Forced to give up my child to accommodate my parents' and society's unnatural way of thinking... thereby setting the scene for 'respectability', for marriage unencumbered by a child.

Compromise myself in the worst way imaginable for a woman. I was stuck just like she was, the same irresolvable issues. It was as if it wasn't possible for either of us to be independent and to live without a man. Especially as a young, unmarried mother with a baby in 1964.

Chapter 22

Mediums and Mixed Messages

Wandsworth Common, London 1977

When do you stop needing a parent, even one 'on hold' in the background, whatever the quality of the relationship? To have at least one of them left helping to hold up the sky, creating the illusion of some sort of protective cover, a kind of safety net so you can't fall any further until the remaining one also dies, leaving you completely exposed to all the elements; to a peculiar kind of freedom, uninvited and scary; to an absence of something so profound it's difficult to articulate, even in your twenties, whatever grown-up stuff you may have done. It's a vulnerability that can't be matched or mended no matter how hard you may search; left bereft looking for something to cling on to, an anchor in the midst of a tsunami. Some sort of certainty.

Sometimes I'd feel like a puppy who'd been removed too early from its mother. I wasn't ready to lose her at 19, become an orphan, as that's what it felt like. I was left with a feeling of emptiness, a feeling as solitary as air. I remember thinking I don't really know where I'm going, what I'm searching for, or why I feel so empty. Nor could I say what exactly it is that I miss. I wonder if I'll ever find it, whatever it is. And will I know it when I do?

Maybe seeing mediums occasionally was my way of recreating a sort of benevolent mentoring situation like a kindly parent might provide – gently advising on a particular course of action, offering a critical but nurturing overview of my life as if the medium knew me in the same way as a loving parent might, having faith in what was being said, receiving advice and guidance as if it were spiritually gleaned from an inviolable source, giving my life some sort of cohesion and reassurance that all will be well. Above all, always hoping I might receive a message from my mum. And information about my daughter.

In darker moments I'd wonder how these 'messages' would help me. In some ways it was a form of prolonged torture, perpetuating the search for God knows what exactly, heightening my sensitivity to things, like always worrying about what had happened to my daughter – things some people, like my father, would regard as best left alone; always reinforcing the notion that there were ways to better myself, things I needed to attend to. Room for improvement. Are searching and avoiding the same thing, I wonder?

I have kept all my readings dating back to the early seventies, but have seldom revisited them. Nothing seemed to fill the void; somehow they never satisfied me. I realise, looking back, that it may have been more about forcing myself to relive the trauma over and over via the readings, at the same time not wanting to keep opening old wounds, and then not knowing how to close them up again. And re-experiencing the disappointment that usually followed.

Looking back, I think the searches were not only looking for answers or information about my daughter, but maybe a confirmation that, in spite of what happened, I am OK as a person.

I've built up quite a file of 'messages' preoccupied with concern and worry about my daughter; it includes psychics, mediums, clairvoyants, channellers, astrological horoscope readers, craniosacral healers, oh, and a cute, Spanish sort-of-Jesus-lookalike wearing a cassock, a ponytail and bare feet who lives in a cave up a Spanish mountain with electric hands-on healing and could tell you your whole life story by simply looking at you or a photo of you in your absence, even passport size. That includes your health and medication!

'You must heal,' he said to me in broken English. 'You have the hands...' then fanned out his fingers in my direction. 'Not just any hands,' he said. 'You are volcano!'

I suppressed a giggle. If only I could heal myself, I thought.

I've recorded all of them through the ages – in the seventies it was in note form, the eighties and nineties it was tape recordings, and finally it was CDs at around the turn of the century! Now you whip out your phone. On average I have seen about one a year, so I guess that's not hugely excessive.

'Maybe deep down I didn't really expect accurate answers from any of them,' I said one day to Martin while we were sitting in front of an early winter fire. 'Why should I believe anything they have to say about my daughter?'

'Maybe seeing mediums was a way of not feeling the grief,' said hubby referring to my visits.

'Well, maybe it was my way of trying to deal with it,' I said. 'I mean... seeing things through a gifted medium's eyes, somehow helps to make it more real, as if they're verifying something that was such a shock at the time you still can't quite believe it really happened.'

It was hard to step back from it all.

'Well... your family disintegrated after your mum died, so you had no one around to discuss these things with nor were you able to confirm what was real for you. Your brother's and sister's experiences were probably very different from yours.'

'I suppose so, but I can't go on pretending everything's fine,' I said. 'And keep longing for what I've lost,' I added silently, noticing how hard it was to form the words judging by the lump in my throat. 'Maybe seeing mediums helps ease things just a little bit. I guess they're all part of the search... but I always think each one might have something for me,' I said.

'How do you mean?'

'Well, maybe they've got something to add,' I said. 'You know... depending on their skills, like new information. Something that I don't know... maybe news of my daughter... something to hold on to. Something real.'

'OK. But how will that help? I mean it's just more of the same thing, isn't it? More and more searching... is that good for you?' he asked.

'It doesn't really matter if it's good for me or not,' I said admitting I'd never thought about it like that before. 'I just need some information about her – something to go on. Something... better,' I said.

'Better?'

'Yes, better than what's stored in my head,' I said. 'A load of fears and fantasies, like she's not loved. I can't bear to think about that... It still gives me nightmares. I just feel hollowed out, empty, that's the worst part, not knowing anything at all.'

Secretly I thought that if I search long enough and hard enough, and see as many mediums as possible, I know they'll help make it happen... I'll find my daughter and we'll finally be reunited, so putting in the effort will pay off. In the meantime I might just find out how she is... whether she's well and happy, maybe even where she is... then I can rest.

'What you focus on is what you get,' according to our meditation teachers. If you say the mantra often enough, they intoned, focus on your goals, you get results. I have got that right, haven't I, after spending 20 years practising it? Maybe I'd attributed to them the same kind of respect and blind faith as I did with mediums, tempered with a little irreverence from time to time to keep things light.

'You used to say they reminded you of Maori elders,' said Martin, 'where you and the wider family would sit in a circle and imbibe their wisdom giving you an identity, a sense of belonging, an awareness of your heritage, the benevolence of your ancestors.'

I blush when I remember how I attributed their 'specialness' to dizzying heights, sneaking a special message under the mattress of our bed that we offered them whenever they stayed with us. Like a message in a bottle except it wasn't bobbing around on the ocean for any old person to discover, it was lying there inert, targeting our teachers and being saturated with their special vibes. Oh, dear. It was a measure of my desperation and my belief that they could help me. 'Please help me find my daughter... get over losing my mum... give me some peace... help me be still.'

But in my heart I knew that no one could repair what can't be mended, heal what can't be fixed.

Battersea, London 1979

It was hard to get out of my head that I needed someone to 'fix' me, help me to improve myself, feel more at ease with myself and I assumed it would take forever, in spite of the parting words of the big boy healer from Battersea. He laid his hands on me while my young daughter Anna looked on anxiously, ready to monitor any untoward move. He had very little to say except when I assumed it would probably take a few sessions to fix me and asked, 'Shall I come back?' to which he boomed, 'Did Jesus say come back?'

St George, Bristol 2012

Although I sought these mediums out I noticed I generally continued to ignore their advice. Unless something stood out or was most unexpected or was complete bollocks.

'You're on a spiritual path this lifetime,' said Dorothy from her converted garage in a distant suburb in Bristol that shimmered with angel light.

'They're telling me I'm going to have fun with you,' she giggled.

'Oh yes, so... who are "they"?' I asked smiling tentatively.

'Well,' she said. 'The room [read garage] is now full: we've got four angels, Gabriel at your feet, Jesus is here and the Virgin Mary.'

'Wow,' I said. 'That's quite a party!' wondering who had

recommended her. 'I feel honoured,' I smiled.

'They do too,' she said. I closed my eyes.

'Many lives, old soul,' she murmured, 'carrying guilt from past lives...'

'Not to mention this one,' I thought.

'Forgiveness is the key... your father left you in your last life as a young child...'

Shame he didn't do the same in this life, flitted the thought.

'You saw it as your fault and there are echoes in this life with a child...' she hesitated and frowned. 'Your child... a daughter.' She paused drew in a deep breath. I held mine.

'You have an agreement with her as she left you in your last life... go to the point of departure with her as well and remember the agreement. She is aware of this, too. She also has the gift... like you.'

She then took another deep breath and went on to say, 'The reason you look so young, dear, is because you shine! But it's important that you let go... have faith... trust. You're capable of healing yourself... at night just surround yourself with white light, open your chakras for five minutes, then close down.'

I suppressed a giggle. It made me sound like a twilight radio station. Capable of healing myself? Really? But the whole experience was rather unsettling; divine intervention on a very grand scale.

Harlow, Essex Summer 1980

Sometimes there was a funny side to these visits, especially one involving my late father. I liked to evoke the image conjured up by Molly the medium or was she a psychic? Vaughn, a good friend, had recommended her. She was lovely, warm and welcoming.

'Family first,' she'd said with a little smile like a benevolent auntie, all sort of round and cuddly, rearranging herself in her armchair as if she was preparing for a party or something.

'Ooh, I'm seeing a man in spirit,' she said in a low voice in the cramped sitting room of her little council flat in Harlow. 'I don't think he's a relative. He's waving a big stick... although...' she added peering and frowning into The Beyond, 'he wasn't crippled.' She had jumped at that point and nearly fallen off her chair exclaiming indignantly that she'd been prodded in the back with it! That always makes me smile. 'Oh,' she exclaimed, 'he says he was your father!'

Medium Molly's credibility soared. I could only gasp and marvel at such a perfect description of my father. So succinct!

'Oh, dear,' she added, 'he says he knows why you've come here and he's not going to help you!'

Then she rattled through my life, saw my first marriage and our seven-year-old daughter Anna, then my imminent, second marriage to Martin. 'A marriage made in heaven... it's in a place with no natural light... mmmn, looks like a crypt,' she said accurately, 'in the middle of a roundabout!'

'Brixton,' I explained, wondering about the wisdom of a marriage made in heaven taking place in a crypt.

'And it looks like the United Nations. Oh, I can hear loud music... reggae... and I smell pot,' she said as she sniffed in a kind of matter-of-fact way. I was impressed.

'Sounds great,' I said, 'want to come?'

We stayed friends for years until sadly she passed away. Her greatest gift was healing.

'You're your own worst enemy,' she told me on that first visit, holding my head. 'Fretting and worrying... all these migraines you get. You need to let things go.'

Then came the bombshell.

'I see you have two daughters!' she said squinting into the mid-distance. 'But... mmmn... there's a great void between the first and the second,' she added turning her head carefully to one side as if she were deaf or might disturb something.

I sat transfixed.

'There's a lot of sadness here,' she added, 'and heartache. You mustn't keep worrying about her. They're telling me she's fine.'

Then she frowned. 'It seems she's oblivious,' she finally said after staring hard ahead of her, like a telephonist trying to decipher crossed lines.

'Oblivious?' I asked, puzzled. 'Oblivious of what?' I moved to perch on the arm of her chair in an attempt to glean as much as possible, anxious not to miss the minutest detail or expression. She blinked several times in quick succession, staring straight ahead, then added '... Of the fact that she's been adopted.'

Molly's reading kept me going for a long time. It was wonderful having some news of my daughter, even a tiny bit. At least she was alive. She did exist. I didn't dwell too much on the information about her not knowing she was adopted. The whole experience allowed me to thaw a little, gave me permission to feel.

Bayswater, London 1985

'Healing is allowing people to have pain,' a gay, ex-London policeman-cum-clairvoyant told me back in the early 1980s. He also gave me some incredible news.

'Your daughter... your first daughter... is well and happy and living in America with her husband and two young children.'

I was speechless.

'She's is a beautiful young woman with dark hair which she sometimes dyes red with henna,' he said.

'Oh my God,' I squeaked, 'that's what I do!'

'But my guides are telling me that she doesn't want to know you...'

I remember overlooking this last piece of information as I skipped excitedly down Bayswater Road swinging my shoulder bag round and round then rushed to the nearest phone box to ring Martin. I decided to ignore Molly the medium's message; it didn't quite fit. And this one was much better!

'I'm a grandmother!' I shrieked down the phone. 'She's alive... she's happy and lives in America!' I burst into tears. I was 38!

Kingsdown, Bristol 1985

Sometimes a reading or pronouncement zaps you in the most unexpected places, like our local pub in Kingsdown. I'd popped in there with a lovely girlfriend Jill and met Moira, a medium, just as she was falling off her bar stool. On the way down she'd declared, 'You'll be together till the end of the chapter!' which I took to mean hubby and me, in spite of a few recent blips, then she lay on the floor looking up at me and said, 'There's a lot of love in your life but also a lot of sadness...'

I helped her to her feet starting to feel slightly unsettled myself when she went on to say, 'You've had to grow up overnight... you were the black sheep of the family – a bit of a rebel, huh?'

She held my hands then said I had healing hands, which my mum used to tell me, and then came the shocker.

'You're surrounded by a lot of love. You have a lovely husband and two children... or is it three?' she said frowning and propped herself back up on the bar stool. 'But you're not really content... and there was a time when you didn't want to keep on living. Your lifeline has a break but joins up again.'

Phew! I want what she's drinking... and asked if she'd like another.

She clutched my arm and said, 'You're artistic, creative. Leave the social work or whatever it is behind! You'll write a book based mainly on fact... about what's happened to you... a heart-rending story that also includes a bit of humour. Stop living in the past and go for it! Let your natural creativity shine, not helping people but inspiring people!'

Redland, Bristol 1985

'This is not a stay-at-home chart,' pronounced Pauline peering at my astrological chart. 'It looks like you need a good cosmic kick up the backside,' she said in a matter-of-fact sort of way, peering over the chart using some measuring device to possibly assess just how big the kick would need to be. 'This is the beginning of a new, very dynamic phase for you where one gives out the best to the world... where you stop looking inward. It's important you move through your emotions, the upheavals... find yourself through self-expression. Emotionally I see a great maturing here,' she said. 'Your path in this life is to do something brilliant! Reshape something – create a book out of your experiences,' she said. 'You will develop confidence, discover self, deal with your fears around expressing power of self otherwise it will limit you...' she declared, reminding me of my mum. 'There's great success ahead, my dear. You're highly intuitive – you shine... a lady with a destiny.'

Wow! I left vibrating with the feeling of, 'Let the challenge begin!' Piped music would have been entirely appropriate! Old habits are redundant, according to Pauline's reading. Time for change! It was as if the past didn't count for much, wasn't really important.

'End old patterns! Live in the present! Be creative instead of searching outside yourself... you won't find it there!'

I was starting a new cycle, becoming something I wasn't before, 'a deep, uncompromising process,' she had said. It sounded a bit like changing from a caterpillar to a butterfly... I hope I don't have to hang around in that gooey chrysalis stage for too long.

Chapter 23

The Birthday

Wandsworth Common, London October 1973

Today is my daughter's birthday. She is nine. There, I said it! Just like that. I didn't dare acknowledge her birthday for the first few years, kept it to myself, but things have changed.

The truth is I never felt released from my own grip on her as if the umbilical cord was never cut. There had been nothing to hang on to over the years: no photos, no information; who was she living with, were they kind and loving, was she well and happy – was she dead or alive? I tried to keep at bay the uncertainty, the fears, the open spaces where anything might have happened...

The irony is that as far as everyone is concerned – family, friends, neighbours, nosy parkers and sticky beaks, it's over – no baby, no past, no present, no future. End of story. Except forever anchoring what I did. Part of me no longer cares what they think, since caring about what others think, or at least my parents caring about what others think, has cost me dear. Cost us dear. And I'm quite sure my girlfriends would agree, those of us who'd been banished and forbidden to return home with our babies.

For me, life was centred in the past, however much I tried to resist it. The lingering impact of grief and regret never went away. The irony is that we were supposed to feel grateful. I mean, it was the swinging sixties after all... we were free now, weren't we? Everyone was happy: infertile couples were assured of a baby should they wish to adopt – there were thousands available – the children free from the stigma of illegitimacy – and, above all, enabling society to continue upholding the sanctity of marriage in the process.

How do you explain all this to the children themselves, especially when they get older – old enough to understand. Understand what exactly?

'I allowed myself to be pressured into giving you away as a baby to strangers because my parents made me?... Because that's how it was back then?' or worse, 'Because you might have jeopardised my chances of getting married!'

'After all, "No one wants soiled goods," I remember my father – yes, your grandfather – muttering in my direction...'

But anyway, that has all changed. I now have a little ritual to help me celebrate my daughter's birthday rather than remembering her with shame. It almost feels like a luxury. A sort of surreptitious luxury because it used to be too painful and upsetting. I'd tried hard not to connect with her: not on her birthday or Christmas or Easter and definitely not everyday things, like seeing other children the same age or getting too close to friends' kids of her age. Keeping everything safely squashed, sealed. My way of managing was learning how to cope with the absence of everything associated with my daughter – no welcome, no funeral, no farewell.

Perhaps my body was trying to protect itself, protect me, I don't know. But sometimes I worried that I might forget when her birthday was. I don't think I have. I desperately hope not, it's my only key to finding her. It's important to me that I remember things as they really were.

So I started to allow myself to sort of reach out to her in my mind and over the years it's just evolved. It sounds a bit odd, but reaching out like that felt almost courageous. Triumphant. Defiant. Maybe because the guilt, shame and sorrow were so deeply embedded seeking forgiveness by complying with the 'rules' was the very least I could do. But now, instead, I was wanting to reconnect with my daughter, with Sarah, wish her well in my mind, let her know I thought about her every day – and hope that she would eventually be restored to me. But it still felt like I was committing a heinous sin.

I always chose a quiet time and sat on the sofa gazing out at the serenity of the common opposite where I had earlier walked with my second daughter Anna asleep in her pushchair. Hubby had already left, cycled off to work up through Clapham Common to Brixton. I was alone. I went to get up and close the shutters and felt a heaviness like old age setting in, a solitary weariness. Maybe it would always be like this – a heavy mantle of grief and regret weighing me down, closing me down.

I lit a candle, my favourite incense that smelled of roses, then half-closed the heavy cream curtains leaving fragments of light filtering through the cracks in the shutters. I sat quietly for a while on the same special, Indian floor cushion with threads of wine and dark inky blues entwined with gold, and thought of her. Just her and me together.

I could see her running around all excited, opening presents, playing with her little friends, stuffing their faces with lollies and cake, wearing black patent leather party shoes and a pretty frock, squealing and shrieking, running round the garden and back into the house. And when it came to the cake, she'd be at the centre of her adoptive family with the parents and siblings surrounding her, doting on her, urging her in unison to 'blow' out the candles. But then I would be filled with doubt.

I wondered if this was the sort of image we were supposed to believe – the house and garden and two loving parents, the security that can only come with marriage and money. Like subliminal advertising, messages hidden from plain sight, but where whole communities and countries were in the grip of these beliefs, possessed by them, so there was no room for anything else – no acknowledgement of love, empathy, for what was natural and full of possibilities: no options.

Instead, banishment was the usual ritual; it symbolised the order of things. Culminating in pressure to surrender your child, if you loved it, to a decent life. That's what all children needed, deserved, should automatically have. As it turned out my daughter's experience couldn't have been further from the truth.

I thought of the family I'd been sent away to stay with while I was pregnant, and wondered how being married automatically made Caroline a better mother, a proper mother, her children happier than my daughter would have been with me.

Sometimes I would be filled with doubts and dark thoughts. I would see my daughter in a loving family surrounded by parents who were overjoyed at finally having the little girl they had always wanted. But in spite of this, there might also be a sliver of disappointment that she wasn't their own natural child. A sliver that may have been there from the moment they first saw her, 'chose' her – is it natural to pretend a child is yours when, plainly, it isn't? About as natural as allowing yourself to be pressured into giving up your own child then pretend it never existed...

She was probably 'matched' to a family, and I used to wonder how that worked. Did it just mean colour of eyes and hair, and don't babies' eyes change colour anyway, and maybe their hair too? And if parents want the baby who looks most like them, why do they then tell them they're not theirs, they're adopted. Maybe it's some sort of game these particular grown-ups played in an effort to be seen to doing the right thing. 'Let's Pretend'. I wondered if that included withholding information about the natural mother, the birth mother – at least the term suggests she did have a mother who gave birth to her – she didn't just land from outer space. Even if she didn't know anything much about me, or have any names, or photos or letters or histories. And needed to be protected from me hidden behind a veil of secrecy and silence.

The sliver grows and festers, has a life of its own. After all, she wasn't their own flesh and blood, was unlikely to have looked like them; she probably wasn't like them in any way. And as she grew older, that sliver of disappointment might become harder to conceal, harder to contain so that even if she did grow up in a reasonably happy family she might always sense she was second best. That something was missing. That she, too, had a sense of something lost.

At other times I couldn't prevent myself from catching glimpses of a family that was far from suitable. This was a less easy vision, like looking through the dirty lens of a camera. I had to stop myself from focusing, try and resist. But sometimes I couldn't. The picture drew me in. In this particular family she felt unloved, was unloved. And worse, believed she herself was unlovable; she didn't belong, was vulnerable, maybe afraid. Or worse, where she was being abused in some way, feeling isolated, hurt and rejected. With no one to look out for her. She was entirely at their mercy, their disappointment and anger. It makes me think of an old Maori saying, no matter how hard I try not to, that when a child is given to an absolute stranger, he or she could end up being 'food for the oven'.

The truth is I am haunted by all these fantasies. And the irony is that these images were being kept alive almost every day in my work as a social worker in the UK working with all sorts of different families including nightmare ones with adopted children that had broken down. Whatever the family, she was at the mercy of strangers and I was at the mercy of nightmares about those strangers leaving me feeling traumatised and panicky, so it was best at the beginning not to dwell. Try not to think of her, or the family she might be living with. Maybe it was nature's way of helping. But it was because of nature that I found it more and more difficult not to dwell, but instead to miss her, worry about her, unable to shake off a deep need to know. It was such a visceral thing, like falling down and breaking your ankle, so that there is numbness at first followed by pain as the bruising comes out. I could feel it weighing heavily all through my body, dragging me down.

How could I know anything at all, find out any information or expect any, when I had to swear on the Bible that I would never try to make contact with her? Even thinking about her made me feel bad, ashamed and guilty. On the other hand, how can I ever have peace when I don't know what's happened to her or where she is? Does she have her own identity, know anything of her background – that her parents were madly in love, her father wrote long, loving letters to me every day that I still have, that we were forbidden to get married, that we lived in a different time when you couldn't keep your own baby if you weren't married… if you didn't have your family's support. That we are still in touch.

She will have been simply grafted on to a family of strangers like a small piece of plant that is made to join an established plant, severed from the original, ironically called a 'clean break', by the authorities. Where she has been assimilated into them, on to them, like a blank canvass in an effort to avoid any contamination or confusion that might arise from knowledge or contact with her birth family, so the adoptive parents could rightfully claim her absolutely as their own. Like a piece of property.

These notes about her birthday are mostly about me. That's because I see her as still being part of me. I need it to be this way, otherwise she'd be lost to me. It's all I've got to hang on to. And I can't write down anything concrete about her, like what has happened to her, because I don't know. All I know is that I feel a deep void, an emptiness that keeps on growing as time passes. Will these feelings ever leave me?

Chapter 24

Falling Apart with the Reynolds Family

Brixton, London late 1981

The Reynolds were starting to have an unsettling effect on me. A general feeling of being unwell, disintegrating at the edges, suspecting I might be coming down with the flu but at the same time managing to soldier on. I tried several different ways to shake off the discomfort that lingered after each meeting keeping a professional, emotional boundary between me and them, especially where the parents were concerned. I thought focusing on this basic technique would help me see how the family operated as a whole system so I could observe more clearly how each member's behaviour affected the others.

But I was finding it hard to relate positively to any of them; they remained entrenched, determined not to budge, yield, even a tiny bit. Each of them immersed in their own frustration and anger. It was as if no one in the family wanted to change anything for the better, even though it formed the basis of our original agreement; or move forward even a little bit: trying to encourage Mr and Mrs Reynolds to at least glimpse the possibility of themselves as a couple as well as parents, trying to sort things out without rowing, making an effort to get on more, starting to respect each other; both kids not having to worry about Mum, Sharon happier with herself and the situation at home, Matthew wanting to please his parents more, go to school regularly, give them less cause to argue... each of them surely wanting things to be better at home bringing with the changes some degree of harmony, affection, trust and hopefully a sense of freedom. Maybe the mantle of anger they all carried meant they could only focus on revenge, didn't trust the process we were engaged in or were simply unable to realise any degree of resolution; perhaps they had never really known harmony. So why the hell were they here?

Working with them was becoming a bit eerie, like stepping out on to a frozen lake hearing cracks cooking just below the surface, knowing at any moment they could suddenly burst open and swallow you up. It was simply uncanny that Mr Reynolds, like me, had been expected to go away and forget a loss that was devastating and shameful, a family secret that was never spoken about again which had caused him huge problems he didn't know how to deal with. Plagued by all sorts of unanswered questions and fantasies going nowhere about what happened to his father. And how did I respond?

'Perhaps this is an opportunity to face things,' I suggested without the slightest hint of emotion in my voice. 'Not try to avoid them, seal them off again...' Ha, ha, who am I to talk? Bloody hypocrite!

But maybe that's where the analogy stopped.

'I'm worried Mr Reynolds might take revenge on his wife or son,' I said to Mike although that wasn't something I myself had experienced with my father, in spite of his unsettling similarities with Mr Reynolds.

'He's been plunged into an unfamiliar position in the family, fallen from his self-appointed top doggie status and become a victim,' I said.

What could be worse for him? Or did he feel, like me, that in some way, some indefinable way, he was responsible for what happened to his father so his fall was partly deserved, self-inflicted?

It made me wonder about my own family's secret. The memory of it sprang to life making me aware that, like Mr Reynolds, I too had felt forced to collude with my family pretending that my daughter didn't exist. Being forced to go to any lengths to preserve a secret you didn't want to be part of in the first place.

I lingered over my own family history zapping myself back

into the family home in Dunedin, slumped on the sofa gazing out at the garden. Then I realised something. There was a complete absence of my parents' wedding photos... not so much as a Kodak brownie. No 'happy ever after' deluded smiling couple bedecked in their wedding gear adorning the walls or photo frames – no veils, frills or lace, no beautiful long gown enveloping the bride, no bouquets or buttonholes... no dress shirt or snappy dark formal suit. No friends, family or confetti... nothing. Did each of their parents withhold their blessing because he was Jewish and she was Presbyterian, or because she was Presbyterian and he wasn't, or because he was Jewish and she most definitely wasn't.

Does that mean they both went against their parents' wishes, way back then, in the dark ages? Or, stretching the imagination to pinging point, maybe I'd got it wrong and they'd eloped! Or even more radical, they weren't actually married! What if they had to get married! But then I remembered my mother saying she had to almost beg him for children. And how would that hypocrisy sit with my father's stance where I was concerned, years later, perched firmly on the moral high ground? Maybe it was driven by what happened to his family's need to assimilate when they immigrated to New Zealand. How much had their situation influenced his decision to pressure me into surrendering my daughter, his first grandchild, because that was the price to be exacted, the price of fitting in.

Chapter 25

A Solitary Session with a Psychotherapist ... and the need for personal reprogramming

London September 1981

Although Mike was very approachable, I decided that talking to him about my 'unsettling' in response to the Reynolds family wasn't really appropriate. It felt too personal, sort of exceeding acceptable boundaries – too much information, too exposing, especially since my own personal experiences were spookily similar to those of theirs! Better to act as if all was well. Mike might start to see what sort of person I really am.

It seemed like there was no escape from the past, maybe there never would be. I needed help to hold on, to keep up a professional face, however hollow and disingenuous, even though I wasn't sure how much of a grip I could continue to keep on my emotions, the situation. I was starting to feel undone.

What would I say to a therapist? Where to start?

'Thinking about this family I'm working with is... um, really upsetting... stirring up old memories of what happened in my family... and I can still feel the shame and pain of it starting up once again... burning and bubbling... over and over as if someone or something forever keeps insisting I'm not good enough, will never be good enough.'

Can I say all that to a therapist without sounding too neurotic? Or is that what she wants to hear. What say she's the type who doesn't say anything and I'm left floundering, filling in the awkward silences? 'Maybe I deserve all this. The heartache I caused is coming back to me. The same twinges are starting to emerge whatever I do. It feels like it's getting harder, not easier, to shake it all off.'

I needed someone who could understand all this, listen and gently suggest some sort of remedy, I'm not sure what for. But it needed to be a female, I know that much. I had a vision of a mid-European woman, maybe German, wearing posh clothes, probably a cowl-neck cashmere sweater, tailored trousers, shiny, black patent leather shoes and a long silk scarf wound loosely around her maturing neck...

Someone suggested a psychotherapist called Julia who lived nearby. I felt quite apprehensive, anxious about what would come out and how I would deal with it all. She wasn't at all as I had imagined. She was quite a bit younger than me for heaven's sake, blond ponytail, casually dressed. What did she know about anything? The thing I remember most is that everything about her was white – the interior of her house, the hallway, the sitting room, the floor, even her clothes, including her scarf. She merged so perfectly with her environment, she almost disappeared. We both sat on white cushions on the floor for an hour and when she asked, 'How can I help?' all I did was cry, pay the £40 and not go back... it was never going to work.

The Endless Self-Improvement Workshop Phase: 1981–

Stumbling along the spiritual path

Eventually I started looking at courses that came my way:

- How to use visualisation and guided imagery: good for calming people down, controlling pain, promoting healing, stimulating the immune response, changing behaviour and building confidence. 'Back by popular demand.' Mmmn, maybe people think they are getting a bargain.
- 'Fast trauma and phobia cure' – do I have a fast trauma?
- 'How to Dispel Feelings of Hopelessness and Gloom.' No

thank you.
- 'How to Use Visualisation to: combat depression, anxiety disorders, addiction, including controlling pain, promoting healing, stimulating the immune response, changing behaviour and building confidence'... Isn't that the same as the first one?

I decided instead to go to one of the workshops that our meditation teacher was offering and scrutinised the list along with other courses to see if anything leapt out at me. There were a lot to choose from:

- 'Dancing in the Fifth Dimension'... mmmn, sounds lovely, perhaps later;
- 'Death, The Great Adventure'... definitely later;
- 'Complete Health'... sounds safe enough;
- 'Creating What You Want in Your Life'... that might take a bit longer;
- 'Healing the Inner Family'... uncomfortably appropriate;
- 'Healing Past Trauma'... ditto;
- 'Working with Resistance: motivation to change'... Am I resisting?
- 'Make it Happen!' Unspecified...
- 'Unifying: The Inside is the Outside'... I hope not!
- 'Purifying Meditations'... Maybe that's what I need;
- 'Seven Steps to Heaven'... I expect that's booked out.

I ended up going to nearly all of them in the search for solutions to my various, often unidentifiable needs and more. About 20 years' worth altogether. I seemed to be always scrabbling around searching, pecking at anything that might just do the job.

'You didn't just peck for 20 years, you also found a community,' said Martin as I screwed up my face. '... OK, a group of like-minded people you could relate to. And you once described our

being like Maori elders, surrogate parents dispensing
member?'

Yes, but why do I resist everything? Why can't I just get
zapped by all the information, accept it and get on with life!
Transform myself!'

Maybe Martin was right. I didn't resist **everything**. Perhaps I
got more from the workshops and the mentoring than I cared to
acknowledge but it felt like the same old patterns kept creeping
in. I was always left with a sense of more to do, more practising
the perfect art of meditating, to attain something better, and
through it all trying to 'become' a better person. And somehow
I was led to believe that if I persevered, this was the path that
would lead somewhere... to enlightenment. But I didn't want
enlightenment. I just wanted to be able to stop the endless
searching, the fretting. It made me dissatisfied and didn't solve
the restlessness; the whole process was like climbing a mountain,
feeling obliged to keep going until you had staggered to the
summit, regardless of your interest in the view.

'What do you really want?' asked Martin.

'I don't know... I think I'm hoping to... sort of start again...
be healed I suppose. Ditch the past, like that medium said I
should,' I said.

'So what's getting in your way?' he asked gently, reaching
out to hold my hand as we sat opposite each other in our local
cafe.

'Well... nothing seems to come to anything... I feel I'm going
round in circles, trying to heal the past, focusing on all these
"perfect outcomes" for myself, the personal goals, the endless
self-care sessions – trying to become a better person,' I said. 'I
think I just want to be at peace with myself... for the shame to
go away, the sadness to dissolve, to believe I am a good person,'
I said. 'And maybe one day even be a little bit pleased with
myself.'

Chapter 26

Time to Start Facing the Music

London 1981

Although I felt I had wasted my time seeing the all-white, silent psychotherapist I couldn't help pondering on the only question she asked me, 'How can I help?' I still could not have given her a clear answer although I have since tried to come up with one. I didn't really know where to start – was I feeling lost because I was failing to get pregnant with my second husband Martin, was it because of guilt and shame surrounding the loss of my first daughter, was I being punished? And my second daughter Anna, how much was this affecting her? Maybe it was it the loss of my mum... and when I think about it more deeply, other losses I hadn't ever acknowledged – my country, my family, my old friends. My increasing inability to cope at work? I hadn't thought of all these things in this way before. Was it guilt, grief... I even started asking myself the same question, 'How can I help?' in rare moments of solitude as if I were her. Once I started to think like this, where I was her as well as me, it became a bit easier to see things more clearly, without so much heat. It reminded me of a saying attributed to the Buddha:

> When the student is ready
> the teacher appears.

I decided to have another go with a psychotherapist who was highly recommended. Mature, cowl-neck cashmere, silk scarf. Perfect.

Therapist: 'So... what can I help you with?'

Me: 'Well, I'm not sure exactly,' I said noticing how well I'd managed to accommodate the question without disintegrating...

have come together all at once... one problem
t another. This family I'm working with... well,
v... but their problems echo my own family's
rting to disturb me. I suppose sometimes the
similarities have been helpful in understanding them but I'm
finding it harder and harder to contain it all... so... ummn, I'm
feeling a bit overwhelmed... and I don't know where to go with
it.'

Therapist: 'Where would you like to start?'

Me: [The pub, a brandy and Babycham, fag, friends and my
feet up...] 'I realise I've never really cared about myself... taken
all sorts of risks, especially when I had a motorbike, never taken
life seriously. Sometimes I don't really care what happens to
me.' [What the hell has that got to do with anything? It wasn't
what I wanted to say at all! It just came out!]

Therapist: 'So, what's going on for you at the moment?'

Me: 'Well... I have a seven-year-old daughter by my first
husband and I've been trying for ages to have a baby with my
second... there's nothing physically wrong with either of us...
but it feels like I can't move forward, something is stopping
me, holding me back... I know it sounds strange but I think
it's something to do with working with this family, like they're
making things worse; they seem to bring my own family alive...
so it makes it hard to focus on everyday things. It's ironic... I'm
the social worker, and supposed to be helping them, but it's not
as clear-cut as that... Actually, it's not clear-cut at all.'

Therapist: 'Maybe you're starting to realise you need to deal
with your own history.'

After a silence in which her statement seemed to reverberate
around my entire body, she said, 'Sounds like there's a lot going
on for you at the moment.'

Me: 'Yeah, I feel a bit overwhelmed by it all. It's like my life
has suddenly been interrupted...' Again, I thought, making
a link with my daughter... 'And I can't seem to... get on with

things, get back on track... move on I suppose.'

I was transported back to 1964 and those exact feelings I had after I returned home... trying to pick up where I left off.

Therapist: 'How would you like things to be?'

Me: 'Well... I'd just like to go back to the way things were **before** I met this family. Where my job and my life were separate not all jumbled up together... Where I'm not being plagued by... upsetting memories.'

Therapist: 'Can you be more specific? What does this family stir in you about your own experiences in your family?'

Me: 'It's hard to know where to start, it's been a sort of gradual thing. The family is nothing like mine. Everything about them is different – the way they live, their aspirations, their education, their beliefs and values... everything! Except the way they interact with each other. That's the spooky bit. In spite of all the differences, there are some incredible similarities that freak me out... remind me of stuff I'd rather not remember.'

Therapist: 'Which similarities stand out to you the most?'

Me: 'Well, the father for a start. He's so dominating, demanding, always needing to be in control – never listens to anyone, just wants things his way all the time. He reminds me of my own father. It really affects how I see him – and I know it shouldn't. He argues endlessly with his wife... and wants to get rid of his son, put him into care because he's not doing as he's told, not going to school, mixing with the wrong kids... And, well... I guess it reminds me of my father.'

Therapist: 'What in particular?'

Me: 'Well... he got rid of me, as well...'

Therapist: 'He got rid of you?'

Me: 'Yes... sent me away because I got pregnant...'

Therapist: 'That's a lot to go through.'

We sat in silence.

Therapist: 'I can see why you might be feeling uncomfortable... and why this family is stirring up memories for you.'

Me: 'I know it sounds silly, but it feels like I'm somehow being forced to relive my past...'

Therapist: 'What are you feeling right now?'

Me: 'Not much, a bit numb and confused I suppose.'

Therapist: 'Maybe some of these feelings are too painful to remember.'

Silence.

Me: 'Umn... it feels like they've just sprung out at me – all of a sudden, like one of those jack-in-the-boxes we played with as kids. Bang! Right in your face if you went too close.'

Therapist: 'Perhaps it's no coincidence that you are "close". Maybe this family you're working with is knocking on your door, because there's something unresolved in your history.'

Me: 'Yes, maybe...'

Therapist: 'Up until now, perhaps you've used your job as an escape from your true feelings. A defence against the pain.'

Me: 'Really? How does that work?'

Therapist: 'Well... maybe you focus on other people's problems as a way of avoiding having to deal with your own.'

Me: 'Mmmn... that kind of makes sense, it's just a bit too... simplistic, I suppose. It feels much bigger than that. And it seems to be popping up all over the place at the moment...'

Therapist: 'Perhaps you could give me an example.'

Me: 'Well... I often feel upset and frustrated at home at the moment, which is not like me... but silly little things set me off, things that normally wouldn't bother me, like being cross with my daughter this morning because she was taking ages to get ready for school. And hubby isn't getting much sleep because I've started having flashbacks again – horrible nightmares and it always gets back to the same thing... anxieties about what's happened to my daughter...'

Therapist: 'You might find there is sadness underneath...'

Me: 'Mmmn... maybe that's it – everything summed up in one word "sadness". Sadness at losing my daughter, my mum, sadness at feeling I can't return home, hold my head up... all buried under layers of crap. All this searching is exhausting me and yet I was still left with an ongoing sense of something lost. Of needing to keep searching... looking out there in the world, outside myself as if someone else could forgive me, heal me, make whole what was fragmented. As if seeing a therapist would make a difference. As if doing good work would stop me feeling like a bad person. As if.'

We sat in silence for the rest of the session, which was fine. It takes quite a lot of perseverance to keep talking about yourself.

Chapter 27

'Make Me One with Everything' (spiritual saying)

Social Services Brixton, London 1981

I made coffee and took it through to Mike's room for my supervision session. He suggested a potentially terrifying task for me to which I responded with a small, feigned smile.

'A really useful exercise for us as family therapists is to identify with each member of the family. It's easy to get out of balance if we over-identify with certain members, and don't identify or understand the others,' he said.

I do this by imagining that I was each one of them in turn. Not an attractive thought especially where Mr Reynolds was concerned. A bit wacky actually, more likely to be his own quirky idea than a conventional family therapy technique. But I liked his quirkiness not just because the ideas were so different from mainstream social work but because they usually brought insights in unexpected ways. And sometimes they were quite fun... well, compared to the traditional casework approach. But this didn't feel like fun, since I might be forced to drag my own family, lock, stock and barrel, out of the closet. And then I'd have to share it all with Mike.

'I don't think I can do the exercise,' I squeaked, 'because I don't really know the family well enough yet.'

'That doesn't matter, you don't need to know them very well. Just use what you've picked up so far,' he said.

'So... how will this help me to work with them?' My resistance was palpable.

'Well, maybe we won't know till you've done it,' he smiled.

Why is everything so bloody easy where he's concerned? Nothing seems to faze him!

The thought of relating to them in this way, imagining I was each family member in turn, was daunting. I had a flash thought about Sharon. She's a blank wall! How can I unify with a blank wall? Maybe she's hiding something... God knows what will come out of this. More family secrets! And what did my own family have to do with the way I worked with them? I mean, their family is the problem family... not mine, right?

I reluctantly started with Sharon, identifying with her position in the family, although I was still really sceptical about the exercise. I had no sense of her. She was barely able to articulate what changes she would like to see at home. And her parents seemed to have difficulty focusing on her, acknowledging what she said. I didn't know what lay behind those arms folded so firmly across her chest. She gave nothing away, had hardly muttered 'hello' or 'goodbye' since our first session – not so much as a hint of a smile or a slight, conspiratorial look even when her parents were behaving so embarrassingly, scrapping like a couple of alley cats.

I decided to imagine myself as her. I sat like her, arms tightly folded, I looked as pissed off as I could and stared hard out the window. I leaned away from the rest of the family but I wasn't completely out of the circle. I was sitting nearest to Mum, furthest away from Dad, my brother a bouncing irritant between me and Dad. I didn't hold eye contact with anyone, certainly not the social worker!

'The first thing I realised being Sharon was how lonely I felt: I wondered if I just didn't "fit" into my family, my behaviour seemed to be the antithesis of theirs. Sometimes I just excluded myself but at other times I feel excluded by them. It's like I don't exist, so much attention is on Matthew. I can't say anything to Dad, he bites my head off. He's always going on to Mum about Matthew. So that means she isn't there for me either, at least not when he's at home. When he isn't there, she's often in bed like she needs a place to recover from him. Recharge her batteries. She doesn't seem to have much energy except on the battlefield with him. Or should I say, against him. So I'm expected to do a lot of stuff around the house. I don't think I should have to, but it's mostly OK. It's just that Dad never seems to notice. But he's the same with Mum, so I don't suppose it matters to him who does what. Sometimes I feel I don't really belong in my family. That I'm somehow on the outside looking in... and nobody seems to notice.

I feel angry that Dad involved Social Services. And even more upset to think he went there to get rid of Matthew! I know he's to blame for a lot, especially their arguments but I don't want to be part of it. And I know life would be a lot quieter without Matthew but who knows when it might be my turn? I mean... anything could happen, even if Dad doesn't want it to... He always thinks he's in charge but he's not. The whole thing is soooo embarrassing. Mum and Dad are more interested in fighting than trying to sort things out with the social worker. They don't seem bothered about who hears them. And there's nothing I can do about it. About anything. I think it's all a big waste of time. I can't see Dad changing. I think he'll always pick on Matthew, blame him for everything...'

I was a bit shocked not only by what came to mind but the speed of it. Almost as soon as I identified with Sharon and her position in the family. It was quite unsettling. She, too, had a mum who was a bit depressed and I imagine, like me and my brother at a similar age, she felt powerless to help. Her response was more passive than mine but the issue was really similar.

I remembered a deep connection to my own mum and her unhappiness. Like Sharon, there wasn't much I felt I could do. I remember I tried loads of times to convince her to leave Dad. We always had a nice time together when he wasn't at home. It was upsetting seeing her stuck in a hole that she didn't seem to have the energy to climb out of. Seeing Sharon in this same way reminded me what this powerlessness felt like and how painful it was. I also remember making the decision never to get stuck in the same way as my mum, never to be dependent on a man. Funny how we make such important decisions as kids often based on 'never!'. I know it was a different time for her, for women. But it wasn't going to be the same for me. I remembered my famous feminist badge bearing the enigmatic message, 'A woman without a man is like a fish without a bicycle.' I wonder what Sharon's take on it is... maybe she feels the same way...

With Matthew I began with a different doubt about the exercise... What could I possibly have in common with a slightly irritating eleven-year-old boy?! Again, while imagining I was him, bouncing up and down in the armchair, never still, looking slightly anxiously from Mum to Dad having placed myself between them, a different identification arose, quick and blinding. It wasn't a conscious thought, it was just there, like a light coming on.

'I know I'm the one causing all the problems at home, upsetting Mum and Dad. And I know they're always rowing about me and getting angry at me – especially Dad, because I won't go to school and stuff. But what would happen if I did? I'm really frightened that my mum might leave... she did it once before... and no one's ever mentioned it. I know she's unhappy... she says she's depressed. Sometimes she just sits in the lounge all day with the curtains closed. Maybe she'll stay 'cos she's worried about me and what Dad might do to me if he hasn't got her to argue with... It's a bit scary... sometimes I get frightened about what's going to happen. Sharon's not going to get them upset and angry... she's not like that.'

This was an amazing exercise! Matthew was identified by the family as 'the problem' and so was I! Although I knew this I could only see it really clearly now by looking back at my family. Somehow it made so much more sense of me being the problem, to be banished, sent away in shame... and even being blamed for my mother's death. Someone's got to be responsible for everything bad that happens. And everyone else went along with it. And this was exactly what was happening to Matthew.

But there was something else that was bothering me about Matthew. I felt anxious about him now that the situation at home had changed, become potentially more volatile since his dad had gambled sharing his long-held secret about his father's suicide with his family. Facts that were not received with compassion by them, particularly his wife who had instead become angry with what she saw as his treacherous, deceitful secret. Perhaps it was the ammunition she'd been looking for to justify her contempt for him or her sense of betrayal. Would her preoccupation with this situation mean that Matthew might suffer in some way, that she'd be so focused on revenge it might blind her to her son's safety? Or even, at some horrible unconscious level, invite it... because she, herself, felt unprotected, especially since her mother died leaving her feeling vulnerable.

It's like Dad's in trouble now because no one's doing what he wants.

Was it the same loss of control that caused my father's behaviour towards me to change after my confession was dragged out of me and exposed to the family? A sort of anarchy that took over where the rules were not so clear-cut and in some ways worse, not knowing what to expect. I could identify with Matthew's precarious situation at home feeling unprotected, vulnerable to his father's anger.

It dawned on me that both Matthew and I were subjected to the same age-old pattern of social control observed by horse whisperers! Where one parent excluded us from the herd by avoiding eye contact, making us both feel vulnerable. We did have difficulties but somehow we'd taken on the role of the 'problem' in the family and that meant once this role was established we were trapped in it – and then most, or all, of the family's difficulties were projected on to Matthew – and on to me. Which, in turn, meant that everyone else could sigh with relief. They didn't have to take any responsibility themselves. I'm sure my father couldn't face how unhappy Mum was with him and it was more likely that it was this sadness, about which she felt powerless to do anything – and not necessarily what I had done – that had contributed to her early departure from us all.

I can see why us 'scapegoats' were needed in the first place, then needed to be got rid of, banished. For a start, we were perceived by our fathers as questioning their authority which must have highlighted their powerlessness to control everything, like Matthew's continued truanting or my getting pregnant. It might have had the knock-on effect of articulating similar feelings of others in the family, giving them silent permission to behave in ways that suited them – like his wife withdrawing and maybe undermining him in the process, deciding she didn't need a man, a husband. He wasn't good for anything. And that was her way of undermining him, castrating him, even. And then what would happen?

Like all good scapegoats I now realise we were voicing something for the others. Maybe I was enacting something for my mum that she would like to have done – experienced the sort of freedom that her generation was denied. And maybe Matthew's behaviour exhibited the sort of tenacious challenge to his dad's authority that his mum would have liked. And both of us provided an ally to our mums which must have set up further feelings in our fathers of impotence and powerlessness which, in Matthew's case, might then easily express itself in Dad's violence. Perhaps the most threatening aspect was that we were able to articulate the despair and gloom in the family, highlighted by our behaviour. But who knows what exactly our behaviour was enabling them to avoid?

It suddenly occurred to me that if Matthew is banished, I have

a sinking feeling it will confirm to the family t
belong any more.

'Being' Mrs Reynolds took me in yet another direction... It wa.
as easy to step into her shoes. I needed to see myself sitting in
the same chair she always chose in the interview room, then try
and feel tense and argumentative, so I thought of being married
to her husband and that seemed to do the trick.

I moved to the edge of my chair, looked in his direction as if
he were there and imagined arguing with him.

'I know I shouldn't ignore the kids but they're used to it by
now anyway... We argue all the time... I just wish he'd agree
with me for a change... He never agrees with anything I say...
like he's always got to prove that he's right. He blames Matthew
for everything, most arguments are about him. He just won't
listen to me. I'm fed up with him, fed up with everything. All
these arguments are wearing me out. I feel tired all the time. And
every day's the same. Nowhere to go any more, now that Mum's
gone. He doesn't care, he's only interested in himself. He wants
everything done his way... He didn't even tell me he was going
to see you lot about Matthew. And he's got a terrible temper...
sometimes I'm... well, anyway... He never even asks me what
I've done all day. Half the time I don't even bother to open the
curtains... unless Matthew does it.'

More uncanny, unsettling parallels, where I was identifying
with someone I thought I had nothing in common with, who,
like me, had lost her mother, a friend... a sister. Again our
reactions were different... hers was to fall into depression and
mine was to press on, to keep on the move so that the feelings
wouldn't surface, mainly an unspeakable grief, a secret grief,
that I thought no one else could understand. A void that could
never be filled. It reminded me of something a healer said years
later when he picked up on my theme of restlessness dating back
to the time I lost my daughter.

'You decided early on in your life not to be depressed,' he said. 'It's not your way. What you've opted for, instead, is the opposite – restlessness.'

I thought about my own mum and witnessing in her a similar sense of powerlessness, having no voice, not being heard. Where arguments were, as Mrs Reynolds said, at least one way of attempting to be heard, attempting to say what it is you want for your child, what you think is best. Mrs Reynolds' husband had made a unilateral decision to get rid of Matthew, banish him from the family by dumping him with Social Services. Similar to my father. He didn't discuss with my mum how he was going to dispose of me either. He just went ahead and organised for me to be sent away to live with strangers.

The more I thought about her, 'became' her – with the help of uncomfortable parallels with my own family – the more I realised how much fear seemed to permeate her life, her being. Just like mine. It struck me that perhaps fear was at the root of this family's problems. They were simply avoiding having to deal with it. But the nagging question remained – what was it they were trying so hard to avoid?

I'm finding this part of the exercise really difficult. It's not just being reminded of my mum. I think I just want to keep a lid on everything. It's a lot easier that way. I'm feeling a bit emotional, a bit fearful, as if I've suddenly been tripped up because I didn't see the obstacle; I wasn't prepared for it. I think it's tied up with doing this exercise realising what little power we women had back then and how different things could have been for me, my mum... and my daughter... different values, different attitudes, human rights. And rather depressingly, how little those rights appear to have changed things for some women like Mrs Reynolds, where the power continues to reside mainly with her husband. Although I could be wrong!

It's quite painful seeing the disintegration of a family being played out in front of you. I wish I could've seen the same process taking place in my own family at the time and been able to do something about it instead of seeing it now, through a different lens. And thinking about both our families, with Matthew and me as the focus of the families' ills, both acting out something we were probably unaware of in an unconscious attempt to make things better. Throwing our families out of balance, where our fathers, instead of trying to sort out what was really going on, then decided respectively which punishment was commensurate with the crime. And the subsequent disintegration of the family that these fathers paradoxically were so desperate to hold on to, so determined to control. In my case, banishment followed by not being allowed to keep my own baby.

And now Mr Reynolds. Surely he couldn't be a part of my psyche too! But now I'd got the hang of this exercise it seemed like I'd allowed myself to open up to something greater than just me, and my mind. I was willing to explore it all... without the usual defences or barriers.

Unfortunately it was easier than I thought 'being' Mr Reynolds. No one wants to see him in themselves, fighting to get their own way regardless of others, shouting to be heard, needing to be in control all the time. Maybe these aspects are in all of us... mmmn, maybe not. Being Mr Reynolds waving his forefinger in your face to make a point, refusing to sit down until heard, talking over everyone, interrupting... It was getting a bit uncomfortable thinking about him in relation to me. I don't think I'm that bad, surely! Not finger-waving anyway!

I'm finding myself faced with a way of dealing with shame and vulnerability, Mr Reynolds' style, where bravado masks vulnerability. Surely not mine, no way! His style of shame is one that must be kept hidden at all costs, never to be exposed. So the vulnerability is never felt, never expressed. Anger is his weapon of choice and he uses it well – maybe dangerously. Being Mr Reynolds it seems unlikely that I would ever admit I'm starting to realise my anger can also mask fear. 'Anger is how I manage to defend my vulnerability – with boxing gloves... always have, always will, because using them means they don't allow for any of those soft sort of feelings to emerge. We all know that the soft stuff means you're vulnerable; we're not stupid, right? Like allowing myself to be taken care of or protected... or sharing the truth of what happened to my father! Never again! No way! I'm telling you – I've been misunderstood and you know why? Because what I defend in myself is so well hidden. It has to be! So... OK, there's never an honest message, not the one I really want to get across to my wife and kids. That's because I'm afraid and ashamed of exposing my... umm, my vulnerability. There, I've said it! So that's why I mostly never say or do what I really mean. Otherwise, what might happen? I'd be left undefended. Unprotected. No... it's too much. So I suppose those I care about get pushed away.'

Hell, shades of my father... and, possibly, tiny, little shades of me. OMG – I can't think straight! Especially when their family's story touches mine.

Ironically Mr Reynolds thinks he derives his power from using anger, but, actually, like my father, I still think it masks their own sense of powerlessness... impotence – glug, can't go there.

The parallels continue: control and vigilance over everything seem more important, more reliable than anything else, and in that way both Mr Reynolds and my father ensured that everything was held in check. Nothing surfaced from the depths. And when it did – after Mr Reynolds 'confessed' about his father's suicide, it confirmed for him just how dangerous it was to open up like that. He took a gamble sharing it with his family, the most intimate gesture he'd ever made towards them, and in the process made himself unusually vulnerable. So he snapped himself shut again. My father on the other hand never braved such a step, he was permanently snapped shut. Should I stay snapped shut as well… or make a choice? It's a tougher route, a pivotal moment not only for Mr Reynolds – but also for me.

This whole experience was really uncomfortable but at the same time strangely liberating. Not only that, it was, well… bonding. I felt compassionate towards all of them, this rather unprepossessing family that arrived on the doorstep. I never thought I'd be saying that when I started this exercise, where part of me wanted to work with them as a family but another more unsettled part quietly cursed them and wondered how come I got landed with them?

Actually, it's been kind of spooky working with them. We have so much in common. Maybe that's why we needed each other. The synchronicity is astonishing: I happened to be the social worker on duty when Mr Reynolds burst into the office, then I happened to be the one to offer them family therapy and they, in turn, got a social worker whose personal experience of family largely mirrors theirs.

Was it a coincidence they turned up on my doorstep at the very same time I'd been realising that I needed to understand my own family, and make sense of my role in it as a way of healing and moving on? Maybe it's not just a random event in a chaotic universe but has some symmetry to it, one that's beyond our normal understanding… a kind of balance. Wow, the right family for the right social worker!? And for them, what is it about me that they need? Mmmn… that question might take a little longer to answer.

Working with them was a bit like being forced to face a distorted mirror, where the silver backing had been rubbed off in parts and worn into strange but familiar shapes that lingered, as if nudging me to stop and look more closely. The images were almost hypnotic, and didn't invite any sort of challenge, as if they were simply inviting me in.

'But perhaps,' observed Martin, 'you were also inviting them in as welcome guests.'

Treat each guest honourably
Be grateful for whoever comes
because each has been sent as a guide from beyond.
Rumi, 13th century poet

Chapter 28

More Mysterious Mirrorings

Brixton, London 1981

It had been unsettling doing the unifying exercise with each of them in turn, where Mike had suggested I 'become' each person. I managed to move from the discomfort of feeling I couldn't relate to any of them to the point where I started over-identifying with each of them for heaven's sake!

As a result it meant I saw Mrs Reynolds in a different way, that somehow she played a part in helping maintain her husband's hostility towards her. That if she had allowed herself to open up, maybe slightly, especially after her mother died, showed some vulnerability, he may have moved a little closer to her. Their relationship was a bit like a dance. Maybe she'd discovered long ago that when she'd tried to get closer to him, showed she needed him, he didn't like it and moved away from her... or maybe he was scared. Or maybe she was scared. And now he was trying to get closer to her and it was her turn not to like it. Maybe that's the dance: 'I'm scared, you're scared... cha cha cha.'

I remembered Mike describing this type of scenario. It stuck in my mind because it was so vivid.

'Each partner's fear and their attempts to manage it plays into the other one's fear,' he explained. 'So she attempts to manage him by controlling him because she fears he'll leave her, abandon her – and he withdraws because he fears being engulfed and overwhelmed by her,' Mike said. 'So he steps away from her, which stimulates her fear of being abandoned and as a result she becomes even more controlling... and this in turn would further stimulate his fear of being controlled and engulfed, and so on.'

Mmmn. Relationships are complex but curiously always trying to find a balance.

Was that what I was trying to do around dealing with the dilemma of obeying my father, allowing myself to be pressured into giving up my child, sent away? Realising that if I didn't concede I risked being abandoned. So like my mum, I acquiesced, became passive, had no voice in the matter. Maybe my mum's fear of abandonment was greater than her fear of his engulfment.

It feels like Mrs Reynolds has already decided to abandon her husband. She has left him once before. So maybe we'll never get to the place of helping them understand this dance of theirs if she's not willing. Now that he has finally exposed his own vulnerability, has risked sharing his innermost hidden secret, she seems to be rejecting him. Not only that but she had challenged him over the lie he had woven around his father's death and humiliated him even further. Surely it must have occurred to him that she had regarded the lie as more important than the truth about what really happened and the profound effects he had carried with him. But in the process of sharing this painful truth she had simply dismissed all the emotional bewilderment, secrecy and shame – negating everything that he had endured as a child, a young man, all his life in fact – by suddenly flicking the switch, abandoning him.

I slipped back into thoughts of my own dilemma, my own family dynamics. Mum, like Mrs Reynolds, was mostly passive, engulfed by Dad and his world and she wouldn't risk abandoning her family in that way by trying to dump him. I, too, was forced into a corner by Dad when I was pregnant knowing that if I didn't comply I would risk total rejection and abandonment.

After the unifying exercise my view of Mrs Reynolds coloured how I saw Mr Reynolds. I was starting to feel empathy for him! It was a sort of visceral thing, a feeling that I felt I had no control over, like an egg slowly cracking open, quietly at first, and revealing something emerging that I couldn't recognise but sort of liked.

Part of me actually wanted to rescue him! To sort of protect him from the wrath of his family and further humiliation; help ease the shame by trying to get his family to understand how hard the whole experience had been for him, carrying the burden of guilt and degradation of his father's suicide.

Perhaps all that bullying and bravado had, after all, masked a profound fear that his family might disown him, never accept the tragedy of what happened, refusing to carry the shame of what his father did, as if they would be forever contaminated in some way. Would it ever be safe to open himself in that way again, a way that was as unfamiliar to him as tropical rain? Somehow he had felt compelled to tell them. Finally expose his darkest secret and in the process make himself as vulnerable as a puppy. What did he really expect, I wonder? What would I have expected?

Maybe he fantasised that their response would, at last, unmask their true feelings for him, a yardstick of their genuine love or affection, an unconditional love that he was never sure about. Never truly experienced. Or maybe this was a bit optimistic. But at least some measure of care or concern about him, maybe sorry that he had been carrying the burden of this secret for so many years not wanting to upset anyone. That he'd been protecting his family as a father should. Unlike his own father. Maybe he, too, carried the shame of it with him, and his family's response was simply a projection of his own feelings including an anger he was never able to express and his guilt about feeling that way. Or maybe, uncharacteristically, he was wanting them to give him permission to finally let go of the secret. Release him from everything that went with it. Accept what had happened. Wipe the slate clean! Or maybe, just maybe, he was hoping to use the sympathy card, his trump card, to win back the diminishing returns of his wife's affection. And at the same time, jolt the kids into line. And then get back to being top doggie.

But the announcement of what Mr Reynolds' father had done, the enormity of it, killing himself and bringing shame on the family, flitted through my body like a snake bite, a hidden enemy suddenly and without warning unleashing its venom, its merciless grip. I could feel myself blushing and burning with the pace of its implacable speed, the story echoing in my head, resounding there like discordant drums. Not only had Mr Reynolds' father gone out and killed himself, which was bad enough. But he had brought terrible shame on the family. And that was what appeared to be so unforgivable.

Like Mr Reynolds, there are things in my life I don't want to remember either, and shame is one of them; the shame I had brought on **my** family and realised in a cold flash how Mr Reynolds' story once again mirrored mine! Where honour based on what others thought and said took precedence over everything. But unlike his father, at least I didn't go and thoughtlessly and selfishly die... in childbirth. My death would probably have been just as awkward for my parents to explain, being 17, pregnant and unmarried, but if I had, I sometimes wondered if the shame of my getting pregnant, never mind the baby of course, the shame I had brought on the family, would have, like Mr Reynolds' father, been greater than the sorrow of my dying?

Chapter 29

Final Family Session without the Family

Brixton, London late 1981

Mrs Reynolds has gone. Abandoned the family, just up and left. Apparently Matthew had come home early from a rare day at school and found a note from his mother on the kitchen table.

I wasn't altogether surprised. It was one of the reasons I had been anxious to discuss the couple's relationship with Mike until the parallels with Mr Reynolds and my father became too intrusive. Poking through like stubborn weeds that kept resurfacing, popping up in unexpected places, taunting me in spite of all my efforts to eradicate them including censoring that bit when I talk to Mike. More hypocrisy... based on a need for self-preservation. More important, it had felt for some time like the Reynolds family was starting to disintegrate. Who could keep up those levels of anger and control that were getting nowhere? And underneath it all I had been left privately wondering how come all this mirroring is going on with my family. It's plain creepy... and set to get worse.

'She's gone!' bellowed Mr Reynolds at our lovely receptionist, charging into the office via the pub waving the note demanding to see, 'that Australian social worker or whatever she is...' Then shoved the now crumpled note in my face shouting, 'Look! She's gone! I hope you're satisfied! This is all your f***ing fault! You and your bloody family work or whatever fancy name you call it... interfering...'

I wanted to say I was sorry she'd gone but decided to say nothing. He was red-faced, sweaty and smelt of booze, in no mood to talk, only shout unabated.

'Let me help you with your troubles, you said! But it's *you* who has caused all the trouble! You!' he shouted in front of a

189

quietly swelling audience of colleagues not to mention a handful of clients now crammed into the reception area, having sprung from the inner sanctum of nearby corridors and offices propelled by curiosity and possibly a wish to protect, but not necessarily in equal measure.

'So...' he continued, having everyone's full attention including the tea lady's, 'What are *you* going to do about it, ay?' he demanded staring straight at me. 'I mean... I've got no choice any more, have I?'

He waved the note again at me. 'I can't work and look after Matthew! He'll just have to go into care after all, won't he!' And with that he stormed out of the office.

I wished I still smoked. I'd been trying to get pregnant and discovered that smoking can affect your fertility. Would one fag really matter? I made myself a coffee and then my mate Maggie appeared. Lovely, tall beautiful Maggie with her long dead-straight hair and soft brown eyes.

'I missed some of the drama then,' she said smiling. 'You OK?'

'Yeah,' I said. 'A bit churned up I suppose. He's such a frustrating bastard! I can see why the wife left him.'

'Did I hear him say he couldn't work **and** look after Matthew? Blimey, just as well mums don't say that – the whole system would collapse!' she laughed.

'Fancy blaming me for his wife leaving! **And** in front of everyone! Not such a great way to advertise family therapy,' I added.

'Hey, we can't be responsible for that – or your part in his wife leaving,' said Maggie. 'I think he did a damned good job all by himself.'

I could see myself blaming him in the same way as he was blaming me.

'I suppose so,' I said. 'I'm sure I would have felt exactly like her – but not abandoning my kids...' I faltered.

The whole scenario was becoming uncomfortably familiar.

I'm pretty sure that's how my mum must have felt too: frustrated and powerless with no voice. But there was something else: I did feel partly responsible for his wife's disappearance. What if I had unconsciously participated in encouraging Mrs Reynolds to leave her husband in the same way as I tried to encourage my own mother to leave my father? And then a chilling thought occurred to me which I can hardly bear to dwell on. What say there was yet another parallel process going on between the Reynolds and me... what if I was partly responsible for encouraging my own lovely mum to leave my father, somehow having planted the same seed... but then she decided that ultimately there was only one way she could leave...

Maybe Mr Reynolds was right after all. I had helped bring about the situation through doing the family tree exercise, encouraged him to make himself vulnerable by sharing his shameful secret with his wife, something he obviously deeply regretted and that softer part of him, that little glimmer of openness and trust and hope that he had allowed to emerge from its precarious and fragile place just once, was now firmly closed, snapped shut, tight as a clam.

Maybe lots of couples take up the 'clam' position in relation to each other, never communicating what they really feel inside. Keeping a safe emotional distance from each other. And somehow it seems to work for them, like the Reynolds. He goes on bullying her, she withdraws but denigrates and undermines him and somehow that keeps them together – until one of them gets fed up, wants to change things. That's when it can all fall apart.

I think I really do need a fag. Or Mike. Help me clarify things. Something else was tugging at me, refusing to let go. Perpetuating those old feelings of guilt and responsibility. Mr Reynolds' family situation had once again reluctantly dragged me back into mine. It was as if he really was a reincarnation of my father! Same blame game: 'Now look what you've done!' Same accusations: 'This is all your fault!' Culminating in Matthew's banishment just like mine years earlier. Will these thoughts and memories ever go away, ever be resolved? Will I ever be free, or will they keep resurfacing, reminding me forever? It's hard to work it all out.

Chapter 30

Prelude to Another Mother

Wandsworth Common, London August 1985

When I came downstairs I found our sitting room heaving with people pressed against the walls and shutters, squatting on the arms of the (new) wine velvet sofa, the armchairs and the large, old, pine coffee table that sometimes doubled up as seating in extreme situations like this. There was a sort of hushed buzz of excitement, a respectful reverence for our guest as she was about to be introduced. She had been invited to our meditation group by Liz, a long-standing member who had given her a star rating when she told us about her at a previous meeting.

'She's a Being of great spiritual advancement,' she announced solemnly. 'A channeller.'

'Mmmn... a channeller,' I thought, 'well, that'll make a change.' I haven't encountered a channeller before but I can't imagine what information she'd be able to channel to me, especially in a crowded room, unless of course it was Dad who elbowed his way through, quick as you like, no doubt giving me misleading stuff, not wanting to help me as he'd declared in a previous reading with a psychic.

'This is Ruby,' announced Liz who brought her, 'but her spiritual name is Angel,' and proceeded to tell us that she was a reincarnation of someone important whose name I have forgotten. She was barely visible in the far corner of the sitting room but I could see that she was rather small and stout and could have been any age. She contemplated us in a quiet, scrutinising sort of way as if someone was about to be plucked out for consumption like a fish in a restaurant tank. And then I heard weird words uttered in a strange, high-pitched squeak, like a small animal might make if you accidentally trod on it, the sort of squeak that immediately makes you cup your mouth with your hand, stifle an overwhelming desire to giggle. But her message was immediately sobering.

'Seek out those who call themselves "Mother",' she squealed in a strange, high-pitched voice craning her neck in my direction.

Suddenly she fixated on me.

'You need to seek out those who call themselves "Mother",' she repeated. 'You are yearning for mother. You are not in truth lost to your mother,' she squeaked while I felt my jaw dropping slightly, tears welling. 'Feel your own motherliness... What you miss is the love that a mother surrounds her child with.' She paused, closed her eyes and took a deep breath as if she were gleaning the information from a divine source.

'You feel you missed the opportunity to be mother to your own child. Imagine a true mother into whom you could sink completely... You are much loved,' she added.

Hell! I take it all back – the surreptitious desire to piss-take, imitate, trivialise... Her words lacerated the air, transforming me in that moment from a giggling squid into a pensive recipient of something exquisite, something privileged, something great. How could I possibly denigrate what she had said, deny the truth of what she said, when it felt so right? I was gobsmacked. It sounds daft but it was as if she had come to the meeting partly for me. I had to act, respond with respect to her words, her message, however squeaky.

Her words have a habit of haunting me, at the same time offering comfort. Somehow she had identified the core of my feelings that centred around the loss of my mother and my daughter. I didn't need to trawl for months or years of therapy through my family's dirty linen to get to the heart of things – there it was, just a simple, yet profound and unbelievably accurate statement. I was almost starting to feel peaceful.

'Why not go the extra mile?' said my hubby some time later.

'And where would that be, exactly?' I asked.

Chapter 31

Visiting the 'Mother'

Somewhere on the Rhine, near Diez, Germany
June 1986

It is 6.30pm. We arrived almost an hour before time and the 'ballroom' of this rural, hillside castle is already full – 300 people who, like us, would have needed to book several months ago to see Mother Meera: internationally-known Avatar who has been offering healing in complete silence to thousands of people for years.

All the chairs face the stage where Mother Meera will eventually sit on what looks like a throne. Our set of rows are shorter than most and run at right angles to the main body. We have a clear view of almost everyone, unfortunately for me.

Martin closes his eyes. We sit in silence for a further half hour, waiting. The stillness is remarkable. All heads face forwards in quiet anticipation. I have to confess I had a couple of glasses of fine French duty-free wine beforehand to help ease the process, should it be necessary. Its effect means I feel slightly removed from the event and am rather more fascinated by my fellow congregation than I ought to be.

'Minders' float around smiling benignly. Pretty boys, tall, pony-tailed, Norwegian or possibly Dutch lookalikes with their beatific smiles and an uncanny ability to smile over everyone's heads without holding eye contact, hands clasped royally behind their backs.

I close my eyes for a couple of minutes and drink in the feelings. What are they? Joy, yes; bliss, possibly... but that may be due to the wine. Twenty minutes to go. A female minder stands on the dais in her native Indian sari, deep colours of wine, gold and reds. She has a beautiful, serene face, maybe from her close proximity to Mother Meera. She too stares mistily into the middle distance and I try to do the same. Then try and close my eyes like everyone else.

Mother Meera is finally about to enter the stage and we all stand in silence, awe and expectation. Some people with their hands clasped reverentially together. She shuffles in, almost childlike, as if the hem of her purple and gold sari were too long making me anxious she might trip. She is petite and quite young, sweet looking. The queues immediately start to form by people sitting or kneeling on the floor of the aisles, shuffling quietly forwards on their bums. Each of us observes the ritual of the 'waiting chair', and the protocol that accompanies it before kneeling in front of her.

I was super-charged by her look. It was like the Day of Atonement with Mother Meera staring hard into your eyes, unblinking, penetrating, beautiful velvet brown eyes that caused me to instantly recant all my sins, my emotions, the things dominating my life. An immediate desire to ditch everything I had thought mattered. Totally surrender. I caught myself tentatively smiling at her then thought better of it. It was a serious moment. I tried to imbibe every single particle until she lowered her eyes signalling the end. Time to return to my chair to digest it all.

Now was the time for reflection. I looked down at my rings and silver bangles and wondered why I needed to wear them, then felt embarrassed at what they represented; I became aware of the paradox between the spiritual quest and the mundane, and suddenly wanted to be free of all these possessions which seemed like meaningless encumbrances. Focus on what's important.

The first question to occur to me was, am I worthy? Am I a fraud? Am I just here because Martin is here? Why can't I just enjoy the moment, let things happen the way he does? Welcome everything: the orchestra of rattly coughs, knee crackles, tummy rumbles, shuffling bums alongside me on the aisle carpet and the nauseating perfumes. But what about the paedophile that looks like Hitler? I can see him rubbing that boy's knee over and over! Has no one else seen it? Why do I get caught up in other people's dramas? Martin has noticed nothing. I don't think I'm cut out for this.

Eventually I became aware of an overwhelming feeling of unity – that we were all here wanting some spiritual input. Some of us hungry for meaning in our lives… all nationalities, ages, sexes. I moved away from seeing most of these people as stern Germans wearing short-sleeved check shirts maybe wanting forgiveness, maybe not, to all of us wanting something else, something better. It was… well, nice.

I thought of Ruby, the amazing channeller and her squeaky message to 'seek out those who call themselves Mother'. I'm not sure what I was expecting. This Mother didn't say anything. The message was all in a look. Not in the form of absolution or advice but a loving gaze… a deep acceptance. Unconditional love like a mother's. I realised after all these years that when my mum died this love went with her, along with my sense of self-worth. A lot of things suddenly made sense.

Maybe 'seeking mother' meant rediscovering unconditional love, but now without my mother. I realise no one else can forgive me, heal me, so maybe there is nowhere else to look except within me… making all the searching futile.

What was it I really came for? My soul healed forever, to be totally cleansed, forgiven especially by my daughter… connect with my own mother as Ruby suggested, feel my own motherliness; focus on what's important… putting things right. But does any of that really matter now… at this very moment?

Finally I close my eyes and draw in a long, deep breath, exhaling almost loudly. I could still feel the imprint where Mother Meera had placed her hands on me; I'm tingly, shivery spine, warm lower legs, seeing purple lights, feeling elation and sorrow, joy and sadness, love filling me up. And a hint of freedom.

Chapter 32

Run-up to Reunion

Village of Leighterton, Gloucestershire, UK June 1985
I heard the familiar squeak of our wooden gate as it opened, then slammed shut on its spring and looked out the cottage window to see the postie trundling up the little cobbled path waving a letter.

'One from home, then, m'dearrrr?' he asked in his strong West Country accent indicating the stamp of a Maori's tattooed face.

I knew straightaway who it was from, I recognised the handwriting. I still have a few of his love letters, not tied together with red ribbon or lace or anything, I wouldn't want to draw attention to them. Actually, it was a manky old rubber band that had perished long ago. I found them at the back of a drawer when we were packing up, moving out of London. He wrote most of them to me when I was sent away. They are full of love. Pages of it. Not a lot else, but then maybe that's all that really matters.

I expect John hasn't kept any of mine. Men tend to be less sentimental than us women, maybe that's how they appear to cope better by not clinging on to the past. They seem to face things more easily, accept things more easily, even those situations that were never accepted at the time, never dealt with or fully faced.

He had sent this letter from home, Dunedin, 22 years after we lost Sarah (21.5.85 to be exact). This letter felt very different. Out of the blue. Instead of tearing it open like I would have done years ago, hungry to hear from him, I immediately felt vulnerable, exposed, as if a stranger had suddenly pierced my skin with a sharp pin and I was bleeding before I knew it. I held it, smelled it as if to imbibe something of him that might be lingering there and to glean some clue about why he'd written to me after all this time. I was curious but also afraid.

The letter was still affectionate but more distant, matter-of-fact, mature. It was years since I had seen him or heard from him. But I knew he still cared about me. His lovely mum told me when I last went home a few years ago. And I still cared about him.

'Susie,' she hugged me. 'We still all think of you as family...' and agreed to act as go-between with any messages and notes. How lovely was that?

She was great, a mother of eight, always chirpy in spite of endless tasks, preparing dinner, cleaning, cooking on her coal range, ironing and taking time to enjoy her children. I really admired her. She knew how to respond to things, and it always felt like the right way to respond. Looking back it was kind of like we'd all stayed trapped in that particular pocket of time in terms of our relationships, the era – the sixties, including his mum. I wondered if she knew he had written to me.

Dear Susie,

I hope all is well with you and your family. I still think of you often, especially lately. Actually I can't get you out of my mind at the moment. I don't know if you've heard or not, but the government is changing the adoption laws. Welfare is going to open up all the records retrospectively! So that means everyone can find each other! And Welfare is offering to help...

What? I couldn't read any more. I couldn't take it in. It was so hard to believe. When did this happen... how... why? It was unheard of! Welfare were the very people who took our babies away, and now they were proposing to help reunite us... it didn't make sense. And a law that was retrospective? Since when were laws retrospective! So that means it includes us! John, me and our daughter. I couldn't get my head round it. I could only relate to UK adoption laws. I'd lived here for so long, and I couldn't imagine it happening here in Britain. It was virtually impossible to find out anything at all, at least legitimately. Never mind getting any sort of help to reconnect with your lost child!

I picked up the letter and went and sat in the little stone walled herb garden we'd created, a peaceful hideaway, to try and calm down. Think things through. Of course I wanted to meet her! Hadn't I wanted this all my adult life? I had imagined over and over what it'd be like, what she'd be like... fantasising about how I might meet her: as her teacher when she was a child, when I could check the register for her birthday... maybe in a pub as a young woman and how I'd recognise her immediately, then somehow get her to tell me her birthday, by suggesting she must be a Libra... and how receptive she would be and embrace me and then at last I could tell her about her family, her father, my father and why she was adopted... and hope she'd understand, forgive me. At those moments I tended to forget I no longer lived in New Zealand. That didn't seem important somehow. Although I always felt I'd meet her one day, there was also the feeling that she might not want to know me. That I didn't deserve her love. I took in a few lungfuls of cold Cotswold air and burst into tears.

Village of Leighterton, Gloucestershire, UK
November 1985

Later, I rang everyone – all my friends! They were ecstatic. Full of questions I couldn't yet answer. I held back on the family, my brother and sister as they had never mentioned her, asked me anything about her or what happened. They hadn't told me that the adoption laws were about to change, even though the coverage had apparently flooded the papers and the news, for ages. I found out that it took seven years to get it through Parliament as a Private Member's Bill and had tremendous coverage during that time, but apparently they told me later they didn't want to 'worry' me about it.

From that moment on I became obsessed with finding her. I could think of nothing else. It was like being in love – that all-consuming feeling that nothing else matters, regardless of what people said. Birth parents being helped to find their lost children? It was unheard of.

I wrote to Welfare. I waited. I wrote again a few weeks later. I lived for the postie. Every day I would greet this diminutive figure as he strutted up our path, restraining myself from grabbing the mail. It was nearing Christmas. I would race home at lunchtimes from my job 40 minutes away in Chippenham, down snowy, winding narrow country lanes in my clapped-out 2 CV Citroen, just in case. Nothing.

I wrote to Welfare again and waited. But not for much longer this time. Eventually I rang them in Wellington to be told, 'We've had thousands of enquiries... so sorry.'

Later that same day my brother rang. He was in Bristol on sabbatical. Had I heard from my daughter? I froze. He'd never mentioned her before and I'd just rung Welfare again to see if they'd had any news.

'Well, she's just rung Auntie Hypatia in Dunedin...'

I was stunned.

'No, she didn't catch her name... No, she couldn't quite catch where she was living – somewhere up north.'

What **did** she catch?

'Better not ring her now,' my brother said. 'She's had a shock.'

I rang her anyway. I'd hardly had any contact with her in the last 20-odd years.

'I didn't know you'd had another daughter!' she exclaimed. 'Why didn't anyone tell me?'

My daughter had said she was a friend of mine and had lost my address.

'After I gave it to her she broke down and said she was your daughter!' my aunt shouted down the phone line. 'And that she'd been in care since she was seven!'

I remember everything stopped. It was like telling me she'd died. And that I had killed her. I felt sick. Then I was.

For a while nothing much affected me after that. I felt numb. I felt tremendously sad. I felt guilty. Horrified. Angry. Outraged. But most of all I felt responsible. Everyone kept saying it wasn't my fault. How was I to know what would happen?

I became paralysed with guilt and grief. I was convinced she wouldn't want to know me, but nurtured the hope that, like me, she'd have a measure of curiosity in her nature. I rang Welfare again and heard the confirmation like a death knell down the phone 12,000 miles away.

'Yes, she had been in care since she was seven,' said the social worker. 'But she has great spirit, she's a survivor. A beautiful, intelligent girl... I've never known anyone like her.'

My daughter had been in care! Had spent most of her childhood in care. The ultimate irony was one that I could hardly bear to acknowledge, even to myself: the chilling irony that I had been a social worker for those same years in the UK only to find out that my own child had spent over half her childhood in care. How could I possibly hope to make any of it better?

The social workers I spoke to immediately offered to trace her for me. They were very kind and caring.

Now the postie assumed even greater importance in my life. My daughter was constantly in my thoughts, my conversations. Every time the phone went I was sure it was her. I became a complete and utter bore.

Then she rang. It was 6.45am on a cold winter's morning. The whole family leapt out of bed simultaneously and hung around on the stairs while I answered.

Her first words to me were:

'Hello. It's Sarah... do you know who's speaking?'

'Of course I do!' I cried. 'I've been waiting 22 years for you to ring me!'

Then we both cried. Then we both laughed at each other crying and sounding exactly the same. She was keen to know everything about me, what I looked like, where she'd got her curly hair from, her nose, her warped sense of humour... all about her sisters.

'I've waited a long time to have my own name,' she said. 'Thanks for giving me such a posh one, Ma.' Then she whispered, 'Thank God you're still alive.'

A week after our first phone call her letter arrived. In spite of all the Christmas Kiwi mail the little postie seemed to know this letter was special and waved it mischievously in the air as he came up the front path. I leapt up, rushed out, grabbed it and tore back inside. I remember sitting down at the kitchen table staring at the envelope, touching it, sniffing it, scrutinising the extremely neat handwriting, the address, her name on the back. A stranger's name. My daughter's.

After a while I opened it. Inside there was a fat letter and some photos. I can still remember feeling almost too afraid to look at them, as if by doing so she would, after all, become real. I know I let out a howl – a long, loud, piercing primitive howl that came deep from within my being. It was 22 years of grief that I'd never really been in touch with, never really knew the intensity that was there. Twenty-two years of silent, forbidden grieving for my baby. Now I was about to see the young woman my baby had become. I turned over the photos. She looked very familiar. She looked very like me.

My two other daughters were at home. Anna, who was 13 at the time and had known about her sister since she was nine, raced downstairs, clutched the photos, then me, failing to hide a look of intense sadness. Little two-year-old Sophie cried in sympathy.

I don't know how long it took me to read her letter. Scrawled along the top, 'Read this one first,' and a smiley face just like I'd have done. Beautiful, neat writing. But the smiley face hid the harsh reality of her life.

Dear Susan,
Yesterday I found out you were my real Mum and it is a dream I have long pursued ever since I was 7 years old…

Reading what had happened to her, how she'd been abandoned at the age of seven, three days before Christmas… it was unbearable, but I had to keep reading, of course I did. It was the least I could do… but it felt like the ultimate betrayal! The ultimate deception! How dare they offer to become her parents, legally adopt her, then dump her. Maybe I could have had her after all! She could have been restored to me. Surely I could have been given a second chance. I was assured she would go to a good home, to a married couple that could give her all the things I couldn't. How could I be so selfish wanting to keep her? How could they be so selfish giving her up like they did? If I loved her, the least I could do was to give her up, I was told… Give her up to what, exactly?

Chapter 33

The Actual Reunion

Auckland Airport, New Zealand January 1987

We arranged to meet at Auckland Airport. I was so excited! I couldn't wait to meet her, couldn't concentrate on anything for more than a minute! I was all over the place. Meeting up was the only possible course of action having finally made contact after 22 years of wondering and worrying. It was a natural response to a profound physical need that could only be quenched by reunion, an insatiable yearning magnified a million times by never knowing what happened to her. It was the only way to explain the circumstances of her birth and ask her forgiveness in spite of well-meaning comments from friends who tried to caution me.

'Perhaps you should wait a while,' said one friend. 'Gosh, you're so brave....' said another. And one or two declared, 'You'll just open up old wounds!'

But how could I allow myself to be consumed by fear? How would she feel if I chose not to meet her?

I told everyone. I showed them her photo I carried round with me. I could think of nothing else. I even told the stranger sitting next to me on the plane for heaven's sake. It was like I'd been thrust into another reality. I used to ensure I never talked about what happened. Sometimes our own stories are the ones we can never tell. It was like keeping a closely guarded secret as if, by revealing it, I was somehow betraying her, betraying us. But when I did eventually mention it to close friends it brought tears to my eyes, and often to theirs, a lump to my throat, even now. Filled me up all over again with shame and guilt and grief. Now everything was going to be different. And suddenly I could talk about nothing else!

Don't stories of adoption and reunion have the quality of fairy tales? Where everything is a struggle but turns out right in the end? Where the ingredients for happiness are put on hold until the odyssey culminates in a magical reunion? I hadn't left any messages like pebbles in fairy tales, no trail through the woods leading to the truth. I wasn't aware that I could except in my dreams.

In many ways this whole journey was like a dream, emerging from a kind of misty, veiled state after 22 years where a fairy godmother had changed me – the very same me – from forever bearing the indelible imprint of a disgraced, undeserving teenager harbouring a dark and shameful secret into a reprieved, respectable and deserving woman; now entitled to openly celebrate her newfound status – all at the stroke of a different, this time a more just, legal pen. Where one day the same world that banished you, shunned you, punished you, pointed the bone at you in retaliation for what you'd done by stepping over the unforgiving moral boundary, later changes its mind! When what people thought of you was so hugely important at the time, pressuring thousands of young women like me into surrendering our precious babies often snatching them away at birth, like my daughter. And then everything suddenly changes, exonerating you! As if all those losses now counted for nothing – the joy of loving her, mothering and protecting her, knowing her, sharing all the events in her life; it's as if the separation need not have occurred.

Most people suffer the 26 hour-long journey by plane from the UK to New Zealand, anxious to reach their destination as soon as possible. But in a strange way I welcomed it although I couldn't wait to meet her. It gave me extra time to prepare myself in the small, solitary space my seat took up when I had time to myself to keep processing everything; it was a bit like the precious time before exams when you cram in as much as you can, preparing yourself for the unknown by throwing yourself into it. But I found myself focusing on regrets and recriminations. I guess I was afraid she might reject me.

Then it dawned on me! I desperately needed to come face-to-face with the fact that in spite of having seen photos of her as a young woman, she was no longer the baby locked in my mind. That sweet, perfect snapshot image that was lodged there would soon need to be gone forever. Instead I had to remind myself that soon I was meeting her as a grown-up – a real person.

I pulled out a newspaper from the tight pocket at the back of the seat in front of me, to take my mind off things. The headlines made grim reading. A young British woman of Pakistani origin whose dismembered body was discovered not long ago in a suitcase on a rubbish dump, had been murdered by her father and brother who, wrongly, suspected her of being romantically involved with a man not of their choosing. Her father stated in court that it was his right, his daughter had 'dishonoured' the family.

I couldn't stop thinking about the young woman on the journey to meet my daughter. Maybe reading her story was synchronistic showing me I had got off lightly in comparison; I should feel grateful. Unlike me, she had no second chance, no reprieve, no legal magician to change the law, reverse the curse, restore a kind of retrospective justice that might bring an end to the shunning, anguish and suffering. Give her back her life.

I wasn't shamed publicly in a formal way, or stoned or burnt to death by my family or community. I was unharmed physically. I wouldn't want to insult the poor young woman's memory, minimise or demean her terrible experience but in some ways it felt like a similar kind of 'cleansing' process, sweeping away us 'fast girls', banished, out of sight, with adoption being synonymous with 'out of mind'.

What is it about young women and their sexuality that so many people are afraid of?

And now, I thought, everything is different, but one thing in particular stood out: it was ironic that the power of one's story, my story, who I think I am, is once again about to reflect what others think of me: now an acceptable, even tragic me, with a beautiful fairy-tale daughter finally about to be restored to me. And with the expectation that I, too, will automatically change my thoughts and feelings about myself and my life accordingly – overnight!

Yet I was unable to suddenly loosen my attachment to the guilt and grief I had carried with me, that never left me, or diminished over the years. And maybe it was hard because the pain, the yearning to know something – anything – about her never went away; it seemed to accumulate over time, like something quietly growing almost independently inside me. How could I change that overnight? Let go of this identity, this label? How can emotional pain simply disappear, dissolve with a change to the law and leave no trace? All these years it was as if I were trapped in this role I had fallen into, allowed it to define me as not being good enough. Where I, too, allowed it to define me as not being good enough. 'You deserved it,' my father would have said. And where, ever since then, I could only occasionally get a glimpse of my true self.

How could I separate myself from all these thoughts, just get off the plane on to the land that was in my bones, the land I grew up in, loved, step out of all the emotion and see myself without thinking, without dragging around the past? I must not allow the past to become more important than right here and now. To contaminate it in any way. The reunion should mainly be about meeting her needs, not mine for heaven's sake! Nothing could be more important! She needs to know that I am here for her, available. But I could feel myself trembling slightly, fearful of what might come.

Unfortunately at least five or six flights arrived all at the same time and I found myself being propelled along the corridors when I was suddenly overwhelmed with anxiety. What say she didn't like me? Or I didn't like her? Or I didn't fit with the gentle, sweet earth-mother she no doubt desperately wanted? Or she wasn't looking for a mother, only for information, for an identity, for answers? She just wants to take what she wants from me? What if we didn't get on, or she couldn't forgive me for allowing her to be taken away and given to strangers who later dumped her in care. That she's brimming with resentment that she didn't get the same chance in life, the same privileges as her two sisters; what's say she's detached and hostile, harsh or overemotional or slightly hysterical... or she sets about deliberately shunning me to show that I have harmed her in every possible way, rejected her, ruined her life and that I don't matter to her... just as she might have assumed that she didn't matter to me? Or she expects me to reject her again, just like her adoptive mother, followed by her adoptive father. Or maybe she expects more of me because her adoptive mother vanished without a trace, just like I had done, and somehow she holds me responsible for this and everything bad that's ever happened to her... or she doesn't trust me, she might never trust me.

Or maybe she has a more philosophical take on it, I thought, trying to slow myself down by breathing deeply, trying to ground myself and realise that restoring relationships is really about forgiving – not about expressing hurt and anger; and that by meeting me I would obviously acknowledge the harm she would have suffered growing up in care, rather than shunning me as a way of proving it, and that this is the best way forward. That maybe she was beginning to realise that her life so far was not who she really is, that she's not just her story, she's so much more. Am I expecting too much? I think I'm scared. And I've just noticed I'm standing under an illuminated sign: 'Anything to declare?'

In spite of the huge, fumbling crowd, I saw her straightaway. She stood out from everyone else looking beautiful and calm wearing a long jade silk dress, my favourite colour! And holding a bunch of 'English' flowers. She was all the women in our family rolled into one. One of us. We clung to each other for a long time. I could've stayed like that forever, holding her for the very first time, touching her. I wanted to squeeze her to bits. I wanted to stare and stare at her, and take in every inch of her. I wanted to touch her wonderful curls that matched my youngest daughter's, stroke her face, ask her forgiveness, explain that I was only a child myself – that I had no choice. Instead she smiled, whispering, 'Come on, Mother, don't let's make a scene,' and gently frogmarched me towards the exit remarking with a squeeze, 'What a little mother I've got!'

We stumbled out into the sunlight and sat cross-legged facing each other under the shade of a Pohutukawa tree in front of the airport. And there we were! Two seemingly strong women, shy and nervous, intrigued and overwhelmed by this powerful bond of estranged intimacy that linked us together, holding hands that were identical, giggling in the same self-conscious way, her smile my mirror-image right down to the same crooked lower front tooth. 'I always wondered where I got my nose from,' she laughed sounding just like me, 'and my warped sense of humour, Mother!'

Wow, she called me 'Mother'! Twice! Three times! Amazing! But I could also feel the tears welling up again. I didn't dare dwell on it. I felt flattered and uncomfortable in equal amounts. She had made it sound as if our time apart had been merely transitory, a pinprick in time and our reunion an inevitability.

Maybe she was right. We had been apart only physically, even though I hadn't been there to comfort her as a child or help tie her shoelaces, or protect her from God knows what. We'd always been in each other's hearts. It was like we'd always known each other in that profound, primitive kind of sense. So when we finally came together there was an almost divine kind of purity of concentration in the way we communicated, the way she communicated, interacted, uninterrupted by her story, or at least before our respective stories inevitably got acted out. I guess that's what is called the 'honeymoon phase', where the love that kicks in and immerses you in a state of bliss is perfect and all-consuming. Unable to be contaminated, diluted by anyone or anything. That's where I wanted to stay, in that warm pool of unconditional love so I could preserve its purity. It made me realise that what I'm most afraid of is hearing about anything horrible or unpleasant that has happened, because I wasn't there to look out for her, protect her... and that, maybe as a result, she really was 'food for the oven', as the traditional Maori saying goes. I can't bear to go there... I know it sounds selfish, it feels too much, too painful at the moment. If only I could face things more easily. Try not to feel flooded by it all. Stay calm!

We reached out and hugged each other again, both making the same little squeals of joy, and just sat there under the tree, still staring at each other, smiling and giggling, mentally computing all kinds of likenesses. And differences. Both exclaiming how unreal it all felt, a dreamlike quality to it.

'Not a nightmare, then,' I ventured and got another hug.

She told me about her friends, how she had spent a lot of time with Maoris, had lived up north with them and loved their values and beliefs – and every time she mentioned one woman in particular, Angie, I felt a pang of jealousy that she was so significant in her life and she clearly loved her. I hoped I wasn't expecting too much even though I knew I probably was.

'So... tell me about my family, Ma. I want to know everything! And all about my father! Are you really still in touch?'

It was hard at that moment to disentangle the present from the past, disassociate myself from it, less easy than I thought to slip into the wonder of meeting her, of having her restored to me, of being thrilled to bits, beyond belief and simply dump the circumstances surrounding her birth. I could feel myself becoming that vulnerable young woman again, could feel the past encroaching, a familiar dark cloud obscuring the brightness and warmth of the sun, then a sudden dawning that my life had, in many ways, stopped abruptly at that point when she came into the world and thereafter felt forever interrupted, empty. A great gaping void.

I was mesmerised by her, our similarities. Our hands melted together, wide capable hands, same long fingers, white-tipped nails, same shape as mine. Her skin, complexion... her dark eyes, her laugh. I couldn't take my eyes off her. Everything about her vibrated with youth, joy, optimism. I didn't really want to tell her I had been sent away in disgrace, that I was banished once the secret of her existence was out. She might think it was all because of her, feel even more rejected, see it as her fault. I would try and explain, 'That that's how it was back then; banishment was an automatic ritual, it was the way people thought, a knee-jerk reaction. My father had immediately shouted, "You'll have to go away! There's no choice!"'

And how to explain that banishment and forced adoption was more important to our parents than their own families for heaven's sake, more important than what happened to their daughters and their children, the grandchildren. It made me think of the young Pakistani woman's mother – did she believe that being seen to conform, being marriageable, took precedence over everything else, including her daughter's life? Just as our parents too were determined to obliterate all traces of what they found most unpalatable – pregnancy and an illegitimate child... for 'honour's' sake.

We stayed there under the tree for hours, till the sun started tipping down towards the horizon, and eventually went back to her house. The interior stunned me. It was very like mine, right down to the framed prints of Klimt with designs in golds and reds and plum-coloured squares on languid figures of ladies that I owned when I was her age! We had the same favourite colours – jade and turquoise, pinks and reds – the same sense of design – the way she set her things out, the same quirks –

amusing little touches like a deceptively lifelike mouse lurking by the cheeseboard on the dresser.

'Now, Mother,' she said settling me down on her sofa with a cup of tea and some lush banana cake she had made specially, 'I want to hear all about my family... and my dad.'

Chapter 34

The Need for Forgiveness

There's no future without forgiveness.
Desmond Tutu

New Zealand – Bristol 1987–1989

I was sure reunion would make everything OK. The two of us reunited. Whole again. Sorting things out, exchanging information, issues, intimacies. Two strong women at last restored to each other; 22 years of wondering and worrying and waiting, both of us surely determined nothing would ever get in the way again. No more obstacles leaving an unfamiliar, exciting taste of freedom.

I still remember those precious hours I spent looking at my lovely daughter as we sat in the shade of the Pohutukawa tree at the airport, neither of us wanting to spoil the moment, interfere with the flow. I saw the look of joy on her face, eager to learn at last about her heritage, her identity, where she came from.

But learning about hers from social workers and others involved in her childhood couldn't have prepared me for the intensity of my feelings – the anger, frustration, guilt and betrayal alongside the utter sadness and powerlessness. And I was caught in my own sticky web trying to unravel my professional perspective of social worker with the personal one of birth mother. I had no template to guide me, neither did anyone else I knew. But when I think of all the case histories I have heard, my own daughter's brought to life the worst managed story of all. And it was set to continue.

While she had been keen to know all about my past, my relationship with her father, my parents, my background, my whole life, I felt the opposite. I hadn't wanted to hear about the adoption breakdown. Or any other failings yet to be aired. But I needed to fill in the gaps. To piece together the fragments of information. To feel I had the whole picture. And Sarah's file had mysteriously disappeared! I tried to get more information and wrote to Welfare a few weeks after my return to the UK.

Dear Susan,

My apologies for not replying to your earlier letter of 28.4.87. Your second letter of 29.12.87 has just arrived. At the time I received your first letter I was particularly busy and put it aside in order to do the necessary research to respond as best we could to your questions. Unfortunately, shortly afterwards we shifted buildings and in the packing and unpacking, your letters got misfiled. I have now 'recovered' it and I've also got your daughter's personal file in front of me now. I am due to go on leave on 15.1.88 and will endeavour this week and immediately after the 1.2.88 to get a reply to you by the end of February at the latest.

Once again my apologies and I am sorry you have had to write again in such an important and delicate matter.

Yours sincerely,

(unsigned)

Social worker on behalf of the Director.

New Zealand 1989

When I was in New Zealand on the second visit to Sarah, a social worker who knew her kindly offered to compile a file of her history, with her consent, because her original file was still 'missing'. (Perhaps the unsigned, fuckwit social worker still had it.) In any case it was impossible for me to read a case history of my own daughter peppered with one disaster after another, mainly local authority failings... 'a series of placements... a lonely child... placement lacking warmth.' I found I couldn't continue reading it.

I decided instead to go in search of the adoptive father. I needed to know details of Sarah's early life and what had happened, information that wouldn't necessarily have been in her file. It was easy finding him, he still lived in Auckland. It's not hard to find anyone in New Zealand, really. And folk tend to just open the door. Invite you in.

I took a girlfriend with me, Helen. We knocked on the door of the address where he lived. A woman resembling a stick insect let us into the kitchen where he was fixing something. He was short and seemed to be draped in gold mayoral-looking chains poking through a wedge of dark chest hair. I announced myself.

'I may or may not look familiar to you!' I said, trying to smile and pace my introduction. 'I'm... Sarah's mother.'

I was greeted as though I'd just popped in for tea. He asked his lady friend to put the jug on and wasted no time in telling me what had happened.

'We never should've adopted,' he said. 'We weren't fit to adopt... but of course **they** didn't know that. And there were so many babies available! We only had to wait for three weeks. But we would have been better off getting a dog. A red setter actually. I never wanted to adopt Sarah in the first place. But the wife was bored – our two children were growing up, we had this big house and I was away on business a lot and having the odd affair...' he smirked. I was stunned. I certainly didn't want him to see the tears that filled my eyes and began plopping on to my lap. I held Helen's hand tight under the table.

'I never liked Sarah. Never wanted to adopt, she was there for the wife. And she spoilt her rotten! Always had her dressed beautifully. She was a pretty little thing, mind... lovely skin. But what a handful. She was so bright we had to take her to a psychiatrist. Boy, she gave us a hard time! Well... I didn't have much to do with her, I wasn't there a lot. Then the wife got bored. I didn't blame her... she went off on a cruise and met this sailor. Well, no ordinary sailor, he was an officer and earned good money. And that was it. The boy went to boarding school and the girl followed her mother a year later to England... that's where I'm from actually, just outside Bristol... anyway, I haven't seen either of them since.'

I couldn't speak. Then, like a typical bloody social worker, always trying to see the best in people, I tried to empathise with his position at the time, being left on his own with a young child.

'It must have been hard for you, trying to work and care for Sarah on your own,' I said quietly.

'I suppose some people thought the wife was callous leaving like that, but I quite admired her really, following her own inclinations.'

There was a brief silence.

'Anyway,' he rattled on, 'we didn't think of the birth mother in those days, although I did know quite a bit about you I suppose, that you were from Dunedin, a good family, a student, and I think I can still remember your family name. But I wasn't going to tell her anything. I thought she might make trouble.'

I remember surreptitiously wiping my nose, trying desperately to cope with what he was saying in an effort to get as much information as I could.

I kept squeezing Helen's hand under the table not daring to look at her in case I distracted myself and missed something.

'Naturally I had to take her back to Welfare... after all,' he repeated, 'that's where we got her from... And as I said, I didn't like the child! I certainly didn't want to take responsibility for her. Yes, I saw her once or twice after that, but she played me up something rotten in a restaurant, and that was that. I wasn't going to put up with that again. I know she wrote to the wife a few times, but she never replied. I don't know where she is. New York, I think.

Sarah called round on me once actually – when she was about 17. Hadn't changed. Wanted to know if I had any photos of her as a child. Of course I said no.'

'And have you?' I asked.

'Not that I know of,' he said shrugging his shoulders. 'Funny you should call today because I'm just in the process of cutting her out of my will. So... would you girls like a cup of tea?'

Helen and I walked numbly out of his house hand-in-hand to the nearest pub and got thoroughly smashed.

Several weeks after my return to the UK I received a roll of unprocessed film posted from New Zealand. There was no note. I had it developed. At first glance they looked like photos of me as a baby. Maybe it was a small gesture of kindness by the adoptive father.

My Social Welfare Report 1964:

Social Welfare Office 1987

Piecing together the past was like putting together a mosaic with only a handful of fragments. I was desperately searching for any shards and snippets of information to help make sense of everything especially the secrecy, the confidentiality, mistakes, abuses, bad policies and practices. One big melting pot. Was I looking for someone to blame to expiate my own guilt? And how satisfying would that ultimately be... And why am I still feeling all this grief? Perhaps it is part of the healing process... but all these years later it still feels unreal, like a dream, someone else's life, not mine. Especially when it came to my father.

My father, 1973

I found out that Welfare got in touch with him after Sarah's adoption broke down when her parents abandoned her.

I was given the original social worker's report in which it states that Welfare managed to contact my father after Sarah's adoption broke down when she was aged seven. She had urged social workers to find me. Not the normal practice at the time, according to the social worker.

'My daughter is married, living in England although possibly returning within two years...' my father wrote. 'She has recently had another child. I doubt her husband knows of Sarah's existence.

I trust you will keep me informed...'

He kept this secret and died two years later without telling me anything.

I had lost my daughter a second time.

'Perhaps the most important point,' emphasised the report in italics, was *'that Sarah's mother did not marry the natural father.'* This led the social worker to conclude he therefore doubted the usefulness of the enquiry.

Would Sarah have seen it this way, having begged Welfare to find me? Perhaps the most important point was that I was not consulted directly. As a consequence my daughter became the legal property of the state and once again I was denied the opportunity to care for her.

I wondered if the same decision would have been reached by a female social worker and my mum. Would they too have continued to exclude me from my daughter's life based ultimately on the assumption that I should be free to live my life? Equated the absence of my child with a 'freedom' I didn't seek in the first place?

I was 26 years old! I'd hitchhiked round the world, had a degree, a driver's licence, was NOW MARRIED, had another child. Did I still need to be 'protected', would I ever be free to make my own decisions where my daughter was concerned? Why did everyone assume that I wanted to erase myself forever from her life and for her to leave no trace on mine?

'The past has got to take a back seat, Mother,' said Sarah rather sternly sometime after we met. 'You must forgive your father. I have.'

Report on a child available for adoption

I was given the original form 'Report on a Child Available For Adoption', a single foolscap page divided into small sections, each less than an inch in depth. It was all handwritten, so the smaller the social worker's handwriting, the more information that was recorded. Poor handwriting could mean disaster, inaccurate information or worse than useless.

Information on the mother was in a section that included: health, education, intelligence, personality and family history.

A description of me was as follows: height (wrong), colouring (wrong), and that I am 'attractive, pleasant, well-spoken and intelligent' (which may also be open to doubt).

At least I wasn't described as 'an easy girl' like some birth mothers I've since spoken to.

Details regarding the father were confined to an even smaller section – the same size I noticed as the space reserved for the question on VD.

'The parents hope to marry when they are older.'

No mention about options like how we might have kept our baby, by fostering.

This assessment, which was designed to determine my child's future, was dated three days after my baby was born, the social worker took about half an hour to complete it. And the adoptive parents got my baby three weeks after applying to adopt.

The Adoptive Mother

I discovered that the adoptive mother had been committed to a psychiatric hospital for shock treatment a couple of years before getting my daughter and that during this time both her children were placed in foster care for around two years.

I still have the letter I wrote her dated June 2, 1987 – a few months after reunion with my daughter.

Dear Diane,

I am writing to let you know that I have recently met my daughter Sarah owing to a change to adoption law in New Zealand. I'm sure you'll be pleased to know that our short time together went very well.

I hope you don't mind my writing to you. I expect you have thought of her over the years. I believe from her file that you had a great deal of affection for her and I thank you for that.

I was very sad and upset to learn that you both felt unable to care for her after your marriage ended. It must've been a difficult decision for you at the time.

Sarah's time in care has been a tragic one and there are many gaps in her early history. It's important for us to try and fill some of these gaps. I hope you'll understand my need to do this.

I look forward to hearing from you…

I realise why I still have the original letter. It was returned unopened.

My daughter managed to ring her a few years later. Apparently she didn't have time to talk, but had enough time to tell her, 'You were a dreadful child and I couldn't wait to get rid of you!'

A Little Loving Kindness

'The system has failed your daughter,' wrote her social worker after we all met. 'Her history is tragic, it reflects her drive for identity, acceptance and self-worth… I believe your daughter is special… she's unlike any other child I've come across in care.'

I wanted to object, to say it wasn't the system that failed my daughter – it was me! Me! I'm the one who's responsible for her tragic history, not the 'system'. I'm the one who should be seeking forgiveness. But then I thought of the part everyone had played, the bigger picture, from government policies including no sex education, no abortion, no state benefits, no voice… perpetuated by the cultural values held tight in the grip of our parents' mindsets. All of them believing, and forcing or pressuring us into believing, that children should only live with their parents if those parents were married. Otherwise we'd have to 'surrender' them (the Canadian term) to the state as if this was the natural thing to do; 'relinquish' them, a much less emotive British term that reflected the whole impersonal process of adoption.

I've always remembered the social worker's words. She had summed up Sarah's life at that point in a few sad words, ending with a glimmer of optimism.

Nevertheless, she was acknowledging how I might be feeling – shocked, upset, excluded, angry, let down and disappointed, and, most important, unfairly disenfranchised. There was something about her taking responsibility to apologise that things hadn't worked out for Sarah, and there was also a kind of dignity about it. I may have been reading too much into the situation, but it felt almost like a covert request for forgiveness.

In any case, they were helpful words, harsh and helpful and I felt that, in talking to me like that, as one adult to another, each of us with a similar agenda, she was sincere. Any feelings I might have had, like anger, frustration or outrage, or the temptation to project all my feelings of failure on to her and the 'system', dissolved.

I had always thought I could never make up for the emotional damage done to Sarah. But the social worker's comments pointed to something deeper, something that maybe can't be damaged, hasn't been damaged, like her spirit. Am I clutching at straws? I don't know, but there's something almost irrepressible about her as if somehow the essence of her remains unchanged... her true nature uncontaminated.

Chapter 35

Short Honeymoon – Long Apocalypse

New Zealand 1987–1997

The honeymoon is over. I thought reunion would have made everything right again, made me right again. It had been my focus for so long I had become tunnel-visioned, as if my life had been on hold all these years. Reunion would surely change all that, bring everything back into balance.

I had two more daughters – delightful, loving and good fun. But they did not fill the void, in spite of trying to convince myself and others that my second daughter Anna was my first and my third daughter Sophie, my second. There was always a gap, a shadow, especially on family occasions and I could sometimes sense myself drifting away from them.

But I assumed reunion would magically fix all that! Heal me. Free me from the guilt and worry of her, liberate me, give me a voice that at last could be heard. I'd be reconnected with my daughter, that lost part of me restored! I'd be able to tell her the story surrounding her birth, why we couldn't keep her. She would forgive me and I would feel whole again... I would be coming home to myself. But it was an elusive panacea expecting reunion would make me happy, it didn't work like that. Even after 12 years.

Where had I gone wrong? Perhaps I was kidding myself imagining things could have worked out well between us, in the same way I needed to imagine she had grown up in a loving family, was happy with her life. She was always part of me, maybe that was why things didn't work out well for her: who knows whether she had inherited my scapegoat script and was regarded by others in the unfavourable light of illegitimacy. Would a good life and reunion have, in turn, healed the trauma, healed me? And her too? Or merely papered over the cracks.

I suppose I could have chosen not to meet her. Instead, spared myself the pain of old memories, the trauma and shame of it all, reliving the shunning, the sense of alienation, the nightmares; the need to seek her forgiveness... but if I had chosen that path, it would remain something I was always caught up with, ironically stuck as a victim forever, instead of remembering in a way that should have liberated me from the torture of never knowing, whatever the outcome. Surely, I thought, all the heartache is worth it. And that includes meeting up with John. Resolution comes when we face things, including the need to forgive, instead of being urged to 'go away and forget'. Right?

Sarah had been desperate to meet her father soon after we met. I was filled with apprehension – how would it go? And would they get on? I felt responsible for everything working out well. We'd exchanged the odd letter but I hadn't seen him for years.

Shortly after our reunion, I had flown down ahead to Dunedin where he still lived. Things were starting to go a bit pear-shaped with Sarah, sabotaging outings, becoming hostile to my friends. I stayed with Sally, a girlfriend from uni days in her cute little house overlooking the harbour.

We shared a bottle of wine on her veranda.

'I feel really nervous about seeing John after so long... What's he like now?'

'Maybe the best way to find out is to hunt him down,' she teased. 'He usually drinks in the Prince of Wales... St Kilda... remember?' she said.

The first thing I saw after a sleepless night was a book Sally had propped up outside my room, *Feel the Fear and Do It Anyway*!

'Ha, ha, very apt,' I said drily.

So off we set the following evening wearing sunglasses for disguise although it was getting dark.

The pub was packed with blokes watching the World Cup on

a gigantic screen. We squeezed our way in and Sally suggested she get us a drink while I looked furtively round at all the blokes. He wasn't here.

'He's over there!' she said, finally returning holding two glasses of wine trying to point several times at the same guy wearing a navy polo and sporting a rather unsightly gut.

'Rubbish! That's not him!' I squawked.

'It is!' she insisted. 'Go over, get closer... trust me, it's him!'

'Jeez... what's happened to my gorgeous John?' I wailed.

'Spent too long in here, perhaps?' she ventured.

It took a couple more glasses of wine to 'do it anyway'. I eased my way through the crowd and ended up standing behind him, a bit too close. I looked over to see Sally waving her hand encouragingly in my direction.

'Hello, John,' I said quietly.

He spun round spilling some beer on me and exclaimed, 'Jesus Christ!' then, 'Oh, my God!' before embracing me still holding his pint while I clutched my wine.

His mates were all looking, waiting for an explanation.

'This is an old friend,' he announced smiling.

'Yeah, we can see that, John,' they laughed.

Then he leaned over and whispered, 'God I can't believe you're here! You still look amazing, darles...'

I couldn't easily return the compliment except to say, 'It's probably living in England... not much sun.'

I could see he was still cute, just a much bigger cute. And suddenly it was as if I was back in time, we were back in time. I could feel myself melting and looked over in Sally's direction for help. She gave me another little wave followed by a thumbs up.

His mates resumed staring at the screen chatting among themselves.

'Why don't we go for a wee walk along the beach,' he whispered. 'Just like old times, ay.'

Sally raised an eyebrow when I told her.

'Mmmn... well I hope you know what you're doing, Suze. Don't suppose you know how long you'll be,' she grinned. 'I've just seen some mates so I'll stay with them for a while... and you – take care! That doesn't mean feel the fear and do it anyway...' she added with a stern, maternal look.

She gave John a little wave as his mates were slapping him on the back, punching him playfully on the arm and making whoopee noises in unison.

The air was cool and fresh after the fug of heat and sweat in the pub. A gentle breeze enveloped us as we headed for the track to the beach. John took my hand and raised it to his mouth.

'I still can't believe you're here!' he said and stopped under the only street lamp to embrace me.

'Aren't you worried someone might see us... tell your wife?' I asked feeling my knees go wobbly, wondering how much I cared about his wife.

'You're special, Susie... you still mean the world to me.'

We walked up the track in silence. I could hear the waves crashing and fizzing in a slow, gentle rhythm. The sea air moistening my face.

'Do you think our special place is still there?' he whispered.

I was half-hoping things were still the same...

I looked up at him and giggled.

'Race you to the top!'

We flung ourselves exhausted into what looked like our hollow.

'It's changed shape,' said John.

'It sure has,' I laughed. 'Seems to have lost its shape, but it's still... um, inviting,' I said and blushed.

I wanted to tell him all about Sarah – every detail from our first contact: her letters, the phone call, the reunion. I thought I should leave out the horrible bits, for the moment anyway. I didn't want him to be filled with guilt and sadness. Sarah had spoken to him on the phone but I wasn't sure how much he knew.

The passion in me fizzled out.

'I should be getting back... Sally will be worrying,' I said quietly.

'I still love you...' he whispered. 'I still want you...'

'I still care about you, too, but... I think I need to go now...' I murmured trying to ease myself out from under him.

'I'll see you tomorrow night at Sally's...'

'It was scary,' I said to Sally when she asked how it went. 'All those old, tempting feelings... It was as if we were picking up where we'd left off, as if they'd been on hold all these years.'

Sarah arrived the next day. She greeted me amicably at the airport which echoed with memories of Dad dumping me there, six months pregnant, en route to New Plymouth. And now here I was meeting her, my daughter! Sadly, unable to share memories, however kindly couched, as anything at the moment invited negativity, blame.

'I could never have given my baby away,' she said the previous week as if I'd had a choice.

'You look so like your mother!' John greeted her at Sally's as they hugged.

Shortly afterwards the nightmare started as Sarah began telling us some details of her childhood – all the worst suspicions of an unprotected child, no one really looking out for her, like a parent would. We were sitting out on the veranda, all of us crying. Sally too.

'It's important that you know the truth,' Sarah said in a matter-of-fact way.

John stayed and we cried all night.

'Maybe it was payback time,' said Martin on the phone from England. 'She wanted you to know how much she'd suffered.'

'You don't believe her?'

'Well... whether the stories are true or not, perhaps it was her way of bringing her anger towards you out in the open.'

'You mean by punishing us?'

'Yes, in the same way she might feel you punished her by having her adopted.'

Chapter 36

Sarah's 35th Birthday

Bristol, UK 1999

Sarah rang me out of the blue with some amazing news.

'Guess what, Ma?' she said. 'I've just won a competition and I'm coming to England! Bonza!' she shouted excitedly down the phone. 'It was for an advertising company. Great, ay! And even better... I'll be there for my birthday! Think of that, Mother, our first birthday together!'

'Oh my God, how exciting! Amazing! Congratulations, darling!' I shouted down the phone. 'I can hardly believe it! All my dreams come true!'

Contact over the last few years had been erratic, pages of emails, then nothing, which always left the same hollowness, the emptiness of not knowing, even after reunion.

My long-held fantasies burst into action: a birthday party! I'd always hoped to formally welcome her back into the family, a little ritual carried out by someone sort of spiritual.

I also fantasised about another gathering where I would invite my closest girlfriends, a lunch feast, showing her off to everyone, a kind of proud parent moment welcoming the usual comments of how alike we are, which had reduced several old friends to tears when they first met her, not long after we were reunited in New Zealand.

I was being thrust, once again, into that other time zone. That other plane of existence. Almost too much to take in.

'At last you can be here with us... see where we live! Oooh, I'm so excited!' I shouted.

'She'll catch a glimpse of our lives, meet up with her sisters again,' I thought. Like we had done a few years ago in New Zealand...

This was excellent news. The last few years our relationship had chugged its way round real and imagined obstacles along a narrow, precipitous, winding track. She started to trust me again, share her problems and ask advice. Sometimes she just wanted me to listen, not get upset.

'You're no good to me all upset, Ma,' she would say.

Three weeks later we rushed to the airport to meet her but she wasn't on her connecting flight from Amsterdam.

'Why didn't they tell me when the flight was leaving?' she demanded to know. After that, it was all downhill. She barely commented on our lovely Georgian house, which I had been feverishly cleaning in preparation for her arrival, the little vase of welcoming flowers on her bedside table picked from the garden, the freshly ironed best linen sheets and pillowcases, the carefully thought-out menus, the slightly exhausting itinerary from Stonehenge to the SS Great Britain. Instead, she chose to sit outside and smoke.

'Happy birthday, darling,' I ventured a couple of tense days later, as I tried to embrace her while she puffed on a cigarette in the rain. She grunted a kind of 'thanks' and continued staring at the ground.

'So... um... what do you want to do on your special day? Still look for something you'd really, really like, then lunch somewhere special?'

She refused to answer. I found myself moving from one foot to another and back again. Why was it all so difficult? Why would she come all this way to sulk and fight when I knew that she had been so excited?

I could see from the garden that the family had gathered in the kitchen, including her two Kiwi cousins who came down from London and Liverpool, waiting for some sign as to what was happening. I caught Martin's eye and mouthed 'help', but he pointed in the direction of the front door as though he had other duties. Sarah had managed to engage him in a loud, lengthy argument on the stairs last night as I lay straining to hear from the safety and comfort of my bath. I needed some respite from all the tension and arguing. I was exhausted and beginning to run out of empathy and wisdom, and maybe Martin was too.

Sarah had her back to the kitchen window and couldn't see the family gesticulating from within. I surreptitiously raised both hands in front of me, palms upwards, to indicate that I had no idea what was happening and felt relieved when I saw them leaving.

'OK, so everyone's wanting to go out and celebrate your birthday,' I said as casually as I could, 'and... guess what... we'd really like you to come with us... so... what's happening?'

She shrugged her shoulders without looking at me.

It was hard to understand. She couldn't wait to be here for her birthday.

'Have I done something to upset you?' I asked gently half-expecting her to say, 'Yes. How could you give me away!' but she just shrugged again and looked blank.

I offered her a cup of tea and went inside. All the presents lay waiting on the table – lovingly wrapped in brightly-coloured paper of turquoise, reds, pink and gold. It made me think of all the presents I hadn't been able to give her... and all the presents she hadn't received.

She stayed sitting on the garden bench stooped forward, cigarette clenched between thumb and forefinger like an old man concentrating hard on something he was trying to remember. Then she suddenly got up and came indoors. Most of the family, except my son-in-law, Neil, had gone out. Someone rang the front door bell and Neil answered. It was Martin's hairdresser for heaven's sake! The one with the PhD. I suggested she come in and wait. Take notes, I thought...

'Where's my f***ing teabags?' Sarah demanded.

I'd had enough of her treatment and decided I needed to try

another tactic.

'Don't speak to me like that,' I said and turned around to look at her directly. 'It's not necessary... just ask me nicely.'

I was standing in the kitchen doorway about to leave when she came up behind me and shoved me. I stumbled but managed to break my fall by grabbing hold of a cupboard door catch. I had not long recovered from an operation and my biggest fear was falling over.

Neil came racing over to restrain her and make sure I was all right.

'It was her fault! Not mine,' she yelled as if I'd pushed myself over. The statement hung in the air, the words echoing back into the past.

Shortly afterwards, the family returned. They all sat round in a circle in the sitting room to discuss what had happened and what to do about it. I sat with them. Sarah had stormed out of the house. I caught glimpses of her in the front garden through the half-shuttered windows, periodically turning round to glare in at us. I uncharacteristically said nothing. My two other daughters and their cousins made a decision. Sarah should go. One of them rang a local bed and breakfast, the others went to pack her suitcase. I still said nothing.

I guess there was something about that day that had an inevitability about it, almost like she was on a course that she couldn't get off, even if she wanted to, like being caught in a spell, in headlights, a hypnotic trance. And maybe it was a bit naïve of me to think she could feel welcomed. It may have had the opposite effect, being with her family at last. Being made welcome with all the little details like flowers in her room may have reinforced her sense of separateness and difference. What she had missed. And no amount of welcoming could ever fix it, make it right. I know I was attempting to repair things, that's what I'd been trying to do ever since we were reunited. Help expiate my feelings of guilt, I suppose. But it didn't work. Maybe it will never work until I stop trying to make things better, stop searching for solutions. Ditch the guilt and the expectations, accept the advice of my mentors, that what's happened has happened for whatever reason – and stop bloody trying! It just makes things worse.

I thought of the family birthday party, the presents, wanting to play the proud mother at the lunch party, showing her off to my friends – all in an effort to what? Make things better, make her feel welcome, assuage my guilt, strengthen our bond. What bloody bond? Would that be the mother-daughter bond? What right did I have to show her off? It was all bullshit, didn't address the real issues whatever they were and maybe that was why she was so angry.

'Resolution comes with the end of the search... and the letting go,' said Martin, suggesting another of his sometimes irritatingly-wise-but-impossible-to-achieve comments which made me feel worse.

'But what about our reunion,' I wept. 'I thought it would make me feel whole again, but I don't. I just feel...broken... all over again...'

He was trying to console me over a late night bottle of wine at our kitchen table soon after Sarah had gone.

'That comment about ending the search came from a book I'm reading written by a woman called Gangaji... she writes about searching and healing,' he said when I stopped crying.

'According to her, our story is expressing the very thing we need to face if we want to deepen our experience of life,' he said.

'Well it doesn't feel like that,' I sniffed. 'It feels like the opposite – and really confusing.'

'Well... it's about facing ourselves in our stories... We can stand back and see our personal stories as part of the bigger whole.'

'How could I possibly do that, think like that or even know what that is with all this emotional turmoil?' I asked still feeling slightly irritated. 'It's impossible to see the bigger picture with all this going on!'

I ran a hot bath, poured in some luxurious Neal's Yard oil of lavender and rosemary, and submerged myself in its velvet warmth still thinking about Martin's words. What was it we needed to face? There were so many things to choose from, things we hadn't actually discussed properly like our feelings about what happened, why I couldn't keep her, why the family rejected her, and me, why I didn't stay in touch with Welfare. It wasn't enough to explain that I wasn't allowed to return home with her, had been made to swear on the Bible never to try and make contact, that I understood this would have been the equivalent of breaking the law. It didn't make sense to her.

'I don't understand why you went along with it, I certainly couldn't,' she said barely disguising the admonition in her voice fuelled no doubt by childhood memories, her sense of rejection etched right through her like the red writing in a stick of Brighton rock played out over and over with all the families she'd been placed with, starting with her own mother: not ever knowing who she was or where she came from. Not belonging anywhere. No wonder she was angry with me, blamed me for everything. Who else could she blame?

I kept going over the last day when we were together. Her birthday when my family rejected her. Suddenly something shocking occurred to me. I realised what had taken place in front of me. Not only had she been rejected by them, but the way in which this had happened was uncanny, almost unbelievable. It had suddenly occurred to me that it was an amazing re-enactment of her birth! From her shove or push of me to her expulsion into the world by the family – a different family this time. They decided she shouldn't return, and uncharacteristically I said virtually nothing. Then somehow went along with the decision. It was painfully familiar!

'Perhaps, unconsciously, she was trying to create in you the same feelings she'd experienced about her adoption, what she went through,' said Martin. 'From her point of view, you'd put her through that, it was your fault, so she was doing the same... giving it back.'

'Re-enacting her birth?'

'Do you remember when we were social workers that some kids in foster homes would push and push the family they were placed with to the limits? Testing them to the end of their tether... pushing to the point of being rejected by them?'

'Yes, but I never really understood why,' I said.

'One idea is that the original rejection is re-enacted as a test – over and over – perhaps in the faint hope of a different outcome,' said Martin.

'OMG – it feels something like that... but it just makes me feel worse,' I said. 'What on earth can I do about it?'

'In a way there's not much we can do. These things run their course. We can only accept the gift that comes hand in hand with the painful re-enactment.'

'The gift?'

'Maybe to fully accept what happened today is to face up to the fact that deep down you believe what she said. That "it's all your fault", including her behaviour, her struggles in life... everything that's happened to her. The gift out of all this is to realise that you still carry that guilt, feel responsible and see yourself as a bad person, and that maybe the time has come to forgive yourself, free yourself,' said Martin. 'Sometimes we say sorry and expect forgiveness before we've forgiven ourselves. So it's not surprising that some people, like Sarah, don't forgive us.'

I guess he knows, being a psychotherapist.

'But how does she know that? How could she know I haven't forgiven myself?'

'It's unconscious, but on that subtle level she knows you still hold the guilt. Your guilt is the coat hook for her to hang her coat on. Without the hook the coat falls to the floor.'

I pondered on ditching the hook, but after Sarah's visit, all I could do was keep wondering where it had all gone wrong and what I'd done to invite that.

'Maybe it wasn't "wrong",' said Martin. 'Maybe it was a natural unfolding. Perhaps things like this don't occur accidentally, they have some meaning. They leap out to give you a chance to resolve things, heal things by encouraging you to release the emotions that keep you trapped, stuck, with nothing ever changing!'

I started to feel excited again! Hopeful. Maybe here was another chance, this epiphany, this crossroad, a new beginning!

Instead, Sarah sent me a very vitriolic email, several pages long. We had all stood round the computer after Martin had called out there was an email from her, expecting a message expressing at least some small regret or something. I couldn't bear to finish reading it, blaming me for everything that had gone wrong in her life, headed up 'Final Closure', like some sort of deal was off. Over.

'But have you considered that *maybe* the email was "perfect" too?' said Martin the following day. 'Perfect for both of you. All that unedited expression of anger and intense feeling... I mean, where's yours? I've never heard you express any anger about what happened. Only sadness. And when you really look at it, the blaming expressed is sort of seen as somewhat absurd, don't you think? It's a bit pointless... perhaps by you both? Her darkest thoughts out in the open for you both to deal with... not as the end point but as a vital stage in the process of forgiveness and reconciliation... a sort of truth but revealed as a story...'

It took me some time before I could take on board what Martin said to me about her email, her 'Final Closure'. I needed time to digest her trip over here, her behaviour when she arrived and what happened afterwards. I went over and over it in my mind, wondering what I could've done differently. And most of all how to ditch the bloody coat hook. In quieter moments I started to wonder if the torment of not knowing her was greater than all this torment of knowing what happened to her... the knowing, it seems, does not set me free.

Chapter 37

Forgiveness of Self: with a little help from Marcus the amazing medium

We have a right to live without pain of the past.
Melanie Higgins, Jungian Analyst referring to Holocaust survivors at a conference on Forgiveness, Bristol 2008

Bristol

Nothing was the same for a long time after Sarah's visit. Everything seemed a bit pointless. I felt powerless, worthless and passive. The feelings permeated everything, my other daughters, my husband, my job. A kind of lethargy set in. Any future with her was now shattered. All our communications were caught in the past and neither of us could change the past, ever put it right. Especially me. So what future could we possibly have together without forgiveness?

Maybe we could change the future, our future. If only we could let things go. Sometimes I wish I could just download it all. Get it over with. Purge myself, a complete cleansing of guilt and shame. Bring it all to an end. Free myself! But the time and effort and patience required to deal with it, to let things go, is almost beyond me. And I'm not sure I know how. The rituals, the recurring nightmares, the thoughts that spike my consciousness all seem to conspire to interfere with the process.

I often think there's nothing else to do but forgive. I need to look clearly into myself, my story, my family dynamics, my role as scapegoat... how I've held myself firmly in place, arrested in time. Maybe now I need to surrender, move on. Find my own freedom. But another part of me thinks the opposite and holds on tight to the sadness and sorrow, always accompanied by shame and guilt. The feelings are a kind of validation of what happened, a loyalty, and I feel almost a sense of duty to honour them.

So much of this entire experience is lodged in my mind, fixed there like a stubborn stain: my reputation in the family, with friends and neighbours, imagined or real that I dragged around with me. Can I really ditch it all that easily, forgive myself? It makes me wonder what **was** real.

I was suddenly made respectable by the NZ Adoption Act 1985. One day the world was telling me that I am a bad person, shamed, unfit to bring up my own child, not deserving enough to have any information about her, and the next day, I'm not! But I am still the same person! So are thousands of other women like me. But now the story was different. Or, at least, people's perception of the story. I was no longer guilty as charged. Now, apparently, it no longer defined me. Maybe it never really did.

Everything had happened so quickly. Help to find each other was suddenly available! Welfare offered to open up all the adoption records retrospectively! And now our status was elevated, fairy-tale notions of adopted children reunited with their long-lost parents. Family and friends, welcoming arms now extended. Suffering surely evaporated. The stuff of magazine articles and television programmes. And books. It was an amazing celebration.

'So why is the shame so hard to shake off?' I asked Martin. 'The guilt too, especially after finding out what happened to Sarah, feeling responsible... even though everyone tells me I couldn't have known what would happen. But it's the shame... It runs right through me, still clings to me like an outer skin.'

'Because the Adoption Act can take away the guilt, but not the shame,' said Martin. 'It's still part of your identity... a reflection of who you think you are. The difference is the Adoption Act now makes your actions OK, but it can't make you OK.'

I want to shake off the shame, shake it out of me. Will I ever be truly free of it? In spite of the Act it doesn't feel very likely. It feels like I am still hiding something.

All the excitement and turmoil around the Act feels like a long time ago, heralding the end of a lifetime of wondering and yearning, the despair of not knowing what had happened to her. Now, I thought, I could start sloughing off that dead, outer layer of myself, encouraged and validated by the Act, more willing to see that everyone was doing the best they could given the context of the time – and their own personal stories. Maybe that's what true forgiveness means. Letting go of blame. And enjoying the freedom it brings. But would my daughter ever feel the same?

Marcus: a most amazing medium
Bristol June 2007

We were sitting at my kitchen table that looks out over the back garden dominated by an enormous, happy New Zealand tree fern. A few friends chatted in the sitting room waiting to see Marcus as well. I can't remember who recommended him but they had been most impressed. It felt like the right time for me to see him. A review was due; where was I going, I wondered? And I wanted to be impressed as well.

'There's a lot of people here who want to say hello to you,' said Marcus whose speciality was communicating with those that have passed over.

'Oh yeah, really?' I ask sceptically. 'Who's there then?'

'Do the names Catherine, Mary and Marion mean anything to you?'

'OMG – that's my mum and her two sisters!' I squealed, absolutely stunned.

'Mmmn… I've got your father here too. Actually, he was here before we sat down.'

I half-laughed still reeling from his previous comment. 'That figures!' I said.

'He apologises for being harsh; he didn't mean to push people away. He hopes you have forgiven him. Was he a bit of a control freak? He was aware his upbringing had problems, his own father enforcing his views on him. But he cares, and he wants so much to get that across here.' Marcus paused then added, 'And who's Martin? Dad wants to make it clear he likes Martin.'

'Dad likes Martin! Wow, that's a first, I didn't think Dad liked anyone!'

'His passing wasn't pleasant, but not sudden, he knew it was coming. His illness was an irritation to him, he was always a very busy person. He wouldn't take his pills. He threw them down the toilet.' Marcus paused. 'There were things he wanted to say to you... I think he kind of tried.'

'Maybe... I received the only quite nice letter from him a few days after he died. I've kept it in case I need reminding.'

'As a father he made too much of things, he was over the top a lot of the time; agrees he was a pain in the arse...'

Marcus looked thoughtful and breathed in and out deeply. Was he pleased Dad had gone or was he seeing something difficult ahead...

'There was a time when you felt lost,' he said. 'Slightly self-abusive, hating yourself. This is to do with your first daughter – I would attribute it to that. But she has brought you recognition of finding yourself; finding the power of yourself...'

I could feel the tears welling up, the sudden overheating of my body, my heart banging.

'I've got your mum here. Such strong mother love for you. She was quite lost towards the end of her life,' he said. 'There's so much love here. But she felt terribly guilty about something – I have to say that. She should have stood up to your father. He could be belligerent. There's public pride here – his "position".'

'She felt she had to stand with him when things went bad for you. She always wanted to heal that aspect of it. She never quite had the strength, always in the shadow of your dad. She does love you deeply as a daughter... and she underlines this point,' he added.

'Another book on the go! Again, I feel the healing aspect is very prominent, because it is very prominent in your life, very prominent energy within you. The healing force comes in many different ways – voice, presence, written word... behind that there has to be compassion and drive. But you doubt yourself! It's strange because you're such a competent person but you have this aspect of coming to terms with spirituality within yourself! Spirit knows you walk the middle ground. You need to "get off that fence!", remove the splinters. You're not going to lose anything by focusing on the spiritual – you're not going to turn into an airy-fairy!' he smiled. 'You're going to write a book that pertains more to that side of things. Just let soul and the moment happen a bit more rather than dissecting, cross-examining everything that goes on: "pile of crap" vs. "great!", that's you! Pursuing truths. Like you're doing, is great!'

'I'm very pleased,' says Marcus. 'I can feel an awful lot of spiritual strength behind you, I can feel them around. You do have moments when you feel really inspired! You have no choice but to write about things. It's why you're here!' said Marcus. 'I'm 100 per cent confident in your ability.

And by the way, your brain is not wanting to let spirit out of your body. You've been through so much emotion, you shut down at one stage. It's safe to open yourself up. You're holding on to stuff – that needs to change...'

'Guilt is a demon. You've done your best. There's nothing to feel guilty about. You still need to get this out of your system. Your daughter has her own journey and it was part of her lesson. She's not purely a subject of rejection. She's made a lot of her own choices. She is processing her own evolution. She'll come to a realisation, when things will change, but it won't be soon.'

Chapter 38

Harold the Hero

Guernsey, UK September 2009

It felt like I was now carrying a different burden, less easy to identify. As if it had changed shape, metamorphosised into something I didn't fully recognise, didn't know how to handle. I wasn't expecting it to be like this. Still feeling lost, incomplete.

I had somehow messed things up again, as if another layer of guilt had been added. But at least we were now back in touch even if contact with her was sporadic.

Around this time someone strongly encouraged me to see 'an amazing craniosacral osteopath called Harold', who practised in Guernsey.

'I don't usually recommend people,' she said. 'But I think you'd really benefit from seeing him.'

I'd never seen an osteopath before – a homeopath, a chiropractor, a neurologist, a psychotherapist, an iridologist, an herbalist, healers and mediums, but decided to bite the bullet, try my luck and hope he wasn't into any surprise manoeuvres. I found out where Guernsey was, hesitated, then made an appointment which happened to be on my birthday, and hubby and I flew there. There was something about Guernsey that reminded me of home. Caught in time, maybe? The vegetation, the friendly community feel...

I warmed to Harold immediately. He was a lovely guy, gentle and respectful and non-judgmental. And he had worked in New Zealand for several years.

'Wonderful place,' he sighed. 'It gets into your bones, doesn't it!'

I immediately felt at ease.

'Do you know anything about restless leg syndrome?' I asked.

I had submitted a very brief medical history to him ahead of my visit including information about my restlessness. 'I've had it for years,' I added, '... since my mid-thirties.'

I was sitting on the edge of his treatment couch with my back to him when he placed one hand on the small of my back and the other on my head.

'Being a premature baby in an incubator for several weeks meant you had to fight for survival on your own. There was no one there. You're not a restless person but you couldn't settle...'

How did he know I was a premature baby? I'm sure I didn't tell him because it didn't seem to be significant when I sent him a brief outline of my medical history. What he said felt right: I was fiercely independent, always on the move. I thought of all the times I'd just up and hitchhiked in New Zealand, the couple of hundred miles up to Christchurch to get away, see friends, or hitched to Queenstown to enjoy the mountains and lakes and sunshine, the summer smells of golden grasses, my motorbike and the calculated risks I took on it; and then eventually hitching over to the UK with my boyfriend who later became hubby number one. We hitched the length of Africa, then Central and South America. And drove to Russia and back in our clapped-out bright pink camper van. 'Crazy Kiwis,' said various English friends. Always on the move. Maybe that's how I managed, by being busy, simply avoiding things.

'This restlessness is still here in your body,' said Harold. 'There's agitation in your sacrum. You've processed a lot of material but there's still agitation there.'

He paused as if he was listening for something before adding, 'You lost peacefulness at 17. Your body needs to know that you were relieved of a baby.'

I turned slowly round to face him.

'Oh,' I gulped. 'Um, I... what do you mean?'

'Your mind has not informed your body that you had a child when you were 17.'

I sat back on the couch stunned.

How could he possibly know anything about that? I was sure I hadn't told him and no one else I knew had had any contact with him. Part of me suddenly felt invaded and vulnerable. What had that got to do with anything now, with the restlessness, all these years later? And how did he manage to glean that information so easily and expose my innermost self, like skinning a fish, a rabbit, revealing everything that needs an outer layer to protect it, to stop it from disintegrating, dying, even. And anyway, what bullshit! How could my own body not know?

What was it that he could feel or 'see' that he'd managed to reveal with such ease as if I were as transparent as glass? Clear as light. A secret hidden away for so many years – a darkened pearl concealed tight within an oyster. How could he pick up on details like the way I'd responded back then, the way I'd somehow managed to deploy a kind of body bypass?

Sitting on the massage couch I was reminded that there were so many things in my life I didn't want to remember, things I regretted, as if the warmth of Harold's hand might gently unleash them, allowing them to rise and bubble to the surface along with me.

Losing Sarah was the biggest regret... being sent away; and shaming the family is another. And not being there when my lovely mum died. And maybe causing my father so much grief he genuinely did believe I was responsible for my mother's death.

So maybe that is how I dealt with all the difficult memories, by denying them. I couldn't internalise what was going on, it was too painful so I separated myself from the situation as if it wasn't happening. Like kids traumatised by abuse of one sort or another where something that was beautiful and natural gets shut down. Maybe I was more like those kids I tried to help when I was a social worker than I realised.

I was alarmed and puzzled and amazed all at the same time by Harold's words. How could my mind behave in such an autonomous way by not involving my body when I'd been over and over what happened – night and day for years as if my whole being, not just my mind, were saturated with guilt and sorrow? Maybe it'd be more accurate to say my mind would take over, usually late at night when I'd hoped that alcohol or sex or whatever would help me forget. Not keep me restless.

Did I really ever want to stop anything? What would have happened if I had let go? Would it have meant I lost my thread to Sarah, the only early memories of her buried deep, in the secrecy of silence; the only link I had with her as a baby?

'You have a deep fear of stopping,' Harold had said. 'It goes against your instinct for survival... Your body still vibrates with your experience of your first few weeks of life as a premature baby in an incubator.'

But in spite of my fears, there was another part of me that felt ready to stop searching! Impatient, almost, for Harold's treatment. The time was ripe. The treatment felt it would be safe and it was – so tranquil, beautiful, full of loving kindness. It was collaborative, a two-way process, a letting go, a melting, after years of holding on, yielding after years of resisting, fighting. Being open to the healing was like a dance where I finally allowed myself to be led.

I wanted to tune in with him, to yield and absorb as much healing or whatever it was as possible. The word 'yield' was somehow perfect: the softening, the melting moment with Harold. A very special moment.

I wanted to stay open to what was happening, be connected with whatever was going on... sort of maximise the moment, partners in somehow solving the mystery of my body's memories and manifestations and how I had dealt with them – wanting to be free of them! And wondering if I would get it right, be as transparent as I needed to be.

'It's like there are two sides to your mind,' said Harold interrupting my thoughts. 'One is your father's voice saying,

"You're not good enough." So even when you're sitting under your olive tree in Spain, sun shining, your mind and body are saying: "Don't just sit there! Get on with something, paint some windows..."'

'Oh yes,' I laughed having told him at the outset that we were driving to our place in Southern Spain. What I hadn't told him was that every time we went there, I spent most of it painting endless windows and shutters!

'There's a lot of fear here,' Harold said after a while. 'You're a bit of a try harder, your mind often turning to things you need to do, dealing with problems at night time, when you should be sleeping – a two- or three-hour session at least! And it's been going on for a long time.'

Harold paused and breathed deeply as if he were resonating with... I'm not sure what... maybe my essence.

'I didn't realise there was so much fear in you until I saw it leaving,' he said quietly.

I had my eyes closed but was aware of him making a gentle swishing motion behind me with his hands as if he were ushering the fear out of me.

'A great burden has been lifted,' he added quietly.

I didn't realise how much fear was in me either, not until I cast my mind back. Fear was everywhere, as pervasive as air. Fear as a child of my father, fear that something might happen to my mum, fear of not doing well enough at school, then fear of getting pregnant, fear that I might die having the baby, fear that things will never be the same again, fear that my reputation would be ruined, fear that I might not be able to marry as a result, fear I might not be able to have another child, fear that my family might shut the door on me forever, fear that my life might be over... all jumbled together so I couldn't identify which fear belonged to me.

'Part of you is concerned to get things right, but the other part of you is light and warm and carefree and full of fun,' said

Harold.

'So maybe you can stop trying so hard and putting in such a great effort and celebrate who you are! You're lovely and loving and a lot of people admire you just as you are...'

I could feel myself melting when he said that. Everything fell away... like meat off a bone... it felt right. And I felt peaceful. Still. I could stay in this place forever, not wanting anything, not searching for anything. Just drinking in the bliss and beauty of that moment.

'No need to change anything,' said Harold, and added a comment that has stayed with me.

'Our parents amplify what we most need to learn.' And I melted again. This time it was the lifelong tensions falling away, all the negativity. A strong feeling of union – not with anyone, more a feeling of love and absolute acceptance, accepting life as it is and as it was, because there was no blame, leaving me with a feeling of well-being, wholeness, completion and oneness. And an overwhelming desire to forgive – even Dad. I became aware that sometimes it's hard to love someone the way they want to be loved when you don't know what that is.

I loved Harold's language, the way he spoke, what he was able to convey in a magical kind of way, words of wisdom bathed in beauty, words that never condemned anyone or anything, no matter how bad, words that reflected love. Sunlight. And as a result they were so wonderfully powerful and memorable. It was like being drawn into a pool of warm, velvety water where my thoughts and beliefs and memories were infused with love. There was a weird kind of feeling of completion and contentment, not imperfection or needing to improve something; none of that seemed to matter. Instead there was a strong feeling of union with everything all at once!

All the tensions and memories I'd dragged around with me, trying to forget them, reminded me of the contrast with the little chambered nautilus in our school song whose sealed past helped keep him buoyant, while mine weighed me down. Until now when they were beginning to surface and fall away. They no longer mattered! I realised I'd been carrying them around because I'd not fully accepted what had happened until this moment. Perhaps the Adoption Act was a turning, triggering the process.

I decided just to let it all go, the fears and prejudices and other people's perceptions of me, and my perceptions of others, particularly when I think of home, to stop actually thinking, stop searching and simply sink into the experience of what that would be like. What that was like! I don't know how much time elapsed but it was blissful as if the world and everything in it was flowing through me. Where I seemed to know nothing and at the same time knowing everything.

'Aaah, there's the still point,' said Harold quietly, having gauged some significant sensation in my body as I lay on his couch. 'There it is.'

I felt as if I was floating away at the same time as being connected to everything around me. Not being separate from who I am. And feeling high with love. Delicious!

Part III

What Can Never Be Lost

Learn to be Still
The Eagles, 1994

Chapter 39

Letting Go

Bristol 2013

The problem with progress is that it suggests there's something to improve. But what if there isn't? What if I'm already OK just the way I am? The irony made me laugh when I thought of the time and expense in going to all those workshops I'd attended over the years, aimed at self-improvement of one sort or another – personal growth (what is that, exactly?), meditation, healing, a silent retreat (just the one), the early morning mentoring sessions (talking at 5am to suit Antipodean time for heaven's sake)... workshops held all over the UK – in Cornwall, Manchester, Wales, Scotland. Oh, and Germany a couple of times. No distance was too far.

I also laughed because I realised that all these attempts at self-improvement hadn't actually changed the core belief I'd always held about myself; I hadn't actually 'improved'. Not really. Even after being made 'respectable' by an Act of Parliament, reunited with my amazing daughter! After 20-odd years or more, I still felt I wasn't good enough, that nothing much in me had changed. Just like some of my social work clients I thought, remembering Mrs Brown in Brixton. But I guess I had learnt a lot about other people in these various workshops, their difficulties, patterns of behaviour, ways we communicate drawn from Neuro-Linguistic Programming, how we interact and the psychological games we play based on Transactional Analysis, Gestalt... our pasts played out in every workshop, how we perceive ourselves, how we are perceived by others... how to 'manage' grief, loss, hope and fulfilment... But has it bloody helped?

I remained unfulfilled despite the reunion, all its joys, delights and sorrows, all the frustrations and feelings of helplessness it induced in me. Like any parenting situation I suppose, except it wasn't like any parenting situation. Once she asked me if she should ring her adoptive mother who had made no contact since abandoning her when she was seven. Not so much as a card. I didn't know how to respond, felt I had no 'legitimate' right to say what I really thought. No real entitlement.

Maybe my daughter and I were both experiencing the same thing, both still left with a sense of rejection and emptiness. I was still restless. Unable to settle at things, experience fulfilment or feel contentment. Instead, those familiar scenarios of always starting things and not finishing them. Wanting to be elsewhere but not knowing where. Maybe return home to New Zealand, maybe not. I couldn't commit myself to anything or see things through to completion. Even as a social worker, I always took on the short-term cases, the ones that seemed to have a clearly defined problem, like the Reynolds family. Who knows, I might need to return home. Whatever I was doing, wherever I was living, I was always wanting to change things. I wondered how I'd managed to sit down and write my books and articles, as I was often left with the feeling of things unfinished. Of needing to move on, always looking for a way out. Where to go next...

'Maybe they're no longer right for you,' said Deborah when we were discussing our meditation teachers.

'How do you mean?' I asked.

'You're looking for something that can't be found with them,' she said.

Her comments resonated with me. Something didn't feel right. Maybe I was looking for a teacher who could make it all OK... Or maybe all the teaching was helpful. It influenced the way I saw the world and my place within it, and I am very grateful. Maybe I needed to learn all that stuff before I could realise that I didn't need it! Like searching for a precious key that was hidden in my pocket all along.

It was becoming clear that I needed to deal with things in

a different way and accept that the 'progressive' school of meditation, to which I had belonged for many years, was like a treadmill, round and round with the same old issues, not really taking me anywhere other than to increase the restlessness I felt by escalating the endless searching. But searching for what, exactly?

I thought of Harold's comments about my restlessness and stopping the search, putting an end to all the trying hard to make things right.

'No need to change anything,' he had said gently. 'There's nothing to change. Just celebrate who you are... your true nature.'

So why couldn't I feel the freedom I was expecting after I was reunited with my daughter? Years later I was still looking for answers. Perhaps it lay in the reams of notes I had zealously recorded at every workshop – notes I never looked back on with enthusiasm or curiosity – in spite of thinking if I collected enough information, I'd find the answer. But nor did I look forward anymore to meditation workshops or practice. It took me a while to notice, see the signals.

Maybe my frustration was more about my own restlessness and disappointment at not experiencing the sense of freedom I had longed for after meeting Sarah. Not being able or ready to take on Harold's comments. Instead, I could feel an increasing sense of alienation from the group and the teachers, and a creeping indifference. I'd taken most of what I'd been taught as true and had hardly questioned the masses of information we were given or the effectiveness of the meditations. Looking back, I don't think I'd ever taken it very seriously, like I should have done.

'Delightfully irreverent,' remarked a friend. 'A healthy sceptic,' remarked another.

And I enjoyed seeing lots of old friends who, like me, attended the workshops fairly regularly. But that changed too as I became aware of feeling separate from the group, with all kinds of doubts surfacing.

'Do you see any correlation between your own family and this situation?' hubby asked.

'Now that you say that, yes, it reminds me of returning home after having Sarah,' I said. 'When I felt different and distant from everyone. Disconnected. Especially my family. I suppose I felt I'd never really belonged in my family... I used to think there'd been a big mistake! And I belonged to someone else... and it was only a matter of time before they claimed me...'

'Why do you say that?'

'I suppose I never really had a sense of belonging to them, being part of them, apart from my mum. I always felt on the edge, tried to spend as little time as I could get away with... I preferred to be with my friends and their families.'

'In a way that's why the search is futile,' said Martin. 'It can't be repaired in that way... from that position – having the sense of being an outsider, or trying to change the story by leaving home. It can't be repaired because there was never anything wrong in the first place.'

'What a load of ****!' I exclaimed. 'Are you saying I imagined all the rows, the shouting, being belted...'

'No,' said Martin. 'But belonging is our natural state... we're part of everything.'

'But that's the point! I never felt I belonged!'

I got up and walked away. It felt as if he had managed to undermine my whole experience as a child, discounted it as if it hadn't happened. It triggered the same feeling of inner loneliness I'd carried with me ever since. Never feeling good enough or 'right' enough, not fitting in, not understood. We'd been sitting in the garden on a rare sunny day in April and, as usual, I'd been distracted. It was all the weeds that had invaded everywhere I looked, the herb garden, the tubs, poking through the gravel that surrounded the two large, circular brick-edged flower beds.

'And how do you think you got those feelings?' Martin called after me.

Sometimes his explanations infuriated me, they were so simple.

'It can't be repaired,' he said referring to my family, 'because there was never anything to repair in the first place.' I rest my case.

Later he had said by way of explanation, 'You've created a set of beliefs... core beliefs, based on painful circumstances, and everything else emanates from them... the way you see the world, the way you live your life. We all do it... our experience can easily become the beacon by which we set our lives.'

I have to admit I like that expression, 'the beacon by which we set our lives', even in the middle of my confusion. It had a ring of truth about it.

'I know all the painful memories are traumatic to the body and mind... and feel very real,' he added. 'And that's because belonging is our natural state... we are part of everything.'

'So what about Sarah? She was separated from me at birth, for heaven's sake!'

'Yes, of course. On the level of body and mind this was a massive trauma. But you cannot be separated from what you are. And that goes for all of us including Sarah.'

'What do you mean?'

'How else would we know what separation feels like if we didn't know union, oneness?' he said. 'It's when it doesn't feel like this, when we feel rejected or abused, when we feel separate from our families or friends, it's because it's unnatural to feel like that. And that's when we sometimes decide to behave in particular ways... and that can only happen through thought, when the mind and body get in the way and you create core beliefs about things, like "I'm never going to be good enough," "I don't belong." That's what separates us from others... when the traumas and so on give rise to beliefs that feel very real and can then act as our beacon.'

'So what do I do? Just dump the thoughts?' I said tutting quietly and feeling my eyes turn skywards.

'No, just observe them... experiment with letting go. You might find the freedom you are searching for. Remember the peace and freedom you felt with Harold when he helped you let go?'

So when we were invited to old friends for dinner I started taking notice of my thoughts and prejudices because the guests included a couple of long-standing irritants. On the car journey there it occurred to me I was doing the same to them as was done to me. I had already judged and rejected them, woven a story around them, anticipated how the evening would go, always confirming my prejudice about them, regardless. So I decided to do the opposite: see them afresh in a new light... in the present moment, not the past.

Letting go the prejudice was strangely liberating! And hopefully for the guests too, no longer caught in the web of my projections.

Conscious decisions and personal memory are much too small a place to live.
Rumi, Persia, 13th century

Chapter 40

Walking the Camino

Spain 2015

All this searching reminded me of a film I saw a while ago, *The Way*, where several people walked the ancient Spanish Camino together and shared their reasons for the journey along the route. A woman wanted to stop smoking, a man to take up writing again, a father in mourning to complete the walk his son had started.

It is only when they arrive at their destination, Santiago de Compostela, that they each discover the true reason they'd walked the Camino which turned out to be quite different from the reason they had set out with. This truth had only emerged in the process of taking the walk. It was as if each of them needed to take the long walk to realise why they'd taken it!

I thought about my own journey, and what I was really searching for; how I might have started the walk, my attention, like the others at the beginning of their journey, initially being drawn to the outside – always looking out there in the world, maybe triggering memories from the 1970s of my long hitchhike from New Zealand to England, or trailing through Africa and South America, driving that clapped-out VW camper van to Russia and back, seeing amazing places on the way, looking for God knows what, driven by a restlessness that was still with me.

As the journey progressed along the Camino my thoughts might have turned to wanting peace, harmony and fulfilment with Sarah. For someone or something to cure my feeling of restlessness. To be a better person. To feel good about myself, as if there were someone out there who could forgive me, heal me, make whole what was fragmented. Make me complete. I thought about the hope I'd had that doing 'good work' and saving people in need would stop me from feeling a bad person seeking penance and redemption through social work by trying to give something back, trying to atone. Become worthwhile.

'The best way to find yourself is to lose yourself in the service of others,' said Gandhi.

I didn't find myself through social work, perhaps I didn't try hard enough; but looking back, maybe my way of helping others is through writing the memoir.

'Keep open to the urge that motivates you,' someone once said. 'The need to express yourself never goes away.'

The Song Inside
So many live lives of desperation
And go to their graves
With their song inside them.
Henry David Thoreau

I thought of my mum and what she never expressed. Then further thoughts along the Camino would have inevitably turned inward to my daughter... all the 'what ifs' and regrets.

I also fantasised that following a spiritual path like past pilgrims on the Camino should have helped wash away the stains, cleanse me. How my husband's unconditional love for me might finally help change the core belief I held about myself. Change everything! That what I did and believed would make a difference; that creating beautiful things which took up a lot of my spare time would, in turn, make me feel beautiful.

'You've made this place really beautiful!' my husband and friends would exclaim after I'd done up a wreck of a place. But nothing rubbed off on me. What was it I was still searching for, for heaven's sake? What holds it all in place?

'What we don't realise,' said the wise husband when I asked why I was still feeling the same, long after reunion with my daughter, 'is that as much as we try choosing to find something different from the original story we are subtly drawn back to the core belief.'

'You mean there's no escape?' I ask disheartened. 'Even though we've been reunited?' It feels as if my story is all I am and that is all there is to me. Trapped in a role, defined by others – including me. Everything seems to flow from there... how I see myself and all the heartache that has emanated from what I did.

'No amount of effort or struggle leads us away from it,' he said. 'It's like quicksand, the more we struggle the deeper we go.'

Maybe he was right. I thought of how all the different workshops I'd attended over the years almost always got back to Sarah. She was always there. I wanted her there but I also wanted to let go. Focus on other things. I remember one workshop Martin ran whose theme was 'In Search of Self' and we paired up to do an exercise, 'Who am I?', in which one person repeats over and over, 'Who are you?', while the other person describes themselves each time so that you start to feel like layers of an onion, the outer layers visible and safe moving down to the nitty-gritty that makes you hesitate...

Who are you?
I am a woman.
Who are you?
I am a wife.
Who are you?
I am a mother...
Who are you?
I am a sister.
Who are you?
Um... I am a friend.
Who are you?
I am... err.

'We see that we are being drawn back to face something, to be reunited with something lost. We can stop the struggle and welcome what comes knocking,' Martin said.

'You mean we face the lessons we most need to learn by recreating them?'

'Well not exactly... what we're recreating is the myth of the core belief – until we realise it's just a story woven around the facts. And no one can fix the core belief other than to see it for what it is.'

Things have changed! There's been a shift inside me. Instead of always trying to find solutions to my restlessness and realising that ultimately I couldn't, that deep down nothing much was ever likely to change, even if I had walked the Camino. No profound insights or revelations, probably just sore feet, aching limbs and total exhaustion. Did I imagine a new ending for myself – completely different, kinder, compassionate, more accepting?

I don't remember consciously doing anything, trying to change the way I thought or acted, engineering a more desirable outcome for myself. I simply stopped searching!

Maybe the time was ripe, in that kind of natural way where you become aware that everything feels just right, like fruit falling suddenly from the tree, a perfect backdrop for something significant to take place. A magical moment, a moment of readiness, when I discovered that there isn't really any walk to take! The freedom is right here, but I needed to take the walk, so to speak, and everything that went with it to fully understand that.

'The fruit falls suddenly, but the ripening takes time,' said an Indian sage, Sri Nisargadatta Maharaj. Ah, I love that!

The ripening happened mainly through writing the memoir. The writing itself became my personal Camino. I felt compelled to continue with it, as I might have done if I were walking the

Camino, wanting to finish but not knowing the ending, just like when I started writing my story over 30 years ago.

The writing back then was infused with a sense of injustice and impotence – the story of a victim, of powerlessness, sadness and guilt. My whole identity was saturated with the story of what happened to me.

But gradually, near the end of my personal version of the Camino, I became aware of a need to let go, to feel a flow running through me, not to go on feeling separate from myself. I realised that having Sarah and all the trauma that followed had become central to my identity. It was how I thought others saw me and how I saw myself. And that's what I wanted to change: loosen my attachment to those memories and the guilt I carried. I wanted to remember what happened but in a way that meant I was no longer consumed with shame and guilt and sorrow. I thought that by freeing myself in this way, I might also free up my daughter. And at last I felt ready.

I wasn't aware that writing about the past and what happened would be my key to freedom! I had spent a long time avoiding it. I could never ponder on the past because of the agitation and restlessness I felt in the present. But I began to find that the more I wrote about my story, the more I realised it was just a story. What didn't change were the feelings of grief and yearning for her.

I'm now aware that when I write, I automatically loosen my attachment to my 'identity', and, instead, become like a witness or observer, and that's what has enabled me to step back, free myself: the amazing thing is that in the process of writing I came to realise that I couldn't be both the storyteller and the story itself. And that's exactly how it happened!

As the writing unfolded, unplanned and without knowing the ending, my personal story became clear: it was a 'guiding fiction', like a script in a play, a story that I, too, had been involved in writing when I was a child, based on messages

I'd internalised from those around me. My beacon. And one, I realised, I no longer needed to follow!

'Why would you let other people decide who you are?' asked Mark, a Kiwi psychiatrist friend. 'They are not the source of your well-being.'

Once I had seen it, it had lost its power. I had a choice. I could discard it, ditch it, dump it. My whole view of myself changed!

What is amazing is that in the process of writing the memoir and reflecting on the direction my life has taken, the 'choices' I made and the things that drew my attention, I could see a pattern emerging that wasn't visible at the time. And now it is clear. It is like standing back from a mosaic and seeing how all the different shaped pieces fit together to form a cohesive whole.

The answer didn't come in a rewriting of the story or searching for healing. It came in the process of identifying with the writer and loosening my attachment to the story! Focusing on the facts of what happened – not in the moral tale woven around it. Instead of fuelling it by focusing on the drama of it, the opposite happened. By observing the main character in my story, I needed to step away from all the drama – and that's what enabled me to realise that that character and all that drama was not who I truly am.

'You need to go through the emotions to the place of insight,' I remembered Harold saying.

It was only by completing the writing, like taking the walk along the Camino, could I know its real purpose... to liberate myself from the inevitable ending of my personal story – to stop questioning my need to go on believing I'm not good enough, and no longer depend on other people's opinions for approval because I now realise that particular belief has outlived its purpose.

'I am as I am,' someone said recently.

I wanted to shout, 'Me too! Take me or bloody leave me!'

And that's how I discovered freedom from my story, a freedom I didn't know I was looking for, until I had exhausted the search in the outside world through writing about it, just as I might have exhausted myself on the Camino, my sore feet finally forcing me to face what really matters.

Ironically I began to feel grateful for all the pain and suffering, all the sadness and sorrow because of what it had taught me and continues to remind me: the ability to stand back, away from the story, away from the fiction and simply observe. So now rather than go away and forget, I am experiencing gratitude for the past. No longer needing to repress memories but actively welcoming it all. That way I could see that hidden in the story are the clues to what I was really seeking.

'Realise what you already are,' Harold had said. 'You're welcome in your life. Love being who you are and the way you are. You're trying hard,' he added, 'putting in great effort when you don't need to!'

He had paused. 'And now celebrate who you are,' he said as I lay on his couch. 'Be pleased to be who you are and then very pleased and then very, very pleased!'

I giggled at the thought of being so pleased and found myself smiling and smiling.

'You're generous, warm, funny, others have a high regard for you, why on earth would you need to try hard? Your nature is enough... Just your being is a great blessing for people... giving good for life on earth; that's who you are. Accept the blessing that you should be this type of person... Look at the story. Little girl wanted to get it right. Always trying hard. You are loving and caring. Be pleased with who you are, all you need to be is who you are! Then you have fulfilled your purpose... life just needs to be lived.'

'Wow, Harold.... um... thank you!'

'I'm only saying back to you what palpates... This clicked with you... You just stopped... your sacrum is easing out...

There is a full range of breath.'

In that moment I could feel a wonderful warmth, an easing, a releasing, deep joy. And enormous gratitude. It was sheer bliss.

Chapter 41

The Voice

Guadalajara, Spain 2015

A very average hotel

How often have you noticed your voice goes unheard? Even when you've said something ingenious. Like in meetings, and your brilliant suggestion is taken up by someone else who expands on it ever so slightly, then gets all the credit for it! Or worse, when your own husband ignores you in a seriously important moment at the hotel reception desk.

Do you unconsciously carry the belief you won't be listened to, and expect that it will influence every situation in which you want to be heard? My husband was engaged in earnest conversation in loud, halting English with a Spanish receptionist (male) and I needed to interrupt to give some vital information about the parking. Both of them completely ignored me, not so much as a tiny glance in my direction, and a huge row with hubby followed, starting uncomfortably close to the receptionist. This scenario is unusual as Martin is quite hard to argue with, unless you really persevere.

Later, in a quieter moment, he tentatively suggested the reason I might've been so upset was that it tapped into an early expectation that my voice didn't count. I didn't expect to be heard and therefore I wasn't. Mmmn, on reflection it felt right. So after the row, a Rioja and a rant, I was ready to listen.

'Maybe this is similar to what we've been talking about,' he said referring to the incident. 'Maybe what happened wasn't just a random event... but part of a bigger picture, something for you to notice and welcome.'

'Welcome?' I squeaked.

'Yes... because it's just a story; maybe your parents didn't listen to you but what you made of that was "I'm not worth listening to..." so it's a really good example of how the story becomes a beacon,' said Martin. 'But maybe there was some other innocent explanation like the fact that you're a twin. I remember you telling me as kids you only got half an orange each not a whole one, half the pocket money your sister got at the same age... and you were in incubators for the first few months of your life. Who listens to a baby in an incubator?'

'Mmmn... that feels a bit far-fetched! Can you be heard in an incubator?'

But there is a flicker of truth around not being heard, being ignored.

What is curious is the way all these little fragments are piecing together as I write – making sense of stuff, the beginnings of a jigsaw puzzle with gaps. It feels like I'm chancing upon these fragments, or maybe they are chancing upon me and they aren't random events. Who knows?

'We have an endless capacity for creativity,' says our Martin. 'We can liberate ourselves by revisiting the story.'

'So basically, we weave our own story from a situation and see it as factual?'

'Yes... that's why it's great you can see the situation for what it is... not just an uncomfortable replay of "old stuff" but a way of releasing you from a story you've carried.'

'Yeah... OK, so that's how it's welcome... if you can manage to step away from the vehicle.'

I realise now that it was writing that gave me a voice. An opportunity to be listened to, even as a child. It felt as though writing 'chose' me as a way of expressing my thoughts and feelings and to tell my story, rather than the other way round.

I sometimes wonder how much my thoughts and expectations were influenced by my mother's experience. She had no real voice in the family either, no authority to speak of, no power to make decisions or monitor them. Like having to agree with Dad about the adoption. It felt like she had to just shut down. Maybe that was part of our special bond; I felt her lack of voice, her powerlessness, her quiet desperation, not only in the family but in the world outside, even though New Zealand was the first country in the world to give women the vote way back in 1893. I guess some things take a long time to change.

When I think of the early days in London in the 1970s I sometimes wonder what my mum would have thought about the emerging feminist movement, the groups of women I joined, gathering together to have our voices heard, our rights aired and affirmed. And ridiculed, usually in the right wing press. Maybe the movement would have articulated for her the thoughts and feelings she'd been unable to express, like her sense of self, being her own person. Like how she really felt about the adoption of her first grandchild. I suppose I always saw her as vulnerable, in need of protection. I wouldn't hesitate to defend her against my father, protect her from his outbursts of anger. After all, she never upset any of us or threatened or hit us; she was the only focal point in the family of any love and tenderness one might hope for. The only reference made to my banishment – and the baby's – by the family shortly after I returned home was an apology by my mum.

'I had no say in the matter,' she'd whispered. 'I couldn't go against your father.'

'Maybe you had the same unconscious expectation you've always had that you weren't going to be heard either. It had a basis in reality, women did not have much of a voice back then, you weren't listened to as a child or around the adoption. The problem is that we take this to be true for the rest of our lives, assume a role and get caught up in the power of the story, how you expect things will be – and then the expectation becomes enmeshed in the beacon we decide to live by... it's like you're following a script,' said our Martin.

'Giving women like me a voice was the aim of my book on birth mothers' experiences [cf. footnote: *Within Me, Without Me*], a voice that somehow had been ignored or overlooked even by the feminist movement – those of once-young birth mothers like me, most of whom were pressured into relinquishing their babies for adoption,' I told Martin when we were discussing the power of women back then.

'When we experience a trauma, we tend to tell ourselves a story about it... one that feels true at the time,' observed Martin, 'but often we rewrite the story.'

Can a woman who has experienced the trauma of a forced adoption ever feel free to live her own life, without the need to rewrite her story, I wondered.

'And what's mine? I got pregnant when I wasn't married, therefore I'm a bad person? Or maybe it's got stronger over the years, more militant, like some birth mothers who feel the state stole their baby! It does have a basis in truth. No one I've spoken to seemed to know they had a legal right to their babies for the first six weeks. Including me.'

'OK, yes, maybe it's how you felt later,' says Martin. 'It's like a lot of people who were abused... it's the same thing, they think they deserved it, that they were bad. And having no voice, not being able to speak out at the time, is a feature of trauma.'

Why should someone who'd been physically or sexually abused feel like that? But I felt like that! So why didn't I feel the same sense of outrage and incredulity about myself as I did about them? How come I've interpreted my experience, my story, as so different from theirs, so that other people's attitudes towards me seemed justified.

'The point is, you are still the same true nature, whatever happens or has happened to you,' said Martin. 'And so are those people who were abused or feel bad about themselves, whatever they see themselves as being responsible for. I mean, look at you. You're still the same lovely person you always were, in spite of what happened.'

I was reminded of an amazing woman who recounted her childhood of neglect and abuse in a workshop to the point where most of us were visibly upset for her.

'Gosh… you must've been so damaged by all that,' said one woman.

'No,' she said emphatically. 'In spite of all that, I now realise although I was deeply affected by my experiences, I wasn't fundamentally damaged by them. My essential nature remains untouched.'

I, too, am still the same person I always was! It was as if my script, one I had decided for myself based I guess largely on identification with my mum, defined my thoughts and beliefs about everything – and maybe deep down I had a fundamentally gloomy outlook in spite of my happy-go-lucky nature: I was a classic birth mother according to my own research! Trust and vulnerability have a lot to do with fear and consequently the need to control. For years I generally found it hard to trust anyone, especially men, to show any sort of vulnerability by being too open, instead to keep a safe, emotional distance, show I didn't need, or feel I needed, other people; to form close relationships in spite of lots of friends, and although I didn't get depressed, I always had a sense of something missing, a feeling of emptiness, of never belonging, a silent yearning.

One amazing thing I've discovered through writing the memoir is a weird kind of shift that is quite hard to explain. A sort of parallel process going on between me the writer and me the birth mother. A shift in perspective where somehow, as a result of having to step back from my story when I'm writing about it, I've begun to see things differently. But there's more to it than that.

'The biggest challenge,' I confided to a girlfriend, 'is not just a simple process of letting go, a pattern of trying to be heard. It's about the challenge of facing an early decision, one that most kids make often based on "never" – in my case I decided to "never surrender", never to end up as unhappy, as powerless as my lovely mum.'

So, these days, I'm finally letting go of the individual voice of the rebel – a fiercely independent position, my position. In the session with Harold the experience felt like surrender even though the original decision was to never let go! Never surrender! (I'm sounding like Churchill!) The surrender is not only letting go a position, a visceral form of self-protection but also of the story itself. In letting go I'm beginning to have no expectations either way. I now understand how the story-less voice doesn't care whether or not it is heard. There's no longer a position to take up, nothing to protect, no hurt feelings taking charge, no primal wound to defend. I often fall back into the old patterns, the self-programming, the 'story' of me but now there is a big difference. I do it with more awareness. When this happens I can sometimes see that this revisiting acts as a further prompt to let go, and as a signpost to the freedom that lies beyond the confines of the story.

Chapter 42

An Ancient Chinese Oracle

Bristol, UK 2010

I love doing the *I Ching* occasionally even if it is usually about an ongoing worry, something I can't seem to resolve. A friend introduced me to it years ago and each time I use it I find it is always uncannily accurate like an infallible, wise parent.

'Just ask a question at the same time as throwing three coins six times and the combination of the numbers gives you a particular response,' she said. 'So first you need to formulate a question, one that doesn't invite a simple yes or no answer because the question is about you in relation to the oracle. OK?'

I decided to ask about the memoir:

'Comment on the function of the past – my memories – in relation to what I'm writing,' I asked.

After throwing the coins and scoring each throw as I went along, the resulting lines formed the Number 47, 'Exhaustion, Oppression'.

The response, states the *I Ching*, is that 'memories can be oppressive, a powerful, negative story that oppresses us throughout life.'

'Wow, how amazing is that!' I exclaimed to my friend. 'It's exactly what I am writing about – the power that memory has to make you believe that you are your story... and the need to understand the effects that such a story can unleash!'

Especially the self-doubt, I thought!

How come we allow these things to seep into our consciousness so that our own essential, loving being is brought into doubt by our selective memory and the story we devise about ourselves? 'Your beacon,' as Martin describes it.

'The oppressiveness and power of that doubt,' continues the

amazing synchronistic reading, 'exhausts our inner resources and may lead to physical illness.'

Why do we doubt our own true nature? And deplete so many of our personal resources attempting to change. I thought back to how exhausting it had been with so much emotion, energy and effort taken up in trying to improve myself... All the time, I now realise, it was about doubting my true nature.

'Such doubts,' states the I Ching reading are, '"creeping vines" that choke out the truth.'

It reminded me of being on Harold's couch. The melting moments in that session were like a stopping, a spontaneous end to all the doubt which meant a complete acceptance of everything that had happened to me... What he described as the 'still point'. Ironically I had spent decades trying to correct myself, improve myself and what made things better was to realise there was nothing wrong in the first place!

It is ironic, I thought, that we need to engage in the search... learning a huge amount along the way only to realise there was never any need to search!

At the reception desk of the hotel in Guadalajara I had felt in the grip of my story, a familiar powerlessness about not being heard and fighting a very old fight. As soon as I stepped back and saw this for what it was it dissolved. Like seeing a mirage is just a trick of the mind:

'Once we perceive it,' said Martin, 'it loses its power and we are able to come to a state of acceptance.'

'That means accepting life just as it is, as well as what has happened? Not so easy... to ditch all the crap, I mean,' I said.

'It's not only about accepting what happened, you also need to accept all the feelings you had at the time: the powerlessness, sadness, shame, guilt... all those feelings you may have carried with you for years but weren't able to express.'

Chapter 43

Coincidence or Synchronicity?

Bristol 2011

Was it a coincidence or synchronistic meeting Dr Jean-Marc Mantel at this point in my life – a delightfully quirky, unconventional, French psychiatrist with a twist? A one-off I'd say, where patients make their own appointments when they feel the need to see him and are very seldom prescribed drugs.

He had stood up in front of a gaggle of psychiatrists at a conference in London at the Royal College of Psychiatrists, and after a lengthy silence announced:

In order to be a psychiatrist, you must completely forget you are a psychiatrist.

Martin was immediately drawn to him and afterwards invited him to speak at a one-day retreat on mental health that he was helping organise in Bristol.

One-day retreat Bristol 2011

The retreat was held at Burwalls, a huge, old Jacobean-style brick mansion – the sort that merchants built on the backs of the tobacco and slave trade of the 19th century – perched on the edge of the Avon Gorge next to Bristol's most famous landmark – Brunel's Clifton Suspension Bridge. The place was humming with curious colleagues keen to hear this legendary man whose reputation had quickly preceded him – a professional colleague who seemed to embody the very philosophy they were trying to promote – bringing together spiritual well-being and mental health.

His opening remarks made quite an impact on me.

'Do we need zis?' he asked Martin who was sitting at the table with him on the dais. He had picked up some pens lying in front of him.

'No,' Martin smiled and removed them.

'And zis?'

'Err, not really,' said Martin and slid the paper down to his bag on the floor.

'And zat?'

Slight squirming and mild amusement in the audience.

'What do we need in life?' he asked us. 'Do we need all zese things we surround ourselves with?'

That's what I liked most about Jean-Marc, his simplicity in everything – his lifestyle, his wants and needs, and most of all his spiritual understanding of the world.

I can still remember my conversations with him during the times he stayed with us which I zealously recorded at the kitchen table once I had got used to his strong French accent alongside his immaculate English.

'You are not a story... We take the story to be the truth of who we are but it is merely a costume,' said Jean-Marc, reminding me of the dream I had about the different sides of my family wearing the costumes they thought identified them as to who they were.

'Yes, of course, to the mind and body the story feels real but the mind and body are part of the story... part of the conditioning,' he said.

'Simply observe your mind and body... this creates some space between the observer and the observed... It can be like sitting in the audience watching our own play, our own drama with all its characters... with ourselves as a character, in a role, living out a story... We do not take the play as reality. It prompts an enquiry into our true nature: if I'm not a story then what? In the story there is often an ongoing drama... a belief about yourself, like not being good enough... a search for healing,' said Jean-Marc.

'I guess I have felt restless all my life and spent years looking for solutions,' I said.

'All searching is agitation, restlessness. Without a story there is freedom, stillness and peace.'

'Then why do we continue to stay caught up in the story?' I asked.

'We are often fascinated by them... addicted to the drama... we often fear the unknown, it's safer to stay with what's known... When free from the story we don't know what happens next... don't know what we or the other person may say or do. And being caught in the story is exhausting,' he said. 'Depression is a good example, a form of exhaustion. But we might welcome the exhaustion of the story! And once we perceive it clearly, it loses its power and we are able to come to a state of acceptance,' he added.

'Why do we keep making the same mistakes over and over?'

'With each repeat of the trauma comes a potential confirmation of the story but also an opportunity to stop identifying with it.'

'Sounds like the story is not even real?' I sort of laughed because part of me knows that stories by their very nature are fiction!

'Yes! The same as the notion of the separate individual – this is an illusion too... We are always part of the whole... We could not be a character in a drama without the other characters... without the stage... without the scenery... or the space,' he said.

I began to feel slightly uncomfortable, squirmy, without knowing why. Was he going to ask me something awkward or too personal?

'Think of a family,' he said, which was exactly what I was doing. 'How could one branch of a plant be separate, independent of the rest?'

I surprised myself by plunging back to Brixton and the Reynolds family I had worked with from way back, as if they

were my only template of fragmentation, separateness –
remembering how the father was determined to dispose of his
son by dumping him in care – before being thrust into similar
memories of my own family.

'Mmmn, well, I was the black sheep in my family. And that
felt real enough.'

'You were or you were perceived as? Was this not just a role?
Not just a part in the family drama? We could say that you
carried something for the whole system, the whole family, that it
was not willing to face. The black sheep,' he continued, 'balances
something that has got out of balance and becomes a projection
exercise for the other characters. These projections, like blaming
you for everything, feel so real that we take them to be true and
then they become part of our identity... who we are.'

It was the same with us young birth mothers. We were
identified as the source of immoral impropriety bringing society
to its knees by threatening the sacred institution of marriage.

Jean-Marc is an amazing man! I'd never met anyone like him.
I love what he says... it feels a real privilege to know him. The
issue of 'balance' in the family hadn't really leapt out at me in
those days. I hadn't appreciated the benign benevolence, no
doubt accompanied by darker, dubious motives, that perhaps
both Mr Reynolds and my father were trying to achieve by
getting rid of us – the black sheep – because the family had got
out of balance and our absence would somehow restore it.

'Oh my God!' I gasp. 'You've just unravelled my life, laid it
out before me and made sense of it in a way that feels right! All
in five minutes! Amazing! So what do I do now?'

'Nothing! All the searching, all the attempts at healing, all
the steps we take are steps away from what we are... stillness
cannot find itself through activity and agitation... Simply
observe this movement, this restlessness and it will dissolve in
your awareness... like sugar in liquid,' he said gravely.

'This pure awareness **is** acceptance... so we can also notice any resistance to what life brings... life as it should be, should have been,' he added.

'So why would we resist what continually points to our true nature?' I asked.

'Well, maybe we are unaware of what our true nature is,' he replied.

We sat in silence for a minute. I wanted to leap up, hug him, offer him tea but I didn't want to interrupt the moment.

'Unless we were freedom how could we know imprisonment?' he went on, leaving me nodding sort of puzzled.

'Unless we were stillness how could we know agitation... Unless we were one how could we know separation and grief?'

So much to digest, it was exciting! As if I was on the edge of discovering something amazing! At last a way of seeing the world – and us in it – that was making sense! Felt right.

'So... what do you mean by pure freedom?' I asked eager to grasp whatever he said. 'Is that like giving up trying to sort it all out?'

'Yes... we need to give up the searching.'

'Mmmn... so how come I feel better when I think I'm in control of things?'

'Control is another illusion,' he said, 'like the child in the back seat who thinks his little plastic steering wheel is steering the car.'

I laughed imagining us adults realising we were often doing the same; the illusion we create by thinking we're in charge and can therefore design our lives... either that or having faith that things will work out, chucking away the handbrake and throwing yourself at the mercy of the universe.

'So, part of the process of letting go of everything is that ability to step back and see the whole experience as a story,' I said. 'And stories by their very nature are not based on fact.

They're a creation around which others – and us – have woven a story. But letting go goes against everything we were taught. How can we attain our goals through not striving?' I ask. 'Give up doubt and inner resistance?'

'You would not have actively chosen the times of pain and suffering in your life but consider how these have had the potential for awakening you to life, love and wisdom... So life is a great teacher, reminding us of the source of our being, by sometimes cutting through illusion...'

I was reminded of how people who are diagnosed with life-threatening illnesses often say, 'I know it sounds strange but it's the best thing that could've happened to me,' as if their illness had forced them to stop leading a life they realised was ultimately an illusion and begin to face what is real; as if the illness itself would enable them to find richness and meaning in their lives. 'Finding who you are beyond your personal history,' says another spiritual teacher Eckhart Tolle.

Welcoming our greatest challenges also reminded me of the *I Ching* reading:

In order to receive help we must return to acceptance and dependence upon the unknown.

'Are you saying that our greatest challenges are also our most profound gifts?' I asked.

'Yes. Consider how you might welcome these challenges as a unique key to your freedom; to what you are really seeking,' he said.

I am blown away! Hearing Jean-Marc's statement that our greatest challenges are also our greatest gift, our greatest teacher, our unique key to freedom from all the angst, all the crap we immerse ourselves in. Such a simple formula yet profound! Possibly a little bit puzzling. But the prospect of letting go, accepting everything, welcoming everything... and experiencing peace, stillness and freedom was there, available! It was another 'still point' for me – similar to my experience with Harold the osteopath, a wonderful melting moment where everything dissolved and I was left feeling free as a bird, in love with the world. This experience, too, was a spiritual 'still point' captured in my mind and held there as a deep truth.

Maybe this is what I have been trying to do all along. Endlessly searching for a template that feels right. And now, having searched for most of my life for clues and answers, it seems there is nowhere to look! There never was. Instead of spending a lifetime searching for answers, trying to release myself from my greatest sorrow, losing my daughter… a sorrow that has now, ironically, become my greatest gift. How very strange this is but it feels sort of right. So do I now say, 'the gift of losing my daughter'? Would she ever understand that? And would she ever be able to see me in the same way? A gift?

I am fascinated with the idea of looking back on our lives and seeing the bigger picture, now being able to see the wood for the trees. A mosaic best viewed from a distance, looking down from above. It is strange to see the way pieces now all fitted together – some big, small, oddly shaped. And seeing patterns, not just in my life but in those of my parents and grandparents: banishment, fitting in, losses. There are always missing pieces, an endless jigsaw of clues that keep popping up. What had seemed like random events and 'choices' on reflection now form part of a greater whole – Harold the osteopath-cum-healer, Jean-Marc, the *I Ching* – Martin! All part of that mosaic that cannot be seen when you are too close.

'So do we need to make changes in our lives?' I ask Jean-Marc.

'No… this would be to create another story… Simply observe your personal patterns and your ego, let go of the identification with these and allow stillness, silence and freedom to be your guide,' he said. 'Let your words and actions arise from stillness.

The expressions of love are then free from conditions and expectations, and others are then invited to be free as well,' he added.

'Circumstances that occur in our life don't come by chance,' he said. 'They are the consequence of a need, conscious or unconscious, to live out some specific experiences. Each experience has its utility, and brings a giving up of some attachments.'

I need to lie down.

Chapter 44

Sarah's Birthday – Aged 50

Auckland, New Zealand calling Bristol, UK

My daughter is 50 today. It still feels unreal, not only having a daughter aged 50, but being in contact! We have now met on four occasions since we were reunited when she was 22, and exchanged lengthy phone calls and letters and loads of emails that ebb and flow. I have photos of her dotted around the house including one of the very few she possessed of herself as a child, wearing a little tartan dress, now encased in a small silver frame on my dressing table which I look at every day. It's not that I need reminding. Even in the absence of any photos of her, I still thought about her almost every day.

She still lives in New Zealand, and has moved around a bit. So I'm not always sure where she's living, even though she usually stays in touch. Unless there's been a fallout and she's gone underground. But not being sure where she is arouses the same feelings I carried with me when she was growing up although back then I didn't know where she lived, or her name. Actually, I didn't know anything. So I suppose I've anchored those feelings in the present because they've stayed with me. It's as if in some ways she is still missing and I'm still searching, still restless; that we are still missing: mother and daughter together as we should have been, would have been in a different context – a few years later perhaps – so in a weird way it feels as if I haven't really found her. And it still feels as if I don't have any real entitlement to a relationship with her; as if I'm still searching to find something I already have.

The same feelings still amount to a quiet panic when I'm not sure where she is living, a hollowness, like time suddenly stopping. And at other times I am not sure I feel justified in knowing her, deserve to know her, have a legitimate right, entitled, even today. So part of me needs to know where she is and another part feels I shouldn't know, although this is gradually dissolving.

These feelings were kick-started again when I emailed her a couple of weeks before her birthday but had no response.

'What would you like for your birthday?' I'd written. 'I want it to be a special present for a special birthday. Something you'd really like, instead of something I think you'd like,' I added, remembering the unsuccessful attempts in the past buying her things that I thought she'd like because they were things I might like, although our tastes are quite similar.

'How about we don't buy things for each other without first checking it out?' she'd said.

Not that I minded what she bought me, it was more about receiving a gift from her although it always helps if you like it. But at least we were now able to agree amicably not to buy things for each other. That was a step forward.

I didn't get a reply from her. My usual response would have been to worry, fret about why she hadn't responded. Was something wrong? Had I done something to upset her? Our contact had become rather sporadic these days, which is fine, with both of us, I think. She used to send me long emails, several pages at a time about people and places I didn't know, so I'd put them on hold to at least try and match the content, and as a result not always get back straightaway. I hoped it didn't feed into her sense of rejection, she's had more than enough. But she seems cool with all that now.

'I think I'll just send her champagne and flowers and hope I've still got the right address,' I called to my husband. 'I know she was living right near the beach, she told me how much she loved gathering mussels from the rocks. I just hope I've got the right beach.'

And this leads to the good bit. The excellent, very best bit! I didn't think it would turn out to be this way, especially since I couldn't contact her. But I decided to just take the plunge, stay cool, bearing in mind that few, read none, of my previous gifts have been much of a success, and just hoped she'd like the champagne and flowers. There was nothing more I could do, not even ensure they would arrive on time, or at all. First, the champagne arrived.

'Hi Ma. Wow, what an awesome mum!' she said down the phone. 'I could see this man at my door and I thought he was a Frenchman selling onions or something. Then I opened it and he was holding a wooden box... I thought it was a dead hamster at first. Mother! What a totally brilliant pressie! I LOVE champagne! How did you know?!'

Then the flowers arrived.

'Mother, have you won the lotto?? OMG, I just got your flowers... they are sooo beautiful. I was chatting my socks off to a girlfriend when this tiny grey-haired man in a hat appeared, rather resembling the French man and he was knocking at the window... I had visions of baskets full of cheese 'n bread I didn't want to buy, so I reluctantly opened the door only to find he was sporting a huge bunch of colourful flowers... wow, thank you mum, with all my heart, and stop making me cry (I say winking, laughing and crying all at the same time)... they are the most beautiful flowers I have ever been given in my life. I really love them. I love them so much I wish I could wear them round whilst dancing and sipping on champagne... oh this is so spooky, it feels like you are here with me. I'm sending you a big hug n my brightest smile...'

Now it's my turn to cry.

'Thank you sooooo much for the lovely funny apt meaningful (and very emotional) card and the mysterious stranger who knocked on my door with a small wooden box... of champas O YEAH & YAY.. I'm stoked! bubbles on me burpday (hic) LOL.

Lots and lots of special love;
Sarah xxxxxxxxx'

Chapter 45

Unhooked

Bristol – Auckland 2014

'You'll never guess what's happened!' I shrieked to Martin after racing to tell him about the amazing phone call. 'It's… like a miracle! She was so delighted and loving… I don't know what I've done to deserve it! I'm bowled over!'

'Well, it's got a lot to do with you – everything to do with you,' said Martin hugging me.

'How do you mean?'

'Remember her last birthday and what happened?'

'Well… yes. Last year I spent a lot of time choosing things I hoped she'd like. But she didn't. Actually, she barely acknowledged the gifts. That's what I don't understand! How come her response is so completely different this year?'

'Because this time you're giving a gift that's not saturated with guilt,' said Martin.

'What do you mean?'

'She's aware of that at some level…' he said. 'That's always "known" by the receiver.'

'What's always known?'

'The giving becomes conditional and can be more for us than for them. "I'm guilty, please forgive me" written in invisible ink all over the gift.'

'OK, well… maybe, but I'm still not clear why her response is so different.'

'When the gift is given without conditions attached, the person receiving it may unconsciously be aware of this so their response is likely to be different. Like her comment, "These are the most beautiful flowers I've ever been given!"'

'So if that's the case,' I said, 'what part does she play in it?'

'I guess it's a bit like a dance where both of you are involved. Some people are easy to give to because they are free from envy and resentment whereas others aren't. When they receive a gift their secret message is something like "you owe me... and whatever you give will never be enough",' he said. 'So now her response is completely different.'

'Really? So how come?'

'Well... look at all the changes you've made over the years: you are released and have released yourself from your guilt through all the personal family stuff you've explored; decades in personal growth and meditation workshops; and facing the changes the way you did with the New Zealand Adoption Act... and the deep acceptance that came with Harold's words and your body's readiness to finally let go of the searching. God, Susie – all the courage over the years to try and face what happened – your perseverance... and it's all meant that now you can forgive yourself... can give freely to Sarah... and this in turn has helped release her, enabled her to receive more freely.'

'Wow... amazing. I didn't realise all that was going on!'

'We can only invite the other person through our release. But before that, they are confined by the unconscious message in the gift: two interlocking stories, where you are playing out "I'll always feel guilty", and she is playing the victim and believing you have ruined her life,' said Martin. 'And now, the letting go has paid off. The gifts, your communication... it feels like they're no longer infused with the story of what happened. You can even welcome what she brings – whatever that is – as a potential release from the story, including ditching the illusion of guilt!'

'What do you mean?'

'Well, if she manages to stir guilt in you, like she did when she sent you that vitriolic email, you can pretty much know there is still some guilt to let go of... This way everything is welcomed,' he said. 'Do you remember Harold saying "look at the story of her adoption and make sure you see every step was right, that was right... that was right..." You did nothing wrong! You had no choice, like so many other young women at the time.'

'It makes more sense to me now,' I said. 'But I don't know if I can take all of that on board. It still doesn't feel quite right to me.'

'Of course not right in the sense of how we would've wanted things to be. Nor right in the sense that people suffer. Sarah and you suffered a great deal. But right in the sense that suffering brings the opportunity to know our true nature beyond the story. Some say this is our purpose in our life.'

I was reminded of a quote I've often pondered on by Holocaust survivor and psychotherapist Viktor Frankl that has lurked in the shadows for years as if waiting for this moment:

Striving to find a meaning in one's life
is the primary motivational force in man.
Man's Search For Meaning, 1992, p. 104

But here was the whole story, exactly replicated, played out: guilt, rejection, ejection but at the same time the story was never true. It was just a story where different people had filled in their own version of events, their own details. I wasn't guilty, I didn't reject her in the way she perceives it, I simply wasn't able to keep her. So what gets recreated is not a fundamental rejection of her as a being, but the impossibility of the situation. What has become clear in a really helpful way is, at last, an understanding that helps articulate what I couldn't: that I didn't reject her and she hasn't rejected me. The fact, which is true, is that I was pressured into relinquishing my daughter for adoption. Along with the facts come personal stories, like Sarah's: 'I'm a reject. My mother didn't want me.' And similarly, my story, 'I'm a bad person, did a bad thing, gave up my child.'

It made me think of the mosaic that was unravelling in the course of writing the memoir – looking back on my life and seeing how all the fragments fitted together: all the fears, frustrations, joys and sorrows, making sense of everything at last.

'... so hopefully Sarah will feel that whatever she does is welcomed; then she herself may feel welcomed, just like you're feeling – which would be very different to her usual experience of feeling rejected – and would be the exact opposite of what she expected would happen!' said Martin.

'Yes,' I said, 'and it's the same with me! Maybe now I can stop looking for her approval and searching for forgiveness.'

'... While we are searching we are caught in the notion that something is missing and that we are not OK as we are,' said Martin. 'The very act of searching, which is a form of restlessness, confirms that we need to find something we don't have... just as the very act of stopping can affirm we have it already and always did... only that the story suggested otherwise. So when you stop searching for Sarah's approval, the story of guilt and blame dissolves and a loving connection is revealed.'

Chapter 46

The Gift of the Story

Ringwood, Hampshire, UK 2015

Not long afterwards, Harold my hero, the craniosacral osteopath, floored me by saying something similar to Martin about gifts.

'I want to give you the gift of someone's story in the same way she gave it to me...' he said and proceeded to tell me about a young woman who saw her life as blighted because of an enormous red birthmark covering much of her face.

'For years she attempted to hide her face with various hairstyles and make-up. She expected people would always stare at her, whisper about her behind her back. But in spite of all that, she could still feel OK about herself even though she doesn't want to have to wake up to that face...' said Harold.

I thought about the young woman, how difficult it must be to bear a disfigurement like that, a permanent reminder, an imperfection she couldn't hide. Unlike mine.

'She's given me a story for you,' he said. 'We're given these opportunities to go through the fear and guilt and she's got a face that's not as good as it could be... Things could have been different, but that's the way it is,' said Harold.

'There's a deep truth in what you've discovered,' he said, 'dumping guilt and shame – and finding your voice... It's a voice of wisdom that you are bringing to this story – and the gift of that is rather like the young woman with the birthmark: we can transcend the suffering. What a gift you are giving to the reader to realise they don't have to suffer the way they are,' said Harold.

'I wonder if that young woman had felt the same as you,' said Martin, 'branded, shunned, helpless, shamed and had not expected to be heard – but had learnt to go beyond the story to a deeper place... That is the gift of inspiration...'

I was left wondering why Harold's comment, 'I'm giving this gift to you,' made me feel tearful. I'd never thought of my story like that – a gift. It was impressively matter-of-fact. Unenviable. But how can you see your own suffering as a gift?

'Many lamps, One light'

One of the things I used to worry about was that Sarah might always feel she had been abandoned and that she would see everything through this lens, always feeling rejected, not part of anything. Separate, different. But in that one precious moment on my last visit to Harold, I felt reassured; truly united with her, with everything. It felt like this was *my* 'awesome' present, at last a true celebration of her birthday – and maybe even my own – and it made me feel like jumping with joy.

'Do you think that's what Harold meant when he said there really is no such thing as abandonment?' I asked Martin shortly after racing to tell him all about the phone call from her.

'Sort of, but I think he meant it more on a spiritual level – that we are all part of everything, all part of nature; we depend on nature to survive – air, water, trees. We all belong to the same planet, so there's no such thing as abandonment. We're all interdependent, interconnected. But because you felt abandoned – and the same with Sarah – it became your beacon, the way you saw yourself in relation to the world.'

'But surely most people wouldn't perceive things in that way... I mean most people would only see things in terms of their own personal experience, whatever story had been woven around the facts of their lives, not the bigger picture where we're all one, all part of the same world,' I said.

'That's right – or as the Taoists would say "many lamps, one light". When you do look at things in that way, you can see there's nothing to fix or heal – there never was, it's a false perception,' said Martin.

'Mmmn... that still doesn't feel quite right,' I said remembering how abandoned I had felt by my family and no doubt Sarah feels by me.

'Remember what Harold said, that of course you *felt* abandoned but there's no such thing. It's a story woven around a situation – a creation of the mind.'

'But how can both be true – I felt abandoned by my family – that was my experience.'

'It's a paradox,' said Martin. 'Not one or the other. How could you feel abandoned unless you knew "belonging"?'

'So you're saying that the problem of, say, abandonment is not what happened but the story we tell about what happened?'

'Yes, it's a similar paradox to searching – we need to search as you have done for years to realise that what you were searching for was never lost. Basically we are not separate from each other. How could we know separation unless we were one?'

This one sentence seemed to sum it all up. When I fully accepted my personal story for what it was: a set of facts around which I and others had woven a moral tale... I could see the story was a fiction and that this fiction drove the search. I could glimpse behind this fiction to what is real. I was letting go the personal story and returning to the universal, to what can never be lost... where we belong and have always belonged. I had felt abandoned and for most of my young life, as Martin pointed out, this had been the beacon that I had followed.

So much has changed in the last few years – or maybe it would be more accurate to say my understanding, my perception is what has changed, influenced by certain key experiences that felt real, that were real, unlike any other. A wonderful feeling of union with everything and, out of that, a deep truth, a knowing that can only really be experienced.

I can now look back on some of those other experiences that have dogged me, stayed with me but I have come to see are not grounded in truth but in fiction: the family scapegoat who was regarded as being responsible for all the family's ills and subsequently banished but transpires to be the same one who possibly had the potential for getting help for the family, for bringing the family together, even a cause for celebration!

When I first started writing I had been influenced by the beacon of the personal story. But that focus has enabled me to find out who I am beyond my personal history because I have had to step back to observe my life, disentangle myself from the story of me, the unreal me: a clear seeing that I've only been seeking the truth about myself.

These days the way I see the world **is** different... I can differentiate between what is real and not real. I no longer feel separate. The writing itself seems to just flow through me rather than from me and emanates from somewhere beyond the personal, from a deeper wisdom – from a freedom born of stillness – a fundamental stillness that can never be lost.

Books by the same author

Within Me, Without Me
Adoption: an open and shut case?
Scarlet Press, 1994
ISBN 1-85727-042-8

Life After Debt: Women's Survival Stories
Scarlet Press (commission), 1997
ISBN 1-85727-043-6

Stop Smoking the Easy Way: 5 simple steps to freedom
New Holland Publishers, 2007
ISBN 978-1-84537-535-5

For further information contact the author at:
sue_wells20@btinternet.com

BOOKS

O-BOOKS

SPIRITUALITY

O is a symbol of the world, of oneness and unity; this eye represents knowledge and insight. We publish titles on general spirituality and living a spiritual life. We aim to inform and help you on your own journey in this life.
If you have enjoyed this book, why not tell other readers by posting a review on your preferred book site?

Recent bestsellers from O-Books are:

Heart of Tantric Sex
Diana Richardson
Revealing Eastern secrets of deep love and intimacy to Western couples.
Paperback: 978-1-90381-637-0 ebook: 978-1-84694-637-0

Crystal Prescriptions
The A-Z guide to over 1,200 symptoms and their healing crystals
Judy Hall
The first in the popular series of six books, this handy little guide is packed as tight as a pill-bottle with crystal remedies for ailments.
Paperback: 978-1-90504-740-6 ebook: 978-1-84694-629-5

Take Me To Truth
Undoing the Ego
Nouk Sanchez, Tomas Vieira
The best-selling step-by-step book on shedding the Ego, using the teachings of *A Course In Miracles*.
Paperback: 978-1-84694-050-7 ebook: 978-1-84694-654-7

The 7 Myths about Love...Actually!
The journey from your HEAD to the HEART of your SOUL
Mike George
Smashes all the myths about LOVE.
Paperback: 978-1-84694-288-4 ebook: 978-1-84694-682-0

The Holy Spirit's Interpretation of the New Testament
A Course in Understanding and Acceptance
Regina Dawn Akers
Following on from the strength of *A Course In Miracles*, NTI
teaches us how to experience the love and oneness of God.
Paperback: 978-1-84694-085-9 ebook: 978-1-78099-083-5

The Message of A Course In Miracles
A translation of the text in plain language
Elizabeth A. Cronkhite
A translation of *A Course in Miracles* into plain, everyday
language for anyone seeking inner peace. The companion
volume, *Practicing A Course In Miracles*, offers practical lessons
and mentoring.
Paperback: 978-1-84694-319-5 ebook: 978-1-84694-642-4

Rising in Love
My Wild and Crazy Ride to Here and Now, with Amma, the
Hugging Saint
Ram Das Batchelder
Rising in Love conveys an author's extraordinary journey of
spiritual awakening with the Guru, Amma.
Paperback: 978-1-78279-687-9 ebook: 978-1-78279-686-2

Thinker's Guide to God
Peter Vardy
An introduction to key issues in the philosophy of religion.
Paperback: 978-1-90381-622-6

Your Simple Path
Find happiness in every step
Ian Tucker
A guide to helping us reconnect with what is really important
in our lives.
Paperback: 978-1-78279-349-6 ebook: 978-1-78279-348-9

365 Days of Wisdom
Daily Messages To Inspire You Through The Year
Dadi Janki
Daily messages which cool the mind, warm the heart and guide
you along your journey.
Paperback: 978-1-84694-863-3 ebook: 978-1-84694-864-0

Body of Wisdom
Women's Spiritual Power and How it Serves
Hilary Hart
Bringing together the dreams and experiences of women across
the world with today's most visionary spiritual teachers.
Paperback: 978-1-78099-696-7 ebook: 978-1-78099-695-0

Dying to Be Free
From Enforced Secrecy to Near Death to True Transformation
Hannah Robinson
After an unexpected accident and near-death experience,
Hannah Robinson found herself radically transforming her life,
while a remarkable new insight altered her relationship with
her father, a practising Catholic priest.
Paperback: 978-1-78535-254-6 ebook: 978-1-78535-255-3

The Ecology of the Soul
A Manual of Peace, Power and Personal Growth for Real People
in the Real World
Aidan Walker
Balance your own inner Ecology of the Soul to regain your
natural state of peace, power and wellbeing.
Paperback: 978-1-78279-850-7 ebook: 978-1-78279-849-1

Not I, Not other than I
The Life and Teachings of Russel Williams
Steve Taylor, Russel Williams
The miraculous life and inspiring teachings of one of the
World's greatest living Sages.
Paperback: 978-1-78279-729-6 ebook: 978-1-78279-728-9

Readers of ebooks can buy or view any of these bestsellers by
clicking on the live link in the title. Most titles are published
in paperback and as an ebook. Paperbacks are available in
traditional bookshops. Both print and ebook formats are
available online.

Find more titles and sign up to our readers' newsletter at
http://www.johnhuntpublishing.com/mind-body-spirit
Follow us on Facebook at https://www.facebook.com/OBooks/
and Twitter at https://twitter.com/obooks